FOOD&WINE
MAGAZINE'S

Wine
Guide
2005

produced by
gonzalez defino
new york, new york

editorial director **Joseph Gonzalez**
art director **Perri DeFino**
volume editor **Tara Q. Thomas**
copy editor **Anne O'Connor**
chief researcher **Colleen McKinney**
researcher **Kae Denino**
tastings coordinator **Fareed Rayyis**
indexer **Andrea Chesman**

AMERICAN EXPRESS PUBLISHING CORPORATION
senior vice president/chief marketing officer **Mark V. Stanich**
vice president, books and products **Marshall Corey**
director, branded services and products **Tom Mastrocola**
marketing manager **Bruce Spanier**
senior fulfillment manager **Phil Black**
marketing coordinator **Richard Nogueira**
business manager **James R. Whitney**
production manager **Stuart Handelman**
newsstand coordinator **Hanif Harris**

cover photograph **Jonelle Weaver**
cover glassware courtesy of Ravenscroft Crystal

FOOD&WINE
MAGAZINE'S

Wine
Guide
2005

by Jamal A. Rayyis

American Express Publishing Corporation FOOD&WINE
New York BOOKS

contents

foreword

by Gray Kunz

When I first learned about wine, I thought of it as a magical ingredient that has an alchemistic capacity to elevate the tasting experience of a dish. I was ten years old and already very serious about my cuisine. It would be a few years before I would discover the true joys of wine as a beverage and embrace its capacity to elevate any experience.

Now, as a committed wine enthusiast and a chef/restaurateur, I often rely on knowledgeable reference books to help me conduct my business and better appreciate this nectar of the gods. But often these sources are hefty tomes far from being convenient or user-friendly. Not so with FOOD & WINE Magazine's Wine Guide 2005. This pocket-size guide is packed with all the pertinent information needed to help make an educated decision when selecting wine.

Besides well-described recommendations for nearly 1,400 wines, the Wine Guide has many other helpful sections such as the "Vintage Chart," the useful "Guide to Grape Varieties," and the "Names You Can Trust" page listing the most consistent importers of excellent wines. And thanks to the "Food & Wine Pairing Chart," the guesswork is taken out of an often confusing and misunderstood subject.

FOOD & WINE Magazine's Wine Guide 2005 does an excellent job of alleviating the fear and elevating the enjoyment of choosing the right bottle of wine for any occasion. I highly recommend this extremely helpful resource.

Gray Kunz,
Chef/Owner & Cookbook Author

introduction

by Jamal A. Rayyis

Wine has inspired philosophers and earned the praises of poets for millennia, from Socrates to Shakespeare, Diogenes to Dante. While the wines these greats preferred have been lost to history, today's world offers far more choices, with quality wines coming from places as diverse as China and Chile. I wrote this book to help you draw your own inspiration from this enormous, exciting world of wine, whether you wish to enliven a midweek meal or pen heroic odes that will entrance generations. From simple, budget-priced quaffers to complex and costly extravagances that deserve reflection, each wine has a place. To this end, I've carefully considered wines of every range, from those that are easy to find and enjoy to others worth your paycheck, and highlighted the standouts. I've also endeavored not to overwhelm with encyclopedic information, but to give you enough of the whats, hows, and wheres of wines to choose wine on your own with confidence. Santé!

key to symbols

This guide is different from most: it's up to date. Recommendations are for the exact wines being released for sale this year. Notes include the following symbols:

Type	🍷 / 🍷 / 🍷	red wine / white wine / rosé wine
Quality	★★★★	**Outstanding** Worth a search
	★★★	**Excellent** Top-notch example of its type
	★★	**Very good** Distinctive
	★	**Good** Delicious everyday wine
Price	$$$$	over $50
	$$$	$26 to $50
	$$	$15 to $25
	$	under $15

the year in wine

Why do wineries put vintage dates on their wine bottles? Because every year brings something different. Indeed, the past year may be counted among the most extraordinary in modern wine history, not only for the challenges presented by Mother Nature, but also because of economic and other factors that affect what people drink.

The weather report The summer of 2003 has gone down as one of the hottest on record for Europe's great wine-producing regions. In France, scores of people perished from the heat—and grapes suffered, too. Weeks of temperatures exceeding 100° F pushed grape sugar levels upward while lowering the acidity that would balance the sugars. There's no question that French wines from 2003 are more powerful than normal, but, given the heat-hastened season, grapes might not have had time to develop the complex flavors necessary for great wine. Regardless of quality, harvest levels came to less than half of normal in some regions. Given the surplus of wines from past years, this might not be so bad.

The sun took its toll in the rest of Europe, too. Spanish and Italian producers are mixed in their opinions of the heat wave vintage. Power they've got; fresh-tasting, complex wines they may not be. In contrast, the brave souls who attempt to make red wine in cool-climate Germany were given reason to celebrate, as warmer temperatures got their grapes actually ripe. With global warming, Burgundy lovers are advised to learn the proper pronunciation of *Spätburgunder*—Pinot Noir in German.

In the United States, uneven weather challenged California vineyards in 2003; a warm, dry October came to the rescue of those who waited that long to pick. On the East Coast, cool, wet weather on the heels of a frigid winter unnerved East Coast vintners. Pacific Northwest winemakers continued their run of very good years with the 2003 vintage, but bitterly cold temperatures in January 2004 damaged vines in eastern Washington. Folks in Walla Walla expect their 2004 harvest to be around a quarter of the previous year.

Mother earth Whatever Mother Nature's mood, Mother Earth expressed a bit of grump in late December 2003 with an earthquake of magnitude 6.5 centered near California's growing Paso Robles wine region. Many vintners lost wine from smashed barrels and broken bottles. Among the hardest hit were the highly regarded Justin Vineyards & Winery and the fabled Turley Wine Cellars, which reported "a river of [very expensive] wine coming out of the barrel room." Those hard-to-come-by allocations of Turley wines have become even more precious.

It's the economy, stupid Drought, frost, and tremors aside, perhaps the biggest news in the world of wine has been the weakness of the United States dollar against other currencies. Between January 2002 and June 2004, the U.S. dollar lost almost 30 percent of its value against both the Euro and the Australian dollar. The result? Prices have risen on wines imported to the U.S., and U.S. wines have become cheaper abroad. Needless to say, California winemakers are happy. Exports to the U.K. have risen by 25 percent in the past year with no slowdown in sight. European and Australian winemakers are keeping prices down by taking smaller profits, but they can only do so for a limited period of time. If your favorite Chianti hasn't yet become noticeably more expensive, consider buying it in quantity before it does. And, speaking of quantity, California's wine glut, which allowed super-discount wines like Charles Shaw (aka "Two-Buck Chuck") to enter the market, has just about dried up. As the U.S. economy improves, count on domestic wine prices to start rising, too.

Vines, not mines California-based Roots of Peace, an organization dedicated to removing land mines in war-ravaged countries and restoring the land to agricultural production, is proving that wine is good for the heart in more ways than one. After helping replant destroyed vineyards in Croatia, the organization is now in Afghanistan, where it has funded the removal of more than 100,000 land mines. In their place they are providing Afghani farmers with the materials and expertise to replant their own vineyards. Several California winemakers and enologists from the University of California at Davis are playing important roles in this effort. But, out of respect for Afghanistan's non-imbibing Muslim culture, table and raisin grapes, rather than wine grapes, are being planted.

guide to grape varieties

There are thousands of different grape varieties, but only about twenty of them dominate American wine racks. Many of these are grown worldwide; others are specific to a certain place. Here's a short guide to the most common grape varieties:

♀CABERNET FRANC

Cabernet Franc adds peppery red cherry flavors to Bordeaux reds, but it stars in France's Loire Valley, where it makes light reds with spicy herb flavors. California and Long Island also make some good examples.

♀CABERNET SAUVIGNON

Cabernet Sauvignon is revered for its cedary black currant flavors bolstered with tannin. It finds its best expression in Bordeaux and California's Napa Valley, though examples show up worldwide.

♀CHARDONNAY

Chardonnay seems to grow everywhere. It reaches its apex in France's Burgundy, where it makes elegant, mineral-laden wines, but it can also turn out corpulent, tropical fruit bombs, toasty Champagnes, and nectarous dessert wines. You'll find an example in nearly every chapter of this Guide.

♀CHENIN BLANC

Chenin Blanc's lush fruit and high acidity make for some of France's greatest wines, like the Loire Valley's full-bodied, long-aging dry wines, dessert elixirs, and sparklers. South Africa and California also make lighter but eminently enjoyable examples.

♀GEWÜRZTRAMINER

Pink-skinned Gewürztraminer offers flamboyant flavors ranging from honeysuckle to lychee, apricot, mineral, and spice. It's especially important in Alsace and parts of Germany. New York State and California also make excellent examples.

♥GRENACHE/GARNACHA

Grenache is essential to many southern French wines for its fresh cherry and spice flavors, especially those from Châteauneuf-du-Pape and the Côtes-du-Rhône. Many Spanish winemakers rely on Grenache (*Garnacha,* in Spanish), especially in Priorat. It is also important in Sardinia (where it's called Cannonau) and shows up in California and Australia.

♥MARSANNE

Most at home in France's Rhône Valley, Marsanne is prized for its honeyed almond flavors and full body. Good versions are also found in California and Australia.

♥MERLOT

Merlot, with its plum and chocolate flavors, has become one of the world's most popular grapes. It makes some of the greatest wines in the world, such as those from Bordeaux's Pomerol and Washington State. There are also terrific examples from California and northeastern Italy.

♥MUSCAT

Muscat comes in many different forms, both red and white, but all burst with fragrant flavors such as honeysuckle, orange blossom, and musk. It's found throughout the world, most famously in Italy as Moscato and in Spain as Moscatel, as well as in France's Alsace region, Greece, California, and Australia.

♥NEBBIOLO

Nebbiolo grows in a few different areas of Italy, but nowhere as well as it does in Piedmont, where its gloriously fragrant black cherry, cedar, tar, and tobacco flavors define the long-lived reds of Barolo and Barbaresco. Nebbiolo is catching the attention of vintners beyond Italy, and today, a few good examples can also be found in California and Australia.

♥PINOT BLANC

Alsace, California, and Italy make wines from Pinot Blanc (also called Pinot Bianco), but this white wine grape is most important in Austria where, under the name Weissburgunder, it takes on richer flavors with more character than the typical medium-bodied, mild-flavored versions.

❢PINOT GRIS/
❢PINOT GRIGIO

In France's Alsace and Oregon, Pinot Gris produces full-bodied, nutty-tasting white wines. All over Italy, where it's called Pinot Grigio, the grape produces light, brisk whites. California makes good examples now, too.

❢PINOT NOIR

Called the heartbreak grape, Pinot Noir is difficult to grow and difficult to make. But when made right, it is as seductive as wine can be, with elegant aromas and flavors like roses, red fruits, and smoke, complemented by a haunting earthiness. Burgundy is held up as its ultimate expression, but excellent, if different, Pinot Noir also comes from Australia, California, the Loire, New York State, New Zealand, and Oregon.

❢RIESLING

Riesling can make wines of incredible complexity with high acidity and lots of mineral flavors, in styles that range from bone-dry to sumptuously sweet. While Riesling is made all around the world, the finest examples are found in Alsace, Germany, Austria, and New York State. Australia is producing excellent examples of the grape as well. Many Rieslings can age for more than a decade.

❢ROUSSANNE

Roussanne finds its home in the northern Rhône, where its nutty, unctuous flavors are often combined with Marsanne for the white wines of Crozes-Hermitage, Hermitage, and St-Joseph. It's also occasionally grown in California, with some good results.

❢SANGIOVESE

Called the "blood of Jove," Sangiovese is the life-blood of Italian winemaking, prized for its tart red cherry, leather, and balsamic flavors balanced by lots of acidity. It's most common in Tuscany, where it makes up large portions of the wines of Chianti, as well as many of the exalted Super Tuscans. Sangiovese has also spread to California, which offers a different take on the grape.

♥SAUVIGNON BLANC

Sauvignon Blanc finds its greatest expression in the lemony, herbaceous wines of France's Sancerre and Pouilly-Fumé, though New Zealand's pungent grapefruit, green pepper, and boxwood-flavored wines have become wildly popular, too. South Africa, California, and Austria also make excellent Sauvignon Blancs.

♥SEMILLON

The second of Bordeaux's great white grapes after Sauvignon Blanc, Semillon finds its glory as the main component of the region's luxurious, sweet Sauternes, but it is presented on its own or blended with Sauvignon Blanc to make some great, full-bodied dry wines in Bordeaux and Australia.

♥SYRAH/SHIRAZ

Typically full-bodied and tannic with berry, pepper, and smoky flavors, Syrah offers power—but is not without finesse. Its most renowned domain is France's Rhône Valley, but California's Central Coast, Washington State, and Australia, where it's called Shiraz, also produce great versions.

♥TEMPRANILLO

Grown throughout Spain, Tempranillo is best known as the grape responsible for Rioja's reds. Tempranillo wines tend to have spicy aromas, full, plummy flavors, and medium body.

♥VIOGNIER

The basis of many of the nectarous white wines of France's northern Rhône Valley, Viognier has become a favorite of California winemakers for the lush peach, citrus, and floral aromas and flavors of its wines.

♥ZINFANDEL

California's own great red grape (by way of Croatia), Zinfandel assumes many different forms, from an off-dry pale rosé and a quaffable spaghetti red to a full-bodied, tannic wine filled with blackberry and spice flavors. Zinfandel also makes thick, Port-style dessert wines.

wine tasting guide

Tasting wine is a bit like going to the gym: the more you exercise your muscles, the stronger they get. Most of us are equipped with all the basic tools needed to taste wine: our taste buds detect sweet, salty, bitter, and sour sensations, plus "umami," the savory flavor found in meat and other foods. Even more impressive—and vital, since taste depends mostly on smell—our noses can differentiate between hundreds of aromas. Using these tools effectively greatly ups the pleasure wine offers, so here are a few tips to help you whip your palate into shape. They can be applied to a single glass of wine sipped with dinner, or an array of wines tasted at one time (the latter is a particularly effective way to learn about wine). As you'll see, exercising your palate is much easier than working out at the gym.

Set the mood For each wine that you want to taste, find a clear, stemmed glass that is comfortable to hold. Choose a well-lit place to sit that's relatively odor-neutral. Leave off the perfume; its scent distracts from the wine. Keep pen and paper handy for note-taking.

Set the scene Pour just enough wine into the glass so that the wine just barely reaches the widest part of the glass. This way, you'll have enough room to swirl the wine without spilling it.

Check the color The look of a wine can tell you a lot. With some exceptions, a light color generally indicates a light wine; a darker color, a richer wine. Also, white wines deepen in color with age; red wines get lighter and take on a brown cast. If you've poured more than one wine, compare the colors and guess which will taste richer. If a young wine looks tarnished, it may indicate poor winemaking or storage.

Swirl & sniff Hold the glass by its stem and swirl it gently to release the wine's aromas. Stop and sniff. What do you smell? Is it pleasing to you? Sniff again. Does it smell like fruit? What kind? It might offer scents that recall herbs, flowers, sweet or piquant spices, vanilla, or wood. Some wines' aromas recall bell pepper, leather, roasted meat, or even manure. Don't worry about being able to pull lots of different aromas from the wine. Just force yourself to articulate what you smell; the effort will make it easier to tell the difference between one wine and another and to share your impressions with another person. Some awful smells like sulfur or must might dissipate with air; if the wine smells bad, give it a few minutes in the glass and swirl it around some more. If it still smells bad, move on to something else. If a wine smells like wet, moldy cork or cardboard, it may be "corked," meaning that it has been infected with an unpleasant-smelling compound called TCA that's fairly common in corks. TCA is harmless, but it makes the wine taste bad, so when you find a corked wine, put the cork back in the bottle and return it to the place of purchase. The store should let you exchange the corked bottle for another one.

Sip & swish Take a sip of the wine and swish it around in your mouth so that every tastebud gets a taste. Try to suck air into your mouth while the wine is still in it (takes practice); like swirling the wine in the glass, this allows the wine to release more aroma. Note how the wine feels: Does it coat your mouth, does it feel prickly, or is it light and refreshing? What does it taste like? Is it bitter or sweet? Does it recall certain fruits or spices? Smell the wine again, deeply. Does it smell like it tastes? Sometimes it does, sometimes it doesn't. Most importantly, do you like it? There are no wrong answers here; it's all about what you perceive.

To spit or swallow? If you're tasting more than a couple of wines at one sitting and you want to be able to get the most out of every glass (not to mention remember them tomorrow), spit—unless, of course, you're at the dinner table.

Get horizontal Try tasting from different angles. For instance, a horizontal tasting is one in which you sample a range of wines that are alike in all but one way, such as a group of wines from the same region and same vintage, but made by different producers, or a lineup of wines from the same producer, same grape, and same vintage, but from different vineyards. Noting the differences between such similar wines will greatly expand your knowledge. To go vertical, you'll taste the same wine from the same producer made in different years. It's a great demonstration of how vintage can make a difference, as well as how age can change a wine's look and taste.

wine tasting terms

Because of space limitations, tasting notes are necessarily brief, offering a quick view of what to expect from a wine. Many notes mention specific flavors, others, the feeling a wine evokes. Please understand flavors as analogies. All the wines in this guide are made from grapes, but grapes have the unique ability among fruits to evoke the flavors of other fruits, herbs, or minerals. A wine said to taste like "pineapple" isn't flavored by pineapple. Rather, it evokes a pineapple's flavors. Though I have consciously avoided fussy wine jargon in this guide, some of the terms commonly used may be unfamiliar. Here is a selective mini-glossary:

Acidity The tart, tangy sensations in wine. Ideally, acidity brightens a wine's flavors like a squeeze of lemon brightens fish. Wines lacking acidity taste "flabby."

Balance The harmony between acidity, tannin, alcohol, and sweetness in a wine.

Body How heavy or thick a wine feels in the mouth.

Dry A wine without perceptible sweetness. A dry wine can, however, have powerful fruit flavors; they just don't taste sweet.

Earthy An earthy wine evokes the soil in which the grapes were grown or related flavors like mushrooms, leather, or damp straw.

Fruity Wines that have an abundance of fruit flavors.

Mineral Flavors that evoke the minerals in the soil in which certain grapes are grown. "Steely" is a subset of mineral.

Oaky Wines that carry the flavors of the oak barrels in which they were aged are said to taste "oaky."

Powerful Full-flavored, heavy in tannin, acid, and/or alcohol.

Rustic A bit rough, unsophisticated—which can be charming.

Tannin A component of grape skins, seeds, stems, and oak barrels, tannin is found most notably in red wine. It gives the mouth a dry, cottony feel, much like over-steeped black tea does.

Terroir Related to *terre*, French for "earth," terroir refers to the particular attributes a wine picks up from the environment in which it was grown, including such factors as soil, climate, topography, sun, and even the plants growing nearby.

pairing wine with food

We used to hear, White wine with fish and red with meat. The modern adage seems to be, Drink whatever you like with whatever you want. Both approaches have advantages, but you're bound to encounter pitfalls by adhering too closely to either. The trick is to pair food and wine so that neither overwhelms or distorts the other. Some suggestions to help you on your way:

Be body-conscious Light-bodied, delicately flavored food goes best with a light and delicate wine; heavy-bodied, full-flavored dishes call for heftier wines. The subtle flavors of sole meunière are going to get lost if washed down with a hearty Napa Cabernet.

Balance extremes If a dish is rich and creamy, you need a tart wine as a counterpoint—and to cleanse your palate. A bit of sweetness in wine balances salty or spicy foods. If you can't wait to drink those young, astringent Bordeaux, Barolo, or California Cabernets, the protein and fat of meat will moderate their tannin.

Dance to the same beat Peppery meat dishes work well with spicy Rhône Valley reds. Dishes with fruit sauces are great with richly fruity wines from southern Italy. California Chenin Blanc and Loire Valley or New Zealand Sauvignon Blanc have the right mineral and herbal nuances to stand up to asparagus and artichokes, which can make other wines taste metallic.

Do as the Romans People have been pairing locally made foods and wines for centuries. Wines from a particular region are often just the thing to drink with foods from the same place.

Mix & match Though the "red with meat, white with fish" rule is too sweeping, tannic reds do taste metallic when drunk with oily fish like mackerel or sardines. If you want to drink red with them, select one that is low in tannin and high in acidity.

For more specific food and wine pairing recommendations, see the Food & Wine Pairing Chart on the next page.

food & wine pairing chart

	antipasti; mezes; salty, assertive foods; hors d'oeuvres	foie gras	sausages; charcuterie	soups; salads	egg dishes
Light, simple whites Unoaked Chardonnay; California and South Africa Chenin Blanc; most Italian whites; Mediterranean blends; Muscadet; basic German Riesling; young white Rioja; Sauvignon Blanc; Vinho Verde	●			●	●
Fragrant, medium-bodied whites Albariño; Australian blends; white Bordeaux; Loire Chenin Blanc; Gewürztraminer; German Kabinett Riesling	●	●		●	●
Rich, full-bodied whites Oaked Chardonnay; white Burgundies; Pinot Gris; Austrian Riesling & Grüner Veltliner; aged Semillon; Scheurebe; Viognier		●			
Light, fruity reds & rosés France's Beaujolais, Cabernet Franc (Bourgeuil), & simple Languedoc reds; basic Freisa, Nebbiolo, & Sangiovese; all rosés	●		●		
Medium-bodied, slightly tannic reds Agiorgitiko; simple Bordeaux; Cabernet Franc (Chinon); Sangiovese from Chianti Classico; Côtes-du-Rhône blends; Dolcetto; Grenache; Merlot; Pinot Noir; Portuguese reds			●		
Rich, dense, tannic reds Aglianico; Barbaresco; Barolo; France's Bordeaux, Rhône Valley, & Southwest reds; high-end New World Cabernets & Syrah/Shiraz; Malbec; Zinfandel			●		
Sparkling white wines Cava, Champagne, Crémant, Prosecco, other sparkling wines	●		●	●	●

There's no single perfect wine for any given dish. In fact, the possibilities are nearly infinite. Use this handy Food & Wine Pairing Chart to help you sort through the options and make delicious matches—at home, in wine shops, and in restaurants.

pasta, rice & other grains			fish & seafood		poultry & game birds		pork & veal	
light; summery; vegetable-based	rich; mushroom- or truffle-based	baked; tomato or cheese sauces	mild varieties; light sauces	rich varieties; heavy sauces	chicken; turkey	duck; game birds	herbed or with savory sauces	fruit-based sauces
●			●		●			
●			●		●			
	●			●	●	●	●	●
	●	●		●	●	●		●
	●	●				●	●	
		●				●	●	
●	●		●	●	●	●	●	●

19

food & wine pairing chart

	beef: steaks, stews, ribs, etc.	lamb, venison, game meats		asian & curry dishes	
		herbed or with savory sauces	fruit-based sauces	fish; seafood; vegetables	meat; lentils; root vegetables
Light, simple whites Unoaked Chardonnay; California and South Africa Chenin Blanc; most Italian whites; Mediterranean blends; Muscadet; basic German Riesling; young white Rioja; Sauvignon Blanc; Vinho Verde				●	
Fragrant, medium-bodied whites Albariño; Australian blends; white Bordeaux; Loire Chenin Blanc; Gewürztraminer; German Kabinett Riesling				●	
Rich, full-bodied whites Oaked Chardonnay; white Burgundies; Pinot Gris; Austrian Riesling & Grüner Veltliner; aged Semillon; Scheurebe; Viognier				●	●
Light, fruity reds & rosés France's Beaujolais, Cabernet Franc (Bourgeuil) & simple Languedoc reds; basic Freisa, Nebbiolo, & Sangiovese; all rosés					●
Medium-bodied, slightly tannic reds Agiorgitiko; simple Bordeaux; Cabernet Franc (Chinon); Sangiovese from Chianti Classico; Côtes-du-Rhône blends; Dolcetto; Grenache; Merlot; Pinot Noir; Portuguese reds	●	●			
Rich, dense, tannic reds Aglianico; Barbaresco; Barolo; France's Bordeaux, Rhône Valley, & Southwest reds; high-end New World Cabernets & Syrah/Shiraz; Malbec; Zinfandel	●	●	●		
Sparkling white wines Cava, Champagne, Crémant, Prosecco, other sparkling wines		●	●	●	●
Dessert wines, white Ice Wine, Muscat, Riesling, Sauternes, Tokaji, Vin Santo					
Dessert wines, red Banyuls, Maury, Port, Recioto della Valpolicella					

barbecue; burgers; pizza	vegetarian dishes			cheeses		desserts		
	stews; gratins	grilled tofu or vegetables	artichokes; asparagus	mild	strong	fruit-based; poundcake	creams; custards; soufflés	chocolate; nuts; coffee
		●	●	●				
		●		●				
		●	●	●				
●	●	●		●				
●	●	●		●	●			
	●				●			
		●	●			●		
				●		●	●	
								●

how to handle a wine list

Few things cause diners as much anxiety as the presentation of a wine list. But you can conquer any list with a few easy steps:

Assess the list A good list is diverse or it specializes in a certain region. There should be wines in different price ranges, with a few priced under $30. If you see a Riesling—not popular in the U.S., but an excellent complement to many dishes—the restaurant is probably serious about wine. A poor list might be limited in selection (not necessarily in number: fifty California Chardonnays and a few other whites can be trouble), have too many wines from one producer, or fail to list vintages. If the list is poor, order the least expensive thing that you recognize as being reasonably good.

Ask questions A wine list is just a menu. You can ask how tannic the Cabernet is just as you inquire how the salmon is prepared. Very few people can look at a list and know exactly what all the wines taste like at that moment. It's the restaurant's job to explain them to you.

Taste the wine When the bottle arrives, make sure it's exactly what you ordered—the vintage, the producer, the blend or variety. If not, say so. If the listed wine is out, you might prefer to choose something else. You may be presented with the cork. Ignore it. I've had fine wines with spoiled corks and bad wines with sound corks. Sniff the wine in your glass. If it smells like sulfur, cabbage, or skunk, say that you think the wine might be off and request a few minutes to see if the odors dissipate. If they remain, the wine is probably bad. Another problem: about 5 percent of wines, in all price ranges, are "corked"—the cork was improperly processed, and the wine tastes like musty cork or wet cardboard.

Send a bottle back if necessary If the wine is off, the server should take it away and offer a new bottle. Restaurants often get credit for bad wines anyway. Disliking a wine is not a reason to send a bottle back unless a server described it quite inaccurately: as light and fruity when it's heavy and tannic, for instance.

how to navigate a wine shop

Wine shops can be intimidating. The dizzying array of wines plus a fear of haughty wine experts is enough to make one wish for the reintroduction of Prohibition. Luckily, this nightmare is usually fantasy. Most wine shops really want to please customers, and most wine sellers can't wait to share their latest discovery. Here's how to make the best of wine shopping.

Scope out a good shop Size doesn't matter: small shops with well chosen wines can trump mega-marts with a random selection. To up your chances of making new discoveries, seek out stores with many unfamiliar bottles. Look for accessible salespeople; a great selection of wines can be useless without guidance. Shops that offer extra information through newsletters or wine tastings are especially worth patronizing. Pay attention to the shop's ambient temperature, too. If it seems too warm, wines might be slowly cooking on the shelves.

Ask questions Most wine-savvy salespeople are eager to share their knowledge and to steer you toward some of their favorites. Tell them your needs, your budget, and anything else that might help them help you find a wine you'll love.

Ask for options No matter what the salesperson recommends, ask for options. This encourages salespeople to be more thoughtful and gives you more interesting choices.

Keep an open mind You may love Merlot, but a salesperson may know of other great wines that share its charms while offering some thrilling differences. However, if you know that you dislike something don't let anyone talk you into it. You're the one drinking it—and paying.

Become a regular The better the store knows you, the better they can choose wines that will excite and please you.

california

California is the Promised Land when it comes to American wine. Warm sunshine moderated by ocean breezes, diverse topography, and the relentless energies of innovative vintners have created a Bacchic bonanza few places in the world can match. With wines of nearly every style and price, the Golden State accounts for three of every four bottles purchased in the U.S.

on the label

California wine labels typically list the winery's name, the grape variety from which the wine is made, the officially designated region, or AVA (American Viticultural Area), in which the grapes were grown, and the year they were harvested. However, under U.S. law a varietally labelled wine need contain only 75 percent of that grape; vintners often blend varieties to make more complex wines. Blends made from traditional Bordeaux grape varieties sometimes carry the moniker *Meritage*. *Reserve* is often used for special bottlings, but the word has no legal meaning.

white wines

CHARDONNAY

Chardonnay is California's alpha grape. The most widely planted wine grape in California, it's also one of the wines that rolls most easily off people's tongues in restaurants across the U.S. For years, California winemakers offered Chardonnays that oozed tropical fruit and butterscotch flavors, reflecting the state's ample sunshine and generous use of oak barrels, but lately, vintners have changed tack to make wines closer to a Burgundian ideal.

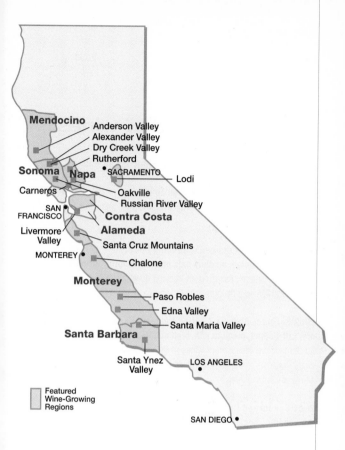

at the table

The flavors of big, oaky Chardonnay can overwhelm light fish, but they can be terrific with grilled, meaty fish like salmon and tuna or even pork loin or turkey. Pair a less-buttery, citrusy Chardonnay with grilled snapper, baked cod, or any number of chicken dishes.

the bottom line For the last several years, prices on California Chardonnay rose as quickly as the NASDAQ average. Fortunately, prices have relaxed somewhat. Chardonnay below $12 tend to be dull, but you'll find a wide range of interesting Chardonnay for $12 to $25. Those costing more—up to $100— can be exceptional, but higher prices often reflect rarity and hype as much as quality.

california **chardonnay**

2000	2001	2002	2003
★★★	★★★	★★	★★

recommended wines

**2001 Au Bon Climat Harmony Nuits-Blanches au Bouge,
Santa Maria Valley** ★★★★ $$$
dry, medium-bodied, light oak, high acidity   drink now–12 years
Great Chardonnay, full of pecan praline, baked pear, and citrus flavors framed
by subtle minerality.

1994 Kalin Cellars Cuvee LV, Sonoma County ★★★★ $$$
dry, medium-bodied, medium oak, medium acidity   drink now–6 years
A rare older vintage, this is worth tracking down for its butterscotch-scented
orange and lavender flavors.

2002 Beringer Sbragia-Limited Release, Napa Valley ★★★ $$$
dry, full-bodied, medium oak, high acidity   drink in 1–10 years
Ed Sbragia oversees a lot of wines at Beringer, but he puts his name on pre-
cious few. This smoky wine earns its pedigree with smooth ripe fruit lifted by
plenty of vibrant acidity.

2002 Cakebread Cellars, Napa Valley ★★★ $$$
dry, medium-bodied, light oak, high acidity   drink now–6 years
A fine tribute to Cakebread's three decades of solid winemaking, this bottling
is full of spicy yet restrained fruit flavors.

**2001 Clos Du Val Carneros Vineyard Reserve,
Napa Valley** ★★★ $$$
dry, medium-bodied, medium oak, high acidity   drink now–10 years
Don't bother with the gym: this bottle's heavy enough to do curls, and the min-
eral flavors are like pumping iron. Citrus flavors cool you off.

2001 Crichton Hall Vineyard, Napa Valley ★★★ $$$
dry, medium-bodied, medium oak, high acidity   drink now–6 years
Autumn in a glass, this Chardonnay is fragrant with almond, pear, and apple
flavors, ripe without going tropical.

2001 Cuvaison Estate Selection, Carneros ★★★ $$$
dry, medium-bodied, medium oak, medium acidity   drink now–6 years
Cuvaison's basic Chardonnay is always reliable, but this vintage is better than
usual, with dense but measured fruit and a nuttiness from well-polished oak.

2002 Flora Springs Select Cuvee, Napa Valley ★★★ $$$
dry, medium-bodied, medium oak, high acidity drink now–8 years
Ever smell a pineapple blossom? Me neither, but that's what a whiff of this indulgent wine brings to mind.

2001 Foley Bien Nacido Vineyard, Santa Maria Valley ★★★ $$$
dry, medium-bodied, light oak, high acidity drink now–8 years
Bien Nacido is famous for a reason: it gives layer upon layer of grapefruit, orange, and lime flavors with light minerals.

2002 Matanzas Creek Winery, Sonoma County ★★★ $$$
dry, medium-bodied, medium oak, high acidity drink now–6 years
Matanzas Creek is known for its Sauvignon Blanc, but its Chardonnay is no second, with delicious fruit and spice flavors.

2001 Morgan Rosella's Vineyard,
Santa Lucia Highlands ★★★ $$$
dry, medium-bodied, medium oak, high acidity drink now–8 years
All of Morgan's Chardonnays are good; this one just stands taller, with dense, spicy fruit and palate-tingling mineral flavors.

2000 St. Supéry Limited Edition Dollarhide Ranch,
Napa Valley ★★★ $$$
dry, medium-bodied, medium oak, medium acidity drink now–6 years
A creamy, dreamy wave of mixed fruit and light spice flavors.

2002 Testarossa Sleepy Hollow Vineyard,
Santa Lucia Highlands ★★★ $$$
dry, medium-bodied, medium oak, high acidity drink now–8 years
Grapefruit and pear flavors are shadowed by minerals for a hauntingly light yet persistent Chardonnay.

2002 Carpe Diem Firepeak Vineyard, Edna Valley ★★★ $$
dry, medium-bodied, light oak, high acidity drink now–6 years
Terrific Chardonnay, worth hunting down for its light citrus blossom and honey flavors with a slip of minerals.

2002 Chappellet, Napa Valley ★★★ $$
dry, medium-bodied, medium oak, high acidity drink now–6 years
Simply delicious, this offers a cornucopia of fruit and spice flavors that will keep you coming back for more.

2002 Clos du Bois Calcaire, Alexander Valley ★★★ $$
dry, medium-bodied, light oak, high acidity drink now–8 years
As the name indicates, this Chardonnay offers plenty of ripe fruit infused with chalky (*calcaire*) mineral notes.

california**chardonnay**

2002 Handley, Anderson Valley ★★★ $$
dry, medium-bodied, light oak, high acidity drink now–3 years
A terrific example of Chardonnay produced in Anderson Valley's cool climate, this is lean and steely, yet full of peach and honey-nut flavors.

2002 Ledson, Russian River Valley ★★★ $$
dry, medium-bodied, medium oak, high acidity drink now–6 years
Satin in texture, earthy in aromas, and luscious in flavors.

2002 Miner, Napa Valley ★★★ $$
dry, medium-bodied, medium oak, high acidity drink now–8 years
This oozes sunshine *and* digs deep into the earth for great mineral flavors.

2002 Beaulieu Vineyard, Carneros ★★ $$
dry, medium-bodied, light oak, high acidity drink now–4 years
BV serves up classic Carneros, with lean fruit, mineral, and almond notes.

2002 Benziger Family Winery, Carneros ★★ $$
dry, full-bodied, medium oak, high acidity drink now–6 years
Pineapple party! Hints of anise keep things interesting.

**2000 Gallo of Sonoma Laguna Vineyard,
Russian River Valley** ★★ $$
dry, medium-bodied, medium oak, medium acidity drink now–3 years
Smoky and sultry, Laguna shows an appealing earthiness with smooth fruit.

2001 Gloria Ferrer, Carneros ★★ $$
dry, medium-bodied, medium oak, high acidity drink now–3 years
From sparkling to still, Gloria Ferrer wines brighten any occasion.

2002 Lolonis, Redwood Valley ★★ $$
dry, medium-bodied, light oak, high acidity drink now–3 years
Well-balanced wine, this is liable to please lovers of California Chardonnay and Burgundy alike.

2002 Markham, Napa Valley ★★ $$
dry, medium-bodied, medium oak, high acidity drink now–3 years
Straight-on Chardonnay, with zingy tropical fruit flavors plus a measure of oak.

2002 R.H. Phillips Toasted Head, Russian River Valley ★★ $$
dry, medium-bodied, medium oak, high acidity drink now–3 years
As the name and fire-breathing California grizzly on the label suggest, here's a warm Chardonnay with lots of toasty oak.

2001 Sequoia Grove, Carneros/Napa Valley ★★ $$
dry, medium-bodied, light oak, high acidity drink now–3 years
Wonderfully zingy orange and nut flavors will really grab you.

2002 The Hess Collection, Napa Valley ★★ $$
dry, medium-bodied, light oak, high acidity   drink now–6 years

An engaging Chardonnay, with appealing fruit and burnt sugar flavors.

2001 Thomas Fogarty, Santa Cruz Mountains ★★ $$
dry, medium-bodied, light oak, high acidity   drink now–5 years

Santa Cruz is loaded with characters—even its wines stand out, with toasty almond, lavender, and orange flavors.

2002 Edna Valley Vineyard Paragon, Edna Valley/San Luis Obispo ★★ $
dry, medium-bodied, light oak, high acidity   drink now–3 years

Subtle grapefruit, walnut, and mineral flavors are a paragon of good taste.

2002 Hayman & Hill Reserve Selection, Russian River Valley ★★ $
dry, medium-bodied, light oak, high acidity   drink now–3 years

Fascinating stuff, this starts off with licorice notes and then goes pure pineapple.

2002 Kendall-Jackson Vintner's Reserve, California ★★ $
dry, medium-bodied, light oak, medium acidity   drink now–3 years

Always reliable for its ripe fruit flavors, K-J's Vintner's Reserve has gotten positively zingy in the 2002 vintage.

2002 Beringer, Napa Valley ★ $$
dry, medium-bodied, heavy oak, medium acidity   drink now–3 years

If you like 'em big 'n' woody, this peppery Chard will serve you well.

2002 Dunnewood Vineyards, Mendocino County ★ $
dry, medium-bodied, light oak, medium acidity   drink now–2 years

Good value, this offers lots of honey and toast flavors for little money.

2002 Echelon, Central Coast ★ $
dry, medium-bodied, medium oak, high acidity   drink now–3 years

Good Chardonnay, perfect for midweek grilled chicken cutlets.

WINES WE WISH WE HAD MORE ROOM FOR

2001 Landmark Lorenzo, Russian River Valley ★★★ $$$ dry, medium-bodied, medium oak, high acidity, drink now–6 years; **2002 Michel-Schlumberger La Brume, Dry Creek Valley** ★★★ $$$ dry, medium-bodied, light oak, high acidity, drink now–10 years; **2001 ZD Wines Reserve, Napa Valley** ★★★ $$$ dry, full-bodied, medium oak, high acidity, drink now–8 years; **2001 Hartford, Sonoma Coast** ★★★ $$ dry, medium-bodied, medium oak, high acidity, drink now–6 years; **2001 Buena Vista, Carneros** ★★ $$ dry, medium-bodied, medium oak, high acidity, drink now–3 years; **2002 Clos Du Val, Carneros/Napa Valley** ★★ $$ dry, medium-bodied, light oak, high acidity, drink now–8 years;

california **sauvignon blanc**

2002 Franciscan Oakville Estate, Napa Valley ★★ $$ dry, medium-bodied, medium oak, high acidity, drink now–4 years; **2002 Meridian Vineyards Reserve, Santa Barbara County** ★★ $$ dry, medium-bodied, light oak, medium acidity, drink now–3 years; **2002 Stags' Leap Winery, Napa Valley** ★★ $$ dry, medium-bodied, medium oak, high acidity, drink now–4 years; **2002 Two Tone Farm, Napa Valley** ★ $ dry, medium-bodied, light oak, high acidity, drink now–2 years

SAUVIGNON BLANC

Light- to medium-bodied, Sauvignon Blanc charms with tangy citrus and succulent melon flavors and a refreshing herbal edge. Vintners often use the term Fumé Blanc for oak-aged Sauvignon Blanc, in an allusion to France's famed Sauvignon Blanc wine, Pouilly-Fumé. It's worth noting, however, that not all Fumé Blancs are aged in oak; neither are all Pouilly-Fumé wines.

at the table

Full of zingy, fresh fruit flavors, good acidity, and fresh, grassy notes, California Sauvignon Blanc makes an ideal house white. It's wonderful with most fish, chicken, and turkey dishes, especially if herbs are a prominent feature. Try it with rosemary-rubbed roast chicken, pan-fried trout, or salads topped with goat cheese.

the bottom line For years California Sauvignon Blanc was one of the state's great wine bargains. You'll still find fine examples for about $12, but the most interesting wines sell for between $15 and $33.

recommended wines

2002 Cakebread Cellars, Napa Valley ★★★ $$
dry, medium-bodied, light oak, high acidity drink now–3 years
This bright, springy Sauvignon Blanc and some herb-marinated grilled chicken breasts would make a perfect Napa picnic.

2001 Dry Creek Vineyard Reserve Fumé Blanc, Dry Creek Valley ★★★ $$
dry, medium-bodied, light oak, high acidity drink now–4 years
This Sauvignon Blanc gets a pinch of cinnamon spice from oak aging and floral notes from a tad of Viognier. Fascinating.

2002 Duckhorn Vineyards, Napa Valley ★★★ $$
dry, medium-bodied, medium oak, high acidity   drink now–6 years
Oak plays a supporting role to honey, melon, and sweet lemon flavors.

2002 Eleven Oaks, Santa Barbara County ★★★ $$
dry, medium-bodied, light oak, high acidity   drink now–3 years
Silky grapefruit and tropical flavors soften up this Sauvignon Blanc's piquant peppery notes.

2002 Flora Springs Soliloquy, Napa Valley ★★★ $$
dry, medium-bodied, medium oak, high acidity   drink in 1–4 years
Time will bring eloquence to this wine's almond, citrus, and stone flavors.

2002 Grgich Hills Fumé Blanc, Napa Valley ★★★ $$
dry, medium-bodied, no oak, high acidity   drink now–3 years
Definitive California Sauvignon Blanc, this offers melon and grapefruit flavors with hints of sweet grass.

2002 Mayacamas Vineyards, Napa Valley ★★★ $$
dry, medium-bodied, no oak, high acidity   drink now–3 years
Crisp as a cold Granny Smith apple, refreshing as a squeeze of lime, this Sauvignon Blanc is delicious.

2001 Murphy-Goode Reserve Fumé, Alexander Valley ★★★ $$
dry, medium-bodied, light oak, high acidity   drink now–4 years
Far from simple Sauvignon Blanc, this impresses with complex mineral, lavender, and light, buttery tropical flavors.

2003 Honig, Napa Valley ★★★ $
dry, medium-bodied, no oak, high acidity   drink now–2 years
A tingling taste of lemon-lime, earthy spice, and herbs. Try the Honig Reserve for Sauvignon that's smokier and more mineral.

2001 Chateau St. Jean La Petite Etoile Vineyard Fumé Blanc, Russian River Valley ★★ $$
dry, medium-bodied, medium oak, high acidity   drink now–3 years
Fruit and minerals provide ample balance to the smoky oak in this hefty Sauvignon Blanc.

2003 St. Supéry, Napa Valley ★★ $$
dry, medium-bodied, no oak, high acidity   drink now–2 years
Zingy, lemony, and fun.

2002 Beringer, Napa Valley ★★ $
dry, medium-bodied, no oak, medium acidity   drink now–1 year
This citrus-scented Sauvignon Blanc stands out for its appealing nuttiness.

2002 Kunde Magnolia Lane, Sonoma Valley ★★ $
dry, medium-bodied, no oak, high acidity drink now–3 years
Citrus, peach, and herb flavors tango together to create one zesty Sonoma Sauvignon Blanc.

2002 Lolonis Fumé Blanc, Redwood Valley ★★ $
dry, medium-bodied, no oak, high acidity drink now–2 years
Three- to four-decade-old vines yield a Sauvignon Blanc with a fascinating floral, stone, and quince personality.

2003 Canyon Road, California ★ $
dry, medium-bodied, no oak, high acidity drink now–2 years
A palate freshener with lime and herb flavors.

2002 Kendall-Jackson Vintner's Reserve, California ★ $
dry, medium-bodied, no oak, high acidity drink now–2 years
A fruit salad of flavors, from tart pineapple to sweet melon and fresh pear, makes a fine supper sipper, especially at the price.

2002 Kenwood, Sonoma County ★ $
dry, medium-bodied, no oak, medium acidity drink now–2 years
A nice summer quaff, with mango and citrus flavors.

2002 Lake Sonoma Winery Fumé Blanc, Dry Creek Valley ★ $
dry, medium-bodied, no oak, high acidity drink now–2 years
New Zealand meets Sonoma, with kiwi flavors mixed with mango and pepper.

WINES WE WISH WE HAD MORE ROOM FOR
2003 Frog's Leap, Rutherford ★★ $$ dry, medium-bodied, no oak, high acidity, drink now–2 years; **2002 Handley Handley Vineyard, Dry Creek Valley** ★★ $ dry, medium-bodied, no oak, high acidity, drink now–2 years; **2002 Rancho Zabaco Reserve, Russian River Valley** ★★ $ dry, medium-bodied, no oak, high acidity, drink now–2 years; **2003 J. Lohr Carol's Vineyard, Napa Valley** ★ $$ dry, medium-bodied, no oak, medium acidity, drink now–2 years; **2003 Geyser Peak Winery, California** ★ $ dry, medium-bodied, no oak, high acidity, drink now–2 years

OTHER WHITE WINES

Many other white grape varieties find a home among the hillsides, valleys, and plains of California. Roussanne, Marsanne, and Viognier claim their origins in the similar climes of France's Rhône Valley. Viognier is especially popular for its floral scents and luscious peach flavors. Alsatian grapes Gewürztraminer and Riesling are fading from the state, while Pinots Blanc and Gris are growing in popularity. Pinot Blanc is appreciated for its easy-to-enjoy pearlike qualities. Pinot Gris shows two faces, with luxurious apricot and spice flavors *à l'Alsace,* or light, zippy citrus flavors *alla* Italian Pinot Grigio. France's Chenin Blanc is made into some charming wines, but its presence is waning. International favorite Muscat also appears in California.

at the table

Viognier's flowery profile nicely complements lightly spiced Asian dishes or fish stews like *cioppino*. Roussanne and Marsanne tend to be heavy, with honey-almond scents that go well with risottos or chicken blanquette. Pinot Blanc or Pinot Gris is terrific with grilled salmon or pan-roasted scallops with wild mushrooms. Pair lighter Pinot Grigio with scampi. Most Gewürztraminers and Rieslings from California are slightly sweet, perfect for curry dishes or fragrant Thai soups.

the bottom line There are a few fine Viognier, Marsanne, and Roussanne for around $10, but expect to pay $15 to $24 for really good examples. Pinots Blanc and Gris sell for $11 to $20, or up to $40 for special bottlings. Riesling and Gewürztraminer can be had for less than $8, though a few dollars more buys superior examples. Chenin Blanc is so far out of fashion that it is a challenge to pay more than $12 for it.

recommended wines

1994 Kalin Cellars Semillon, Livermore Valley ★★★★ $$
dry, full-bodied, light oak, high acidity drink now–8 years
Proof that Semillon can age exceptionally well, this white is rich with mineral notes and dry fruit.

2002 Claiborne & Churchill Dry Riesling, Central Coast ★★★★ $
dry, medium-bodied, no oak, high acidity drink now–10 years
An Alsatian-style Riesling, this offers substance melded with finesse, with notes of minerals, smooth citrus, and nuts.

2002 Austin Hope Roussanne, Central Coast ★★★ $$$
dry, medium-bodied, light oak, high acidity drink now–6 years
Golden in hue and flavor, this Roussanne is full of spiced autumn fruit and waxy herb notes.

TOP 10 PICNIC WINES

Whether filled with ham sandwiches and potato salad, fried chicken and coleslaw, or a chunk of cheese, crusty bread, and dry sausage, what's a picnic basket without a bottle of wine? You can pick any wine, but a picnic's informality suggests something modest, refreshing, and fun. Here are some suggestions, from a cheerful sparkler to three light, easy-drinking whites, a gutsy pink, and a handful of red wines big enough to take on a cold roast beef sandwich.

1. 2000 Huguet Reserva Brut Nature, Cava, Spain

2. 2003 Selbach Piesporter Michelsberg Riesling Kabinett, Mosel-Saar-Ruwer, Germany

3. 2002 Hugel Cuvée Les Amours Pinot Blanc, Alsace, France

4. 2003 Anselmi San Vicenzo, Veneto, Italy

5. 2002 Bonny Doon Vineyard Vin Gris de Cigare, California

6. 2002 Perrin Réserve, Côtes-du-Rhone, France

7. 2001 Château d'Oupia, Minervois, France

8. 2002 Hedges CMS, Columbia Valley, Washington State

9. 2002 Planeta La Segreta, Sicily, Italy

10. 2002 Shenandoah Vineyards Reserve Zinfandel, Amador County, California

---

2002 Chalone Vineyard Chenin Blanc, Chalone ★★★ $$$
dry, medium-bodied, medium oak, high acidity drink now–8 years
Chenin built for aging, with nutty flavors in a rich, waxy texture that will only get better with time.

2001 Clos Du Val Ariadne, Napa Valley ★★★ $$$
dry, full-bodied, light oak, high acidity drink now–12 years
Named after the wife of Dionysus, this Bordeaux blend could well be offered to the gods for its mix of fresh and glazed fruit plus mineral flavors.

2002 Trefethen Viognier, Napa Valley ★★★ $$$
dry, medium-bodied, no oak, high acidity drink now–3 years
This is as fragrant as a basket overflowing with heirloom apples, Meyer lemons, and wildflowers.

2002 Beckmen Vineyards Purisima Mountain Vineyard Marsanne, Santa Ynez Valley ★★★ $$
dry, full-bodied, light oak, high acidity drink now–8 years
It's rare to find unblended Marsanne. This indulgent, peach- and almond-scented wine begs why.

2002 Cold Heaven Sanford and Benedict Vineyard Viognier, Santa Barbara County ★★★ $$
dry, medium-bodied, no oak, high acidity drink now–6 years
Pretty wine, Cold Heaven charms with summer fruit, spring flowers, and all-season mineral flavors.

2002 Conundrum, California ★★★ $$
dry, medium-bodied, light oak, high acidity drink now–3 years
With the many layers of fruit, flowers, minerals, and nuts, your tongue might be confused, but it will be happy.

2003 Havens Albariño, Carneros ★★★ $$
dry, full-bodied, no oak, high acidity drink now–3 years
Lush in body, with peach, grapefruit, and sea-breeze-like minerality, this Albariño would make any Spaniard proud.

2002 Qupé Bien Nacido Vineyard Roussanne, Santa Maria Valley ★★★ $$
dry, full-bodied, medium oak, medium acidity drink in 2–10 years
Give this Roussanne some age to soften the oak and bring out its delicious baked apple, orange, and spice flavors.

2003 St. Supéry Virtú Meritage, Napa Valley ★★★ $$
dry, medium-bodied, light oak, high acidity drink now–3 years
A Bordeaux blend bright with notes of grapefruit and fresh-cut grass.

2002 Tablas Creek Vineyard Côtes de Tablas Blanc, Paso Robles ★★★ $$
dry, medium-bodied, no oak, high acidity drink now–3 years
From the Central Coast outpost of France's Château de Beaucastel, this zippy wine captures the sun through its mixed citrus, herb, and mineral flavors.

2002 Treana Mer Soleil Vineyard Marsanne-Viognier, Central Coast ★★★ $$
dry, full-bodied, medium oak, medium acidity drink now–6 years
Sea and sun: lots of mineral knit finely into ripe peach and pear flavors.

2003 Babcock Pinot Grigio, Santa Barbara County ★★★ $
dry, medium-bodied, no oak, high acidity   drink now–3 years
Handfuls of fresh, peppery herb flavors pick up a background of citrus.

2001 Bedford Thompson Pinot Gris,
Santa Barbara County ★★★ $
dry, medium-bodied, light oak, high acidity   drink now–3 years
A confit of citrus and strawberry flavors with notes of nuts and honey.

2002 Chappellet Dry Chenin Blanc, Napa Valley ★★★ $
dry, light-bodied, no oak, high acidity   drink now–3 years
California's Chenin master turns out another beauty with light pineapple, mineral, and almond flavors.

2001 Borgo Buon Natale Primogénito/First Born,
Santa Maria Valley ★★★ $
dry, medium-bodied, light oak, high acidity   drink now–6 years
Made from three northern Italian grape varieties, this is a treasure of smoky fruit, mineral, and spice flavors.

2002 Beringer Alluvium Blanc, Knights Valley ★★ $$$
dry, medium-bodied, medium oak, high acidity   drink now–6 years
A river of citrus and tropical flavors, with some oak running through it.

2002 Moon Mountain Vineyard Reserve
Sauvignon Blanc-Semillon, Edna Valley ★★ $$
dry, medium-bodied, medium oak, high acidity   drink now–6 years
Semillon brings a Bordeaux-like texture to this wine's honeycomb and baked quince flavors.

2002 Stags' Leap Viognier, Napa Valley ★★ $$
dry, medium-bodied, light oak, high acidity   drink now–6 years
Light peach and flower flavors are nice now, but give this a little age so the oak can deepen and enrich its flavors more.

2003 Estancia Pinot Grigio, California ★★ $
dry, medium-bodied, no oak, high acidity   drink now–3 years
Blimey, this is limey. Zingy, too.

2003 Frog's Leap Leapfrögmilch, Napa Valley ★★ $
off-dry, medium-bodied, no oak, high acidity   drink now–1 year
Few Napa Valley wines are as fun as this fruit-and-flower dance on the palate.

2002 Valley of the Moon Pinot Blanc, Sonoma County ★★ $
dry, full-bodied, no oak, high acidity   drink now–3 years
Lovely Pinot Blanc, with the soft flavors of ripe, slightly spiced pear and lemon.

2003 Fetzer Vineyards Echo Ridge Gewürztraminer, California ★ $
off-dry, medium-bodied, no oak, medium acidity   drink now–3 years
Fun, fruity, flowery wine.

2002 Peju Province Carnival French Colombard, California ★ $
off-dry, light-bodied, no oak, medium acidity   drink now
A blast from the past, French Colombard appears in this light, easy white.

WINES WE WISH WE HAD MORE ROOM FOR
2001 Cline Viognier, Sonoma County ★★★ $ dry, medium-bodied, light oak, high acidity, drink now–3 years; **2002 Iron Horse Vineyards T bar T Cuvée R, Alexander Valley** ★★ $$ dry, medium-bodied, no oak, high acidity, drink now–3 years; **2002 Gallo of Sonoma Reserve Pinot Gris, Sonoma Coast** ★★ $ dry, medium-bodied, light oak, high acidity, drink now–3 years; **2003 Handley Gewürztraminer, Anderson Valley** ★★ $ dry, medium-bodied, no oak, high acidity, drink now–6 years; **2003 Echelon Esperanza Vineyard Pinot Grigio, Clarksburg** ★ $ dry, medium-bodied, no oak, high acidity, drink now–2 years; **2002 R.H. Phillips EXP Viognier, Dunnigan Hills** ★ $ dry, medium-bodied, no oak, medium acidity, drink now–2 years; **NV Rosenblum Cellars Vintners Cuvee Blanc IV, California** ★ $ dry, medium-bodied, no oak, high acidity, drink now–2 years

rosé wines

Demeaned by associations with sugary, insipid White Zinfandel, California rosé wines have a hard time in the world. This is a shame, since there are several dozen excellent winemakers producing eminently enjoyable dry, spicy rosés from a number of different grapes.

at the table

A cool glass of rosé on a warm summer's night is an ideal way to start an evening, but you can bring it to the table, too. Dry rosés match a wide range of foods, from chicken to a Moroccan-spiced fish tagine, or even roast ham. Use it as a peacekeeper at restaurants when one person orders fish and another, meat.

the bottom line
White Zinfandel can be found for $6, but you'll do far better with rosés from other grape varieties for $8 to $15. The few that cost more are exceptional.

recommended wines

2003 SoloRosa, California ★★★ $$
dry, medium-bodied, high acidity drink now–1 year
A deep, bright rosé filled with cherry flavors, a hint of toast, and a flinty edge, from a winery dedicated solely to rosé.

2003 Frog's Leap Pink La Grenouille Rouganté,
Napa Valley ★★★ $
dry, medium-bodied, high acidity drink now–2 years
An embarrassment of tart cherry flavors.

2003 Iron Horse Vineyards T bar T Rosato di Sangiovese,
Alexander Valley ★★★ $
dry, medium-bodied, high acidity drink now–1 year
A cornucopia of peachy fruit, nut, and spice flavors.

2003 Bonny Doon Vineyard Vin Gris de Cigare, California ★★ $
dry, medium-bodied, medium acidity drink now–1 year
A parade of fresh flavors, with a trombone of strawberry, a piccolo of floral flavors, and a snare drum of citrus.

2003 Ojai Vineyard Vin du Soleil Rosé, California ★★ $
dry, medium-bodied, high acidity drink now–1 year
The southern California sun provides loads of mixed fruit flavors, earth, some almond, and spice, all very dry.

red wines

CABERNET & KIN

Though many of California's other wines can match its quality, Cabernet Sauvignon is the grape variety that secured the state's place among the world's greats. Once modeled after the elegant Cabernet-based wines of Bordeaux, California "Cab" has assumed its own identity: muscular in body, bulging with dark berry and earthy herbal flavors supported by firm tannin. Depending on where it's grown, Cabernet Sauvignon can take on different profiles: dense, with black fruit and smoke from mountain vineyards, or lusher, with more red and dusty mineral flavors from flatter areas. Not fully abandoning the Bordeaux ideal, many winemakers blend Cabernet Sauvignon with other

Bordeaux grapes like Merlot, Cabernet Franc, and Malbec, in the hopes of adding complexity to their wines. Unconcerned with meeting the minimum 75 percent threshold for labeling wines by single grape variety (see p. 24), these Bordeaux-blend wines frequently take the moniker *Meritage*, though some wineries prefer to use their own proprietary names like Mondavi's Opus One. These other Bordeaux varieties are also often bottled separately and labeled by variety. Peppery Cabernet Franc, in particular, is made into wines reminiscent of those from France's Loire Valley. You'll find recommended Bordeaux blends in the tasting section following this one, p. 44

at the table

A good word of advice for pairing wines with food: follow the locals. In steak houses around America, the preferred wine is California Cabernet, whose heavy tannin and juicy berry flavors cut right though the fat of a well-marbled sirloin. The match doesn't have to be steak, though: grilled or braised, any red meat sings with a glass of Cabernet Sauvignon, as does aged Cheddar. Enjoy Bordeaux blends in a similar manner. Lighter-bodied Cabernet Franc is a good choice with lamb chops rubbed with cracked pepper.

the bottom line
It"s possible to find some enjoyable Cabernets for around $10, but to have something truly distinctive, you'll need to pay $30 or more. Fifty dollars will bring you excellence; $100 or more, the sublime—though, scandalously, some $100-plus bottles still fall short.

what to buy CABERNET SAUVIGNON

1999	2000	2001	2002	2003
★★★	★★★	★★★★	★★★	★★★

recommended wines

2001 Arns, Napa Valley   ★★★★ $$$$
dry, full-bodied, heavy tannin, high acidity   **drink in 2–15 years**
Be ready to lose yourself in the soft perfume of violets and roses and the lushness of this wine's black fruit.

california cabernet sauvignon

**2000 Diamond Creek Vineyards Gravelly Meadow,
Napa Valley** ★ ★ ★ ★ $$$$
dry, full-bodied, heavy tannin, high acidity   **drink in 3–25 years**
Legendary wine, Diamond Creek Cabernet lives up to its repute with profound
flavors of cassis and stone. Try Volcanic Hill, too, for beautifully smoky mineral
notes backed with dark fruit.

2000 Peju Province Reserve, Rutherford ★ ★ ★ ★ $$$$
dry, full-bodied, heavy tannin, high acidity   **drink now–12 years**
Fascinating sage, bay, and lavender aromas mingle with juicy, delicious fruit.

2001 Miner, Oakville ★ ★ ★ ★ $$$
dry, full-bodied, heavy tannin, high acidity   **drink in 2–15 years**
A motherlode of cassis, coffee, and spice flavors.

2001 Caymus Vineyards, Napa Valley ★ ★ ★ $$$$
dry, full-bodied, heavy tannin, high acidity   **drink in 2–10 years**
One of the standards in Napa Cab, Caymus delivers ripe fruit flavors with a jolt
of coffee and oak.

2001 Far Niente, Oakville ★ ★ ★ $$$$
dry, full-bodied, heavy tannin, high acidity   **drink in 2–12 years**
A wine as complex as its detailed label, this is colorful, multitextured, and
wonderfully old-fashioned.

1999 Freemark Abbey Sycamore, Napa Valley ★ ★ ★ $$$$
dry, full-bodied, heavy tannin, high acidity   **drink in 2–15 years**
Lots of oak, espresso, and dried herb flavors enrich this wine's dark fruit.

2000 B.R. Cohn Olive Hill Estate Vineyards, Sonoma Valley ★ ★ ★ $$$
dry, medium-bodied, heavy tannin, high acidity   **drink now–10 years**
In a world of high-proof Cabernet, here's one that proves full flavor can be
found at lower alcohol levels.

2001 Clos Du Val, Napa Valley ★ ★ ★ $$$
dry, full-bodied, medium tannin, high acidity   **drink now–8 years**
A steak-house favorite, always elegant, always delicious, with just enough
fruit, spice, and tannin to make a steak sing.

2001 Flora Springs, Napa Valley ★ ★ ★ $$$
dry, medium-bodied, medium tannin, high acidity   **drink now–8 years**
A fount of fruit, flower, and mineral flavors with great finesse.

2001 Frog's Leap, Napa Valley ★ ★ ★ $$$
dry, full-bodied, heavy tannin, high acidity   **drink now–8 years**
Frog's Leap jumps over a higher bar this year, with concentrated fruit and herb
flavors firmed up with plenty of tannin.

**2001 Geyser Peak Winery Block Collection Kuimelis Vineyard,
Alexander Valley** ★★★ $$$
dry, full-bodied, medium tannin, high acidity **drink now–10 years**
Indulgent stuff, this Cabernet is rich with lush fruit and spicy tannin.

2000 Grgich Hills, Napa Valley ★★★ $$$
dry, full-bodied, heavy tannin, high acidity **drink now–15 years**
Mike Grgich's legacy of great Cabernet continues with wines like this,
superbly balanced between fruit and earth.

2001 Lolonis Winegrower Selection, Redwood Valley ★★★ $$$
dry, full-bodied, heavy tannin, high acidity **drink in 1–12 years**
Nature gone wild, with heavy berry, bramble, and spice flavors.

**2000 Louis M. Martini Monte Rosso Vineyard,
Sonoma Valley** ★★★ $$$
dry, full-bodied, medium tannin, high acidity **drink now–12 years**
Thick, juicy, dark fruit flavors and fine tannin from a great old California name.

**2001 Terra Valentine Wurtele Vineyard,
Spring Mountain District** ★★★ $$$
dry, full-bodied, heavy tannin, high acidity **drink in 3–15 years**
Give this a few years, and it will be so delicious you might leave your heart on
Spring Mountain.

2000 Trefethen, Napa Valley ★★★ $$$
dry, full-bodied, medium tannin, high acidity **drink now–8 years**
Gracious wine, with luxurious dark berry and bitter chocolate flavors.

**2001 Vita Nova Purisima Mountain Vineyard,
Santa Ynez Valley** ★★★ $$$
dry, full-bodied, heavy tannin, high acidity **drink in 2–15 years**
Known more for Rhône varieties than Cabernet, Purisima offers an earthy red
with profound Cabernet fruit. Terrific.

2002 Babcock, Central Coast ★★★ $$
dry, full-bodied, medium tannin, high acidity **drink now–5 years**
A lighter Cabernet, full of cherry fruit and light spice.

2001 Beaulieu Vineyard, Rutherford ★★★ $$
dry, full-bodied, heavy tannin, high acidity **drink now–8 years**
BV's Rutherford is classically constructed, with elegant fruit and mineral fla-
vors. Try the Georges De Latour for more of everything.

2001 Laurel Glen Counterpoint, Sonoma Mountain ★★★ $$
dry, full-bodied, medium tannin, high acidity **drink now–10 years**
Laurel Glen's second-tier wine oozes mixed fruit and mineral flavors.

california **cabernet sauvignon**

2000 Gallo of Sonoma Barrelli Creek Vineyard,
Alexander Valley ★★ $$$
dry, full-bodied, heavy tannin, high acidity drink now–8 years
With night-black fruit and smoky spice, this Cabernet is built for the long run.

2001 Hanna, Sonoma County ★★ $$$
dry, full-bodied, heavy tannin, high acidity drink now–8 years
Complex herb and spice notes give this fruity Cabernet extra personality.

2001 Sequoia Grove, Napa Valley ★★ $$$
dry, full-bodied, heavy tannin, high acidity drink now–8 years
Chunky Cabernet, this is chewy with cassis, cedar, and green pepper.

2001 Stonestreet, Alexander Valley ★★ $$$
dry, full-bodied, heavy tannin, high acidity drink in 1–10 years
Dense minerals infuse dark fruit and bitter chocolate flavors.

2001 Alexander Valley Vineyards Wetzel Family Estate,
Alexander Valley ★★ $$
dry, full-bodied, medium tannin, high acidity drink now–6 years
Solid Cabernet, chock full of peppery bramble-berry flavors and fine minerals.

2001 Clos du Bois Reserve, Alexander Valley ★★ $$
dry, full-bodied, medium tannin, high acidity drink now–5 years
Smooth berry and spice make everything nice.

2001 Clos LaChance, Napa Valley ★★ $$
dry, medium-bodied, heavy tannin, high acidity drink now–6 years
The hummingbird on the label indicates sweet nectar, but it seems this one's
after dry, dry spice and tart berry.

2001 Dynamite Vineyards, North Coast ★★ $$
dry, medium-bodied, medium tannin, high acidity drink now–3 years
Straight-on Cabernet, perfect for steaks or burgers on the grill.

2000 Kendall-Jackson Vintner's Reserve, California ★★ $$
dry, full-bodied, heavy tannin, high acidity drink now–6 years
Consistently solid, with juicy berry and slight green-pepper flavors that show
why K-J's Vintner's Reserve Cabernet is so popular.

2000 St. Supéry, Napa Valley ★★ $$
dry, full-bodied, heavy tannin, high acidity drink now–8 years
Classic Napa Cab: cassis, minerals, peppers, and hints of violet.

2001 Canyon Road, California ★★ $
dry, full-bodied, medium tannin, high acidity drink now–3 years
Light, enjoyable Cabernet Sauvignon, with tart berry and herbal flavors.

WORMY WINES

Splice the genes of a silkworm to Merlot and what do you get? Researchers in Florida are hoping to get the beginnings of a fine wine industry for their state. Grapevines are being genetically modified (GM) in the hopes of improving a vine's ability to withstand temperature extremes, disease, and pests. In Florida, a silkworm's genes might make wine grapes impervious to Pierce's disease—one factor that inhibits the growth of the Sunshine State's wine industry.

You might think Californians would welcome such research, but reactions have ranged from hopefulness to hostility. Critics have various worries: Might the genetic mutations spread to non-GM vines, eliminating genetic diversity? Could GM vines have unforeseen health problems? Will their resistance to disease and pests inspire stronger vectors? Opposition to GM vines reached a critical point in Mendocino, California, where a countywide initiative against GM agriculture was passed in March 2004. In France, a coalition of winemakers has called for a ten-year moratorium on GM organizations, and wine industries in Australia and New Zealand have issued statements against GM wines until they can be proved absolutely safe and acceptable to consumers.

Opposition or not, it might be some time before GM wines enter the market—though GM yeasts are already in use. Unfortunately, unless a wine is certified organic, there's no way to tell if it was made with GM yeasts or grapes—turning on its head the old adage, *In vino veritas.*

2000 Jekel Vineyards Winemaker's Collection, Central Coast ★ ★ $
dry, full-bodied, medium tannin, high acidity   **drink now–6 years**
Cabernet's herbal side, rounded out by ripe cassis notes.

2002 Esser Cellars, California ★ $
dry, full-bodied, medium tannin, medium acidity   **drink now–3 years**
Simple, clean berry flavors make for happy drinking.

WINES WE WISH WE HAD MORE ROOM FOR
2000 Dalla Valle Vineyards, Napa Valley ★ ★ ★ ★ $ $ $ $ dry, full-bodied, heavy tannin, high acidity, drink now–20 years; **2000 Altamura, Napa Valley** ★ ★ ★ $ $ $ $ dry, full-bodied, heavy tannin, high acidity, drink

in 2–15 years; **2001 Cakebread Cellars, Napa Valley** ★ ★ ★ $$$$ dry, full-bodied, heavy tannin, high acidity, drink in 1–12 years; **2000 Simi Reserve, Alexander Valley** ★ ★ ★ $$$$ dry, full-bodied, heavy tannin, high acidity, drink in 2–12 years; **2000 Sterling Vineyards Reserve, Napa Valley** ★ ★ ★ $$$$ dry, full-bodied, medium tannin, high acidity, drink now–10 years; **2001 Chappellet Signature, Napa Valley** ★ ★ ★ $$$ dry, full-bodied, heavy tannin, high acidity, drink in 1–10 years; **2000 Clos Du Val Oak Vineyard, Stags Leap District** ★ ★ ★ $$$ dry, full-bodied, heavy tannin, high acidity, drink in 2–15 years; **1999 Marcelina Vineyards, Napa Valley** ★ ★ ★ $$$ dry, full-bodied, heavy tannin, high acidity, drink now–8 years; **2001 Matanzas Creek Winery, Sonoma County** ★ ★ $$$ dry, full-bodied, medium tannin, high acidity, drink now–8 years; **2001 Benziger Family Winery, Sonoma County** ★ ★ $$ dry, full-bodied, heavy tannin, high acidity, drink in 1–8 years; **2001 Hess Select, California** ★ ★ $ dry, medium-bodied, medium tannin, high acidity, drink now–3 years; **2001 Beringer Founders' Estate, California** ★ $ dry, full-bodied, medium tannin, high acidity, drink now–2 years

recommended bordeaux blends

2000 Dalla Valle Vineyards Maya, Napa Valley ★ ★ ★ ★ $$$$
dry, full-bodied, heavy tannin, high acidity   drink now–20 years
If Maya were a watch, it would be Patek Philippe: perfectly calibrated, simple, and beautiful.

2000 Lail Vineyards J. Daniel Cuvée, Napa Valley ★ ★ ★ ★ $$$$
dry, full-bodied, medium tannin, high acidity   drink now–15 years
Charming but also substantial, this offers a harmony of soft berry, nuts, and light spice with smooth, silky tannin.

2001 Ridge Monte Bello, Santa Cruz Mountains ★ ★ ★ ★ $$$$
dry, full-bodied, heavy tannin, high acidity   drink in 2–25 years
Heaven in a glass, Monte Bello seduces with floral, cassis, plum, and pepper flavors and great minerality.

2000 Dominus, Napa Valley ★ ★ ★ $$$$
dry, full-bodied, heavy tannin, high acidity   drink now–15 years
The Bordeaux pedigree shows in this elegant, dark, peppery fruit.

2001 Flora Springs Trilogy, Napa Valley ★ ★ ★ $$$$
dry, full-bodied, heavy tannin, high acidity   drink in 2–15 years
Simply delicious, with layers of fruit, floral, spice, and mineral flavors.

2001 Joseph Phelps Insignia, Napa Valley ★ ★ ★ $$$$
dry, full-bodied, heavy tannin, high acidity **drink in 2–20 years**
Broad-shouldered, yet with great finesse, Insignia is like an all-star linebacker who studied ballet.

2000 Mount Veeder Winery Reserve, Napa Valley ★ ★ ★ $$$$
dry, full-bodied, medium tannin, high acidity **drink now–12 years**
Five Bordeaux varieties, all mountain-grown, make a Napa classic.

2000 Rudd Oakville Estate, Oakville ★ ★ ★ $$$$
dry, full-bodied, heavy tannin, high acidity **drink in 2–20 years**
Beautiful Napa wine, full of dark fruit, coffee, pepper, and fine mineral flavors.

2001 Clos du Bois Marlstone, Alexander Valley ★ ★ ★ $$$
dry, full-bodied, heavy tannin, high acidity **drink now–12 years**
A combination candy store, fruitmonger, and spice market, with great minerality to hold it all up.

2000 Geyser Peak Winery Reserve Alexandre Meritage, Alexander Valley ★ ★ ★ $$$
dry, full-bodied, medium tannin, high acidity **drink now–12 years**
Powerful and graceful, with dark berry fruit embroidered by violets and stones.

2000 Havens Bourriquot, Napa Valley ★ ★ ★ $$$
dry, full-bodied, heavy tannin, high acidity **drink now–12 years**
Spicy yet soft at once, this blend takes pepper from Cabernet Franc and adds it to Merlot's plush fruit. Delicious.

1999 J. Lohr Cuvée St. E, Paso Robles ★ ★ ★ $$$
dry, full-bodied, heavy tannin, high acidity **drink now–12 years**
An orientalist fantasy painted in two Cabernets plus Merlot, full of spice, mulberry, and tamarind flavors.

2001 Archipel, Sonoma County/Napa County ★ ★ $$$
dry, full-bodied, heavy tannin, high acidity **drink in 2–10 years**
Despite the sleek label, let this get dusty in the cellar for a while so the oak can melt into the dark berry and coffee flavors.

2000 Dry Creek Vineyard Meritage, Dry Creek Valley ★ ★ $$$
dry, full-bodied, heavy tannin, high acidity **drink now–8 years**
From the peppery school of Bordeaux blends, with dark fruit flavors to round things out.

2000 Valley of the Moon Cuvée de la Luna, Sonoma County ★ ★ $$
dry, full-bodied, medium tannin, high acidity **drink now–8 years**
Tart berry, herbs, high acidity, and lamblike meaty flavors make this Bordeaux blend beg for food.

MERLOT

Easy to love for its velvet texture, plummy flavors, and violet-scented charms, Merlot is in many ways a victim of its own success. In the late 1980s, word got out that Merlot was a softer alternative to the sometimes too tannic Cabernet and the public embraced it. To meet increasing demand, winegrowers planted it all over California—ignoring the fact that quality Merlot thrives in only certain conditions. Happily for them, much of the public hasn't noticed, but certain wine-savvy consumers—and their imitators—have unjustifiably turned their backs on what is surely one of the world's most noble grapes. Chosen correctly, Merlot can be as seductive as ever.

at the table

You can enjoy Merlot in much the same way as Cabernet, but its softer tannins make it a fine choice with many other foods. Try complex versions with roasted duck or a lamb stewed with dry fruit. Simpler Merlot makes a great picnic wine, perfect with burgers or cold cuts.

the bottom line

Take $10 as your bottom line for drinkable, everyday Merlot; $18 for anything really special. Certain exalted bottles cost $100 or more, but are rarely of much higher quality than those costing half the amount.

what to buy MERLOT

1999	2000	2001	2002	2003
★★★	★★★	★★★	★★	★★

recommended wines

1999 Beringer Private Reserve Bancroft Ranch, Howell Mountain ★★★ $$$$
dry, full-bodied, heavy tannin, high acidity drink in 2–10 years
Howell Mountain is tough to scale in youth. Let age soften this up, so the berry flavors have a chance against the wine's formidable minerality and tannin.

2000 Sterling Vineyards Three Palms, Napa Valley ★★★ $$$$
dry, full-bodied, medium tannin, high acidity drink now–8 years
A California Merlot with Bordeaux-like finesse, juicy yet subtle.

2000 Chalk Hill, Chalk Hill ★★★ $$$
dry, full-bodied, medium tannin, high acidity drink now–10 years
Beautifully balanced dark fruit flavors, profound minerals, and earthy herbal flavors make this Merlot a classic.

2001 Duckhorn Vineyards, Napa Valley ★★★ $$$
dry, full-bodied, heavy tannin, high acidity drink now–12 years
Every Duckhorn Merlot is delicious. Even its simplest cuvee has abundant fruit with demure lavender and pepper flavors.

2001 Michel-Schlumberger Benchland Wine,
Dry Creek Valley ★★★ $$$
dry, full-bodied, heavy tannin, high acidity drink now–10 years
This strikes a delicate balance between dark fruit and elegant minerals.

2001 Nickel & Nickel Suscol Ranch, Napa Valley ★★★ $$$
dry, full-bodied, heavy tannin, high acidity drink now–12 years
Graceful in every way, this Merlot's dark fruit and fine mineral flavors will live up to any elegant repast.

2001 Peju Province, Napa Valley ★★★ $$$
dry, full-bodied, medium tannin, high acidity drink now–8 years
Mediterranean-scented Merlot, this is full of herbs and flowers.

2000 Thomas Fogarty, Santa Cruz Mountains ★★★ $$$
dry, medium-bodied, medium tannin, high acidity drink now–8 years
Mountain minerality and violet aromas kick into strawberry fruit flavors for an impressive Merlot.

2000 Atalon, Napa Valley ★★★ $$
dry, full-bodied, heavy tannin, high acidity drink in 1–10 years
With time for the oak to melt into the dark berry and mineral flavors, this will bring great pleasure.

2000 Gloria Ferrer, Carneros ★★★ $$
dry, medium-bodied, medium tannin, high acidity drink now–6 years
Sparkling wine is the house specialty here, but Ferrer also makes a Merlot with seductive fresh fruit and plum-pudding flavors.

2001 Taz, Santa Barbara County ★★★ $$
dry, full-bodied, medium tannin, high acidity drink now–6 years
Lip-smacking, with ripe fruit, sweet oak, and spice.

2001 Cakebread Cellars, Napa Valley ★★ $$$
dry, full-bodied, heavy tannin, high acidity drink now–8 years
Stalwart Merlot, with polished blocks of dark fruit cemented with minerals.

california **merlot**

2001 Frog's Leap, Napa Valley ★★ $$$
dry, full-bodied, medium tannin, high acidity   **drink now–5 years**
Herbal flavors balance jammy, brambly fruit for a delicious Merlot.

2001 Kendall-Jackson Grande Reserve,
Mendocino/Sonoma/Napa Counties ★★ $$$
dry, medium-bodied, medium tannin, high acidity   **drink now–6 years**
A study in black cherries, berries, and plums, with a dark mineral underside.

2001 Alexander Valley Vineyards Wetzel Family Estate,
Alexander Valley ★★ $$
dry, full-bodied, medium tannin, high acidity   **drink now–6 years**
Deliciously juicy, this oozes berry and spice flavors with palate-cleansing acidity.

2000 Arrowood Grand Archer, Sonoma County ★★ $$
dry, medium-bodied, medium tannin, high acidity   **drink now–3 years**
The second-tier wine in Arrowood's quiver, Grand Archer's aim is dead on,
with clear berry flavors and pointed acidity.

2000 Benziger Family Winery, Sonoma County ★★ $$
dry, medium-bodied, medium tannin, high acidity   **drink now–3 years**
A bouquet of violet scents joined by dark fruit flavors makes this delightful.

2000 Havens, Napa Valley ★★ $$
dry, full-bodied, medium tannin, medium acidity   **drink now–5 years**
Like a dandy who was tossed in the mud, this has a certain elegance underneath all its earthiness.

2001 R.H. Phillips Toasted Head, California ★★ $$
dry, full-bodied, medium tannin, high acidity   **drink now–4 years**
Measured Merlot, this is made up of a handful of berries, a dash of spice, and
two shakes of tannin.

2001 J. Lohr Los Osos, Paso Robles ★★ $
dry, medium-bodied, medium tannin, medium acidity **drink now–3 years**
Los Osos isn't bearlike, but you could imagine that these wild nut and berry
flavors would please one.

2001 Beringer Founders' Estate, California ★ $
dry, medium-bodied, medium tannin, high acidity   **drink now–3 years**
Easy-to-drink cherry flavors make this a great by-the-glass pour.

WINES WE WISH WE HAD MORE ROOM FOR
2001 Provenance Vineyards, Carneros ★★★ $$$ dry, full-bodied,
medium tannin, high acidity, drink now–6 years; **2001 Stags' Leap Winery**
Reserve, Napa Valley ★★★ $$$ dry, full-bodied, medium tannin, high

acidity, drink now–8 years; **2001 Wild Horse, Paso Robles** ★ ★ ★ $$
dry, full-bodied, medium tannin, high acidity, drink now–3 years; **2001
Matanzas Creek Winery, Sonoma County** ★ ★ $$$$ dry, full-bodied,
medium tannin, high acidity, drink now–6 years; **2001 Chateau St. Jean,
Sonoma County** ★ ★ $$ dry, full-bodied, medium tannin, medium acidity,
drink now–6 years; **2001 Dynamite Vineyards, North Coast** ★ ★ $$
dry, full-bodied, medium tannin, high acidity, drink now–3 years; **2001
Lolonis, Redwood Valley** ★ ★ $$ dry, full-bodied, medium tannin, high
acidity, drink now–6 years; **2001 Seventh Moon, California** ★ ★ $ dry,
full-bodied, medium tannin, high acidity, drink now–3 years; **2001
Dunnewood Vineyards, Mendocino County** ★ $ dry, medium-bodied,
medium tannin, medium acidity, drink now–2 years

PINOT NOIR

Cabernet Sauvignon might have brought fame, but for many a
vintner Pinot Noir represents the Holy Grail. Difficult to grow well
even in its native Burgundy, California vintners have struggled
with the grape for decades. Grown in cooler parts of the state
like the Russian River Valley, Carneros, Santa Barbara, and
Mendocino, Pinot Noir can be divine—full of graceful cherry,
smoke, and spice flavors, echoing, if less subtly, its Burgundian
inspiration. Pinot Noir from warmer regions tends to be more
robust, sometimes a little clunky.

at the table

Pinot Noir is among the easiest wines to pair with food. It complements milder cuts of beef like tenderloin, a rosemary-laced
spring lamb, and duck. It's also a good choice with fish, especially when served with a mushroom or red wine sauce. The
leathery notes of an older Pinot Noir are just right for game.

the bottom line
A vintner's labors are costly, and
you'll pay for the difficulties of growing Pinot Noir. While there are
some passable examples for between $10 and $15, count on
spending $20 to $30 for ones that will grab your attention and
over $50 for the truly memorable.

what to buy PINOT NOIR

1999	2000	2001	2002	2003
★ ★	★ ★ ★	★ ★ ★	★ ★	★ ★

recommended wines

2001 Etude Heirloom, Carneros ★★★★ $$$$
dry, full-bodied, heavy tannin, high acidity   drink in 1–15 years
Full-bodied Pinot Noir sounds like an oxymoron, but this is big California Pinot done right: big fruit, big minerality, big future.

2001 Au Bon Climat Knox Alexander,
Santa Maria Valley ★★★★ $$$
dry, medium-bodied, medium tannin, high acidity   drink now–12 years
This has an elegance that comes purely from substance (though this is pretty stylin', too), with enchanting berry and floral flavors.

2000 Gloria Ferrer Rust Rock Terrace Vineyard,
Carneros ★★★★ $$$
dry, full-bodied, medium tannin, high acidity   drink now–12 years
Minerals and more: this beautiful Pinot Noir is as earthy as it is filled with ripe, sunshine-filled fruit. Try Ferrer's basic Carneros bottling for a more affordable yet delicious option.

2001 Goldeneye, Anderson Valley ★★★★ $$$
dry, full-bodied, medium tannin, high acidity   drink now–12 years
Bull's eye: this aims with confidence straight down the center with fine fruit, spice, mineral, and floral notes.

1994 Kalin Cellars Cuvee DD, Sonoma County ★★★★ $$$
dry, medium-bodied, medium tannin, high acidity   drink now–8 years
Given the time good Pinot deserves, this gorgeous Pinot Noir shows mature flavors of tawny cherry, mushroom, leather, and smoke.

2002 Acacia Field Blend Estate Vineyard,
Carneros District ★★★ $$$
dry, medium-bodied, heavy tannin, high acidity   drink now–8 years
Deeply flavored Pinot Noir, this is full of minerals, dark cherry, and bitter almond flavors without feeling heavy.

2001 Babcock Grand Cuvee, Santa Ynez Valley ★★★ $$$
dry, medium-bodied, medium tannin, high acidity   drink now–10 years
A silky smooth texture with fine berry and slightly wild, earthy notes makes for pure drinking pleasure.

2001 Belle Glos, Santa Maria Valley ★★★ $$$
dry, medium-bodied, medium tannin, high acidity   drink now–10 years
If Catherine Deneuve were a wine, she'd be this—graceful and elegant, but with a distant mystery.

2001 Clos Du Val Carneros Vineyard, Napa Valley ★ ★ ★ $$$
dry, medium-bodied, medium tannin, high acidity   drink now–12 years
Surprising for a wine in such a heavy bottle, this Pinot Noir offers a balletic
display of fruit, spice, and minerals: light and graceful.

2001 Cuvaison Estate Selection, Carneros ★ ★ ★ $$$
dry, medium-bodied, medium tannin, high acidity   drink now–8 years
Beautiful in color, velvety in texture, and succulent in its smoky fruit flavors.

2002 Ledson, Russian River ★ ★ ★ $$$
dry, full-bodied, medium tannin, high acidity   drink now–8 years
Thoroughly delicious, with lush cherry and cedarlike flavors.

2001 Morgan Double L Vineyard, Santa Lucia Highlands ★ ★ ★ $$$
dry, medium-bodied, medium tannin, high acidity   drink now–8 years
Double L for double luscious, with dark wild berry and tobacco flavors.

2002 Sea Smoke Southing, Santa Rita Hills ★ ★ ★ $$$
dry, full-bodied, medium tannin, high acidity   drink now–12 years
Indulgent Pinot, Sea Smoke's dark fruit and herb flavors roll across the palate
like a giant ocean swell.

2002 Testarossa Garys' Vineyard, Santa Lucia Highlands ★ ★ ★ $$$
dry, medium-bodied, medium tannin, high acidity   drink now–8 years
Pepper, light clove, and fennel flavors spice up a sea of cherry and orange fruit
in this light, exotic Pinot Noir.

2002 Cambria Julia's Vineyard, Santa Maria Valley ★ ★ ★ $$
dry, medium-bodied, medium tannin, high acidity   drink now–8 years
Bright, acidic orange peel and red berry flavors make for a Pinot Noir that
could be enjoyed at any time, from aperitif through to the cheese course.

2001 Hartford, Sonoma Coast ★ ★ ★ $$
dry, medium-bodied, medium tannin, high acidity   drink now–8 years
Earthy but elegant, this offers an abundance of smoky, tarlike flavors infused
with an equal measure of smooth berry fruit.

2000 Thomas Fogarty, Santa Cruz Mountains ★ ★ ★ $$
dry, medium-bodied, medium tannin, high acidity   drink now–6 years
It's coming up flowers in the Santa Cruz Mountains, with violets and cherry
blossoms mixed with fine fruit.

2001 Iron Horse Vineyards, Sonoma County/Green Valley ★ ★ $$$
dry, medium-bodied, medium tannin, high acidity   drink now–6 years
This starts out simple and quickly grows complex, adding intriguing herb and
spice flavors to its tart red berry fruit.

california **pinot noir**

2001 Landmark Kastania, Sonoma Coast ★★ $$$
dry, medium-bodied, medium tannin, high acidity   drink now–8 years
Like a double raspberry latte (but better), this is full of fruit and roasted coffee flavors in a creamy texture.

2002 ZD, Carneros ★★ $$$
dry, medium-bodied, medium tannin, high acidity   drink now–6 years
ZD's basic Pinot has spicy, minerally, refined cherry flavors; the Reserve soars.

2002 Beaulieu Vineyard, Carneros ★★ $$
dry, medium-bodied, medium tannin, high acidity   drink now–6 years
Classic Carneros, with vibrant cherry flavors and the finesse that comes from the area's cool climate.

2001 La Crema, Anderson Valley ★★ $$
dry, medium-bodied, medium tannin, high acidity   drink now–6 years
If you like your fruit spicy and smoky, La Crema's for you.

2001 Wild Horse, Central Coast ★★ $$
dry, medium-bodied, medium tannin, high acidity   drink now–3 years
Good, solid Pinot, full of vervy berry flavors and a little spice.

2001 Seventh Moon, California ★★ $
dry, medium-bodied, medium tannin, high acidity   drink now–3 years
Good quaffing Pinot—perfect for midweek baked salmon.

2001 Dunnewood Vineyards, Mendocino County ★ $
dry, light-bodied, medium tannin, high acidity   drink now–2 years
You'll have a hard time finding better Pinot Noir for less than ten bucks.

WINES WE WISH WE HAD MORE ROOM FOR
2001 Carpe Diem Firepeak Vineyard, Edna Valley ★★★ $$$ dry, medium-bodied, medium tannin, high acidity, drink now–10 years; **2001 Cheval Sauvage Bien Nacido Vineyard, Santa Maria Valley** ★★★ $$$ dry, medium-bodied, medium tannin, high acidity, drink now–10 years; **2000 LinCourt Vineyards, Santa Barbara County** ★★★ $$ dry, medium-bodied, medium tannin, high acidity, drink now–8 years; **2002 Alexander Valley Vineyards Wetzel Family Estate, Alexander Valley** ★★ $$ dry, medium-bodied, medium tannin, medium acidity, drink now–4 years; **2001 Anapamu, Monterey County** ★★ $$ dry, medium-bodied, medium tannin, high acidity, drink now–3 years; **2002 Beringer, Carneros** ★★ $$ dry, medium-bodied, medium tannin, high acidity, drink now–5 years; **2002 Orogeny, Sonoma County/Green Valley** ★★ $$ dry, full-bodied, medium tannin, high acidity, drink now–6 years; **2002 Kendall-Jackson Vintner's Reserve, California** ★ $ dry, medium-bodied, medium tannin, high acidity, drink now–3 years

SYRAH

Syrah, sometimes called Shiraz, is California's most ascendant grape. In the past ten years, Syrah plantings have increased 30-fold with no end in sight. The basis of the famed smoky reds of France's northern Rhône Valley—Hermitage, Cornas, and Côte-Rôtie—Syrah thrives throughout California, at home in both the cooler and warmer reaches of the state. California vintners take one of two paths with Syrah: French or Australian. French-styled Syrah is generally full-bodied though demure, with smoky wild berry and spice flavors. Aussie-styled Shiraz is full-bodied and rambunctious, screaming with dark fruit and spice.

at the table

Whichever style you choose, Syrah/Shiraz is great with hearty braised meats like short ribs, brisket, and lamb shanks. Thicker, sweeter sauces benefit from the stronger flavors of an Australia-style Shiraz; lighter dishes like mushroom lasagna or roast duck breast might find a better match with the lighter flavors of Syrah. Anyone will adore it with aged Gouda.

the bottom line

Happy news: with more Syrah in the market, average prices for the wine have fallen. Made for popular consumption, California "Shiraz" sells for $8 to $13, or slightly more in a few cases. Syrah starts around $10, but the sweet spot for high quality and reasonable price is between $15 and $25. Syrah in the $35 to $50 range is normally superb—though for that price you might also look in the French aisle.

what to buy SYRAH

1999	2000	2001	2002	2003
★★	★★★	★★★	★★★★	★★★

recommended wines

**2001 Edmunds St. John Bassetti Vineyard,
San Luis Obispo County** ★★★★ $$$
dry, full-bodied, medium tannin, high acidity **drink now–10 years**
This Syrah is so laden with fruit and minerals that it's hard to resist now, but wait if you can, because it has an incredible future ahead of it.

california **syrah**

2001 Arrowood, Sonoma County ★★★★ $$
dry, full-bodied, heavy tannin, high acidity drink now–12 years
Fine Syrah, reminiscent of France's Cornas, with dark, gamey fruit, floral notes, and profound mineral flavors.

2001 Austin Hope, Paso Robles ★★★ $$$
dry, full-bodied, heavy tannin, high acidity drink in 1–10 years
Toasty and smoky, this espresso-thick Syrah will certainly awaken any palate.

2001 Babcock Black Label Cuvee, Santa Barbara County ★★★ $$$
dry, full-bodied, heavy tannin, high acidity drink now–10 years
Black is beautiful in this Syrah, dark with black cherry, mineral, and spice.

2001 Beckmen Vineyards Purisima Mountain Vineyard, Santa Ynez Valley ★★★ $$$
dry, full-bodied, medium tannin, high acidity drink now–10 years
Definitive California Syrah: powerful dark fruit with a smoky, tarry edge.

2000 Havens Hudson Vineyard, Carneros ★★★ $$$
dry, full-bodied, heavy tannin, high acidity drink now–12 years
Minerals, game, and smoke mix beautifully with spiced blackberry flavors.

2001 Geyser Peak Winery Shiraz, Sonoma County ★★★ $$
dry, full-bodied, heavy tannin, high acidity drink now–8 years
An Aussie's clearly behind this wine, full, rich, and spicy with Shiraz's dark fruit.

2001 Martella Hammer, California ★★★ $$
dry, full-bodied, heavy tannin, high acidity drink now–12 years
Indulgent wine, this Syrah's perfumed, plush, dark fruit is irresistible.

2002 Qupé Bien Nacido Vineyard, Santa Maria Valley ★★★ $$
dry, full-bodied, medium tannin, high acidity drink now–10 years
Bien Nacido provides the backdrop, Robert Lindquist the masterful winemaking in this elegant, fruit- and earth-laden wine.

2001 Jepson, Mendocino ★★ $$
dry, full-bodied, medium tannin, high acidity drink now–6 years
Dry mixed berry flavors seem infused by wildflower honey. Charming wine.

2001 Morgan, Monterey ★★ $$
dry, full-bodied, medium tannin, high acidity drink now–6 years
Solid Syrah, with all the requisite flavors of earth and fruit.

2002 Rosenblum Cellars Abba Vineyard, Lodi ★★ $$
dry, full-bodied, heavy tannin, high acidity drink now–8 years
This Syrah is exceptionally floral, but lacks none of the grape's plummy fruit and mineral edge.

2002 Edna Valley Vineyard Paragon, Central Coast ★ ★ $
dry, full-bodied, medium tannin, high acidity   **drink now–6 years**
Juicy, dark fruit with a drop of smoke, great with barbecue ribs.

2002 Sterling Vintner's Collection Shiraz, Central Coast ★ ★ $
dry, full-bodied, medium tannin, medium acidity   **drink now–3 years**
Just pure, juicy fruit.

2001 Fetzer Vineyards Valley Oaks, California ★ $
dry, medium-bodied, medium tannin, high acidity   **drink now–2 years**
Light, smoky Syrah flavors for a low price.

ZINFANDEL

Zinfandel is the quintessential California grape. Though descended from an obscure Croatian grape and cousin to southern Italy's Primitivo, Zinfandel rarely appears outside California, and nowhere does it express the same bold personality. Don't be misled by the insipid pink form known as White Zinfandel: Zinfandel is a red grape with intense purple color and explosive mixed berry and spice flavors. Some vintners exploit the grape's tendency toward super-ripeness and make wines with impossibly rich flavors and dizzying levels of alcohol (if it's 15 percent or higher, beware). Others treat the grape more gently, making gracefully balanced, flavorful wines that can fill in for any claret. Long a part of California's wine industry, patches of "old-vine" Zinfandel are found around the state. While the term "old vines" has no legal definition, some of the vines exceed eighty years in age and produce wines of unique intensity.

at the table

Simple, zesty Zins are great companions for Italian-American classics like eggplant parmesan or baked manicotti. More complex wines—though not alcoholic monsters—are wonderful with double-cut pork chops or veal saltimbocca. As American as wine can be, they're also a great choice for Thanksgiving birds. Heavy, high-octane Zins need rich foods like osso buco or a chunk of Stilton cheese.

the bottom line
Eight to eleven dollars will buy simple Zinfandel. Things can get more interesting at $15 to $30; above that, you can find exceptional, small-production wines.

california **zinfandel**

what to buy ZINFANDEL

1999	2000	2001	2002	2003
★★	★★	★★★	★★★	★★★

recommended wines

**1999 Haywood Estate Rocky Terrace Los Chamizal Vineyard,
Sonoma Valley** ★★★★ $$$
dry, full-bodied, heavy tannin, high acidity drink now–12 years
Fascinating Zinfandel, the "Rocky Terrace" shows in smoky, stony flavors that
infuse the wine's pomegranate and mulberry fruit.

2002 Ridge Lytton Springs, Dry Creek Valley ★★★★ $$$
dry, full-bodied, heavy tannin, high acidity drink now–15 years
More robust than in years past, with piquant berry and loads of minerals.

2002 Cline Ancient Vines, California ★★★★ $$
dry, full-bodied, heavy tannin, high acidity drink now–12 years
A spice bazaar in a glass, with intensely gamey, minerally flavors.

2001 Clos Du Val Reserve, Stags Leap District ★★★ $$$$
dry, full-bodied, heavy tannin, high acidity drink now–12 years
Heavy-duty Zinfandel, weighted down by tobacco, minerals, and dense black-
berry flavors, this was designed for aging—or double-thick steaks.

2001 Fife Dalraddy Vineyard, Chiles Valley ★★★ $$$
dry, full-bodied, heavy tannin, high acidity drink now–10 years
Rad Zin, full of wild, spicy fruit and tons of stones.

**2001 Kunde Estate Century Vines Shaw Vineyard,
Sonoma Valley** ★★★ $$$
dry, full-bodied, heavy tannin, high acidity drink now–12 years
Super stuff: those century-old roots pull a treasure of minerals out of the
earth—a perfect complement to the luscious berry fruit.

2001 Lolonis Winegrower Selection, Redwood Valley ★★★ $$$
dry, full-bodied, heavy tannin, high acidity drink now–10 years
These mixed fruit and sweet spice flavors can provide all your holiday cheer.

**2001 Murphy-Goode Ellis Ranch Snake Eyes,
Alexander Valley** ★★★ $$$
dry, full-bodied, heavy tannin, high acidity drink now–6 years
Fruits and nuts rolled together make a delicious wine.

2001 Rancho Zabaco Stefani Vineyard,
Dry Creek Valley ★★★ $$$
dry, full-bodied, medium tannin, high acidity   drink now–6 years
This is rich in full-on crushed berry flavors, yet its lively acidity keeps it graceful.

2002 Rosenblum Cellars Monte Rosso Vineyard,
Sonoma Valley ★★★ $$$
off-dry, full-bodied, medium tannin, medium acidity   drink now–12 years
Big Zinfandel, this offers such thick, perfumed berry flavors it feels like Port.

2001 Alderbrook OVOC, Dry Creek Valley ★★★ $$
dry, full-bodied, medium tannin, high acidity   drink now–8 years
Old vines, old clones (OVOC) lead to loads of wild berry and spice flavors.

2001 Fife Redhead Vineyard, Redwood Valley ★★★ $$
dry, full-bodied, medium tannin, high acidity   drink now–10 years
Lovely wine, with soft *dulce de leche* flavors wrapped around berry fruit.

2002 Rosenblum Cellars Planchon Vineyard,
San Francisco Bay ★★★ $$
dry, full-bodied, heavy tannin, high acidity   drink now–10 years
Smoky, rich Zinfandel from one of the great names in Zinfandel, perfect for smoked brisket or ribs.

2002 Trinitas Old Vine, Contra Costa County ★★★ $$
dry, full-bodied, heavy tannin, high acidity   drink now–6 years
Ninety-year-old vines give a Zinfandel with lively dark berry flavors and peppery wit. Try the Russian River bottling, too.

2001 Clos LaChance Twin Rivers Vineyard, El Dorado County ★★ $$
dry, full-bodied, medium tannin, high acidity   drink now–5 years
Nuggets of mineral flavors stud this Zinfandel's fresh, sweet cherry flavors—a delicious combination.

2000 Mazzocco, Dry Creek Valley ★★ $$
dry, medium-bodied, medium tannin, high acidity   drink now–6 years
Floral, spicy wild berry flavors give this Zinfandel an Italianate twist; use it to fill in for any Chianti.

2001 Beaulieu Vineyard, Napa Valley ★★ $
dry, full-bodied, medium tannin, high acidity   drink now–3 years
A classic name in California winemaking makes a classic California Zin.

2001 Beringer, Clear Lake ★★ $
dry, medium-bodied, medium tannin, high acidity   drink now–3 years
Clear Lake gives a Zin of elegance, with tart red fruit and smoky minerals.

2001 Foppiano Vineyards, Dry Creek Valley ★ ★ $

dry, full-bodied, heavy tannin, high acidity drink now–3 years

A tasty muddle of berry and sweet spice flavors, this would be great for a mid-week stew.

2001 Hayman & Hill Reserve Selection, Dry Creek Valley ★ ★ $

dry, full-bodied, medium tannin, high acidity drink now–3 years

Just delicious Zinfandel, Hayman & Hill's Reserve Selection scores with pure berry fruit flavors.

2001 Ravenswood, Lodi ★ ★ $

dry, full-bodied, medium tannin, high acidity drink now–3 years

A big name in Zin makes a big wine, with intensely ripe fruit edged in herbs.

2001 Wild Horse, Paso Robles ★ ★ $

dry, medium-bodied, medium tannin, high acidity drink now–4 years

Light and juicy cherry flavors gallop across the palate.

2002 Cline, California ★ $

dry, full-bodied, medium tannin, high acidity drink now–2 years

Tasty, toasty, and juicy fruit flavors make it easy to see why this affordable Zinfandel is so popular.

2001 Seventh Moon, California ★ $

dry, medium-bodied, medium tannin, high acidity drink now–2 years

Simple, Beaujolais-like Zin, this has the bright, easy-drinking cherry fruit flavors and light weight to make it appropriate for any sort of simple occasion.

WINES WE WISH WE HAD MORE ROOM FOR

2002 Ridge Geyserville, Sonoma County ★ ★ ★ $$$ dry, full-bodied, heavy tannin, high acidity, drink now–15 years; **2001 Carmenet Evangelho Vineyard, Contra Costa County** ★ ★ ★ $$ dry, full-bodied, medium tannin, high acidity, drink now–8 years; **2000 Haywood Estate Los Chamizal Vineyard, Sonoma Valley** ★ ★ ★ $$ dry, medium-bodied, medium tannin, high acidity, drink now–6 years; **2000 Ravenswood, Napa Valley** ★ ★ ★ $$ dry, full-bodied, medium tannin, high acidity, drink now–8 years; **2002 Frog's Leap, Napa Valley** ★ ★ $$ dry, full-bodied, medium tannin, high acidity, drink now–4 years; **2002 Handley, Redwood Valley** ★ ★ $$ dry, full-bodied, medium tannin, high acidity, drink now–3 years; **2001 Dry Creek Vineyard Heritage Clone, Sonoma County** ★ ★ $ dry, full-bodied, medium tannin, high acidity, drink now–3 years; **2001 Woodbridge by Robert Mondavi Fish Net Creek Old Vine, Lodi** ★ ★ $ dry, full-bodied, medium tannin, high acidity, drink now–3 years; **2001 Canyon Road, California** ★ $ dry, medium-bodied, heavy tannin, high acidity, drink now–2 years; **2002 Rancho Zabaco Dancing Bull, California** ★ $ dry, full-bodied, medium tannin, high acidity, drink now–2 years

OTHER RED WINES

California's Mediterranean climate attracted legions of Italian and other southern European settlers, many of whom brought with them a thirst for wine and the vines that could quench it. As a result, Italian grapes like Sangiovese, Dolcetto, and Barbera, and southern French grapes like Grenache, Mourvèdre, Carignane, and Petite Sirah were widely planted, sometimes separately, sometimes all mixed together. These were largely ignored until the 1980s, when some winemakers noticed that California resembled the Rhône Valley more than Burgundy or Bordeaux. Dubbed the Rhône Rangers, they started making wines from Mediterranean varieties they found and planting those they couldn't. With bright fruit and earthy herb flavors, these wines seemed the perfect match for an emerging "California cuisine" that favored fresh, local ingredients over all else. Despite much talk, Cal-Ital varieties have yet to come into their own, though they are still responsible for some fine wines.

FUELED BY ZIN

It might not be too long before bumper stickers that read "Fueled by Zinfandel" will not be an invitation to get pulled over for a DUI, but a sign of a fuel-efficient car. Research shows that grapeseed oil added to gasoline can boost an engine's performance by about 8 percent. Vintners have long looked for useful ways to use every part of the grape: the skins and stems left over after fermentation are often distilled into grappa or marc, or used as mulch in the vineyard. In a slightly more upmarket application, some spas are offering grape-skin baths, on the premise that the skin's antioxidant properties are a tonic against aging. And while you might not want to fill your tank with grapeseed oil until a few more studies are completed, you do want to cook with it. Grapeseed oil can withstand higher temperatures than olive oil, has similar cholesterol-lowering properties, and is high in antioxidants. So far, grapeseed oil tends to be pricey in the U.S., but with more market development it may well become as common a cooking oil on this side of the Atlantic as it is in France.

california **other reds**

at the table

Simple, inexpensive Barbera, Dolcetto, and Sangiovese will enliven simple dishes like spaghetti with red sauce, meatloaf, or even chili (but not three-alarm recipes). More complex versions are good with veal chops or wild mushroom pastas. Grenache and Carignane will deliciously wash down grilled lamb sausages or garlic-and-herb-marinated chicken. Heavier in tannin and body, Mourvèdre and Petite Sirah have the power to cut through braised oxtails or thick rib-eye steaks.

the bottom line Rhône-style blends are bargains at $9 to $13; more serious versions climb to $40. Most single-variety Grenache, Barbera, Mourvèdre, and Petite Sirah cost $15 to $25. You'll find good Sangiovese for $18 to $40.

recommended wines

2002 Rosenblum Cellars Pickett Road Petite Sirah, Napa Valley ★★★★ $$
dry, full-bodied, heavy tannin, high acidity   drink now–12 years
Century-old vines give a vibrant, earthy Petite Sirah, loaded with dark minerals and dry, peppery spice.

2000 Lolonis Heritage Vineyards Petros, Redwood Valley ★★★ $$$$
dry, full-bodied, heavy tannin, high acidity   drink now–12 years
You'd expect stoniness from a wine named Petros, but this adds an ambrosial mix of fruit, mineral, and spice.

2000 Altamura Sangiovese, Napa Valley ★★★ $$$
dry, full-bodied, medium tannin, high acidity   drink now–8 years
Cal-Ital at its best, this Sangiovese shows the vibrancy of a good Chianti.

2000 Murphy-Goode Murphy Ranch Petit Verdot, Alexander Valley ★★★ $$$
dry, full-bodied, medium tannin, high acidity   drink now–12 years
The purple berry flavors of this Petit Verdot go as deep as its intense color.

2000 Stags' Leap Ne Cede Malis Reserve, Napa Valley ★★★ $$$
dry, full-bodied, heavy tannin, high acidity   drink now–8 years
Seven Rhône varieties create a diabolic brew of wild berry, scrub, and animal flavors with a dash of charcoal. Impressive.

2001 Treana, Central Coast ★★★ $$$
dry, full-bodied, medium tannin, high acidity   **drink now–12 years**
Cabernet, Merlot, and Syrah are rolled together for one lovely wine, velvety smooth and full of mixed berry and light pepper flavors.

2002 Trinitas Petite Sirah, Russian River Valley ★★★ $$$
dry, full-bodied, heavy tannin, high acidity   **drink now–10 years**
There's nothing diminutive about this Petite Sirah's explosive flavors of black berry, floral notes, and minerals.

2001 Beaulieu Vineyard Beauzeaux, Napa Valley ★★★ $$
dry, full-bodied, medium tannin, high acidity   **drink now–5 years**
Pronounced "bozo," this jumble of unique grape varieties makes fun drinking.

2000 Bedford Thompson Thompson Vineyard Grenache, Santa Barbara County ★★★ $$
dry, medium-bodied, medium tannin, high acidity   **drink now–6 years**
Earthy and smoky Grenache, with delicious red fruit.

2002 Cline Ancient Vines Mourvèdre, Contra Costa County ★★★ $$
dry, full-bodied, medium tannin, high acidity   **drink now–8 years**
A taste of Provence *profonde* in a glass, full of wild herb, meaty fruit, and lamb flavors, plus bright sunshine.

2000 Fife Redhead Carignane, Redwood Valley ★★★ $$
dry, medium-bodied, medium tannin, high acidity   **drink now–6 years**
Earthy and appealing, this is one of California's best Carignane wines.

2002 Qupé Purisima Mountain Vineyard Grenache, Santa Ynez Valley ★★★ $$
dry, medium-bodied, medium tannin, high acidity   **drink now–6 years**
Glorious Grenache, this has all the red cherry, dry spice, and mineral flavors you'd expect from the grape.

2001 Tablas Creek Vineyard Côtes de Tablas, Paso Robles ★★★ $$
dry, medium-bodied, medium tannin, high acidity   **drink now–6 years**
California's Central Coast becomes *Côte Centrale* in this cherry- and herb-scented wine from France's Perrin family. Give it time to breathe.

2001 Clos du Bois Reserve Tempranillo, Alexander Valley ★★ $$
dry, medium-bodied, heavy tannin, high acidity   **drink now–3 years**
This rare California Tempranillo has much of the bright fruit and spice of the Spanish original.

FOOD & WINE MAGAZINE AWARDS 2004

Just as Hollywood has its Oscars, American vintners have the FOOD & WINE Magazine American Wine Awards. In spring 2004, FOOD & WINE editors polled wine writers, sommeliers, and past award winners to nominate the year's outstanding wines, as well as the best vintner, new winery, new wine shop, and importer. The winners in the latter categories are:

Winemaker of the Year JOHN KONGSGAARD

For a quarter of a century, wine maestro John Kongsgaard has conducted one landmark winery after another: Newton, Harrison, Livingston-Moffett, Stony Hill, and Luna, playing works from Chardonnay to Sangiovese. Today, he leads Arietta, producing two harmonious Bordeaux blends, and Kongsgaard, for masterful Chardonnay and Syrah. He also directs Chamber Music in Napa Valley.

Most Promising New Winery COPAIN CELLARS

Since 1999, California winemaker Wells Guthrie has been applying experience gained at M. Chapoutier in France's Rhône Valley to Rhône grape varieties grown in the U.S. Specialties include a smoky, spicy Syrah that has been likened to Hermitage. Pinot Noir and Zin are great, too.

Best New Wine Shop FERRY PLAZA WINE MERCHANT

Smack in the middle of San Francisco's Ferry Building Marketplace, amidst the dazzling array of food purveyors, Ferry Plaza Wine Merchant offers small-production wines from California cults to obscure Spaniards. Taste before you buy at the wine bar, or gather some lunch and enjoy your bottle on the spot for a low $6 corkage fee.

Best Wine Importer/Distributor LAUBER IMPORTS

For twenty-five years, Lauber Imports has provided the New York tri-state area with vinous treasures large and small, from Ravenswood Zins to Kistler Chardonnays. Its greatest strength, however, may be bringing to market the stunning wines of outstanding importers like Cape Classics, Classical Wines, Dreyfus Ashby, and Vin Divino. For a complete listing of the 2004 American Wine Awards, visit www.foodandwine.com.

2001 Foppiano Vineyards Sangiovese,
Alexander Valley ★ ★ $$
dry, medium-bodied, medium tannin, high acidity   drink now–3 years
Delicious and easy to drink, this Sangiovese has zingy berry and spice flavors
that would be great with sausage and peppers.

2000 Gallo of Sonoma Barrelli Creek Vineyard Barbera,
Alexander Valley ★ ★ $$
dry, full-bodied, medium tannin, high acidity   drink now–3 years
Savory wine, this Barbera offers roasted meat flavors mixed with dark, juicy
fruit, a good combination to have with pasta in a beef ragú.

2002 Jade Mountain La Provençale, California ★ ★ $$
dry, medium-bodied, medium tannin, high acidity   drink now–5 years
A juicy Mediterranean blend that cries for lamb braised with white beans.

2001 Kempton Clark Petite Sirah, Dunnigan Hills ★ ★ $
dry, full-bodied, medium tannin, high acidity   drink now–3 years
For $10, this Petite Sirah packs a punch.

WINES WE WISH WE HAD MORE ROOM FOR
2001 Stags' Leap Petite Sirah, Napa Valley ★ ★ ★ $$$ dry, full-
bodied, heavy tannin, high acidity, drink now–10 years; **2000 Bedford
Thompson Thompson Vineyard Mourvèdre, Santa Barbara County**
★ ★ ★ $$ dry, medium-bodied, medium tannin, high acidity, drink now–5
years; **2000 Fife L'Attitude 39, Mendocino** ★ ★ ★ $$ dry, full-bodied,
heavy tannin, high acidity, drink now–10 years; **2001 Joseph Phelps Le
Mistral, Monterey County** ★ ★ $$ dry, full-bodied, medium tannin, high
acidity, drink now–8 years; **2001 Westside Red Garnet, Paso Robles**
★ ★ $$ dry, full-bodied, medium tannin, high acidity, drink now–4 years;
2002 Beckmen Vineyards Cuvée Le Bec, Santa Ynez Valley ★ ★ $
dry, medium-bodied, medium tannin, high acidity, drink now–3 years

pacific northwest

Washington and Oregon now number second and fourth respectively in the list of America's top wine-producing states—and second to none in quality. Pacific Northwest winegrowers are putting out some of the best Syrah, Merlot, and Pinot Noir in the U.S., and some excellent white wines, too.

oregon

Generally cool and often rainy, Oregon is not an obvious place to look for fine wine. But the Beaver State' grows some of the best, most elegant Pinot Noir in the U.S., especially in the cool, damp Willamette Valley. The warmer and drier Rogue and Umpqua Valleys in the state's southern half and, in the northeast, the Columbia and Walla Walla Valleys (shared with Washington State) claim some excellent Bordeaux-style wines, too. In every region, the last few years have been unusually warm, ripening grapes to levels previously unknown, and the wines are better than ever.

on the label

As in California, Oregon's vintners normally label their wines by grape variety. However, in most cases, Oregon requires varietally labelled wines to contain at least 90 percent of the named grape variety rather than the federally mandated 75 percent. The exception is Bordeaux varieties like Cabernet Sauvignon and Merlot, which may be blended with up to 25 percent other Bordeaux varieties and still take a varietal label. As in California, the term Reserve is not defined by law, but Oregon's wineries normally use it for wines they consider superior to their normal bottlings.

Featured Wine-Growing Regions

Washington

• SEATTLE

SPOKANE •

• OLYMPIA

Columbia Valley

Yakima Valley — Red Mountain

Columbia River

Walla Walla Valley

• PORTLAND

— Yamhill Valley

• SALEM

Willamette Valley

• EUGENE

Oregon

Umpqua Valley

Rogue Valley

white wines

With the high praise given to Oregon's Pinot Noir, it's no surprise that its winemakers put faith in other Pinot grapes as well. Much enthusiasm is showered on Pinot Gris and Pinot Blanc, the former for its waxy pear, orange peel, and almond flavors, the latter for its crisp citrus and apple notes. Ever-popular Chardonnay is still the most widely planted grape here. From the right clone (see p. 67), Oregon winemakers produce a Chardonnay closer to the citrusy, mineral-laden whites of Burgundy than to California's luscious tropical Chards. Riesling, Gewürztraminer, and Müller-Thurgau, which range between dry and off-dry, do well in the state, too, but they are losing ground to the Pinots.

at the table

With both appetite-whetting high acidity and palate-tickling minerality, Oregon's white wines match well with a wide range of dishes, from fish to chicken to turkey. Enjoy Pinot Blanc with trout or perch. Richer Pinot Gris—sometimes a touch off-dry—is beautiful with lobster or Southeast Asian fish dishes, especially those with a slightly sweet edge. Chardonnay is wonderful with halibut or Cornish game hens. Pull Riesling or Gewürztraminer out for spicy Asian or Creole dishes. Müller-Thurgau makes a fine aperitif.

the bottom line Compared to California's, Oregon's whites are a bargain. Few Chardonnays cost more than $30; most are in the $13 to $22 range. Pinot Blanc usually runs less than $15, and Pinot Gris hovers between $12 and $25, making it a good buy compared to many of Alsace's versions. Many Rieslings, Gewürztraminers, and Müller-Thurgaus barely scratch $10, though a few exceptional bottlings reach $15 or higher.

recommended wines

2001 Domaine Serene Clos du Soleil Vineyard
Dijon Clone Chardonnay, Willamette Valley ★★★★ $$$
dry, medium-bodied, medium oak, high acidity   **drink now–12 years**
Citrus and smoky oak flavors would be enough to love, but the minerals in here make this Chardonnay glisten.

2000 The Eyrie Vineyards Reserve Chardonnay,
Willamette Valley ★★★★ $$
dry, medium-bodied, light oak, high acidity   **drink now–10 years**
A few years of age yields a mélange of fruit confit flavors with a snappy, fresh-cut-apple edge.

2003 Adelsheim Vineyard Pinot Gris, Oregon ★★★ $$
dry, medium-bodied, no oak, high acidity   **drink now–6 years**
Pinot Gris is rarely expressed with such vibrant tones in Oregon, with spicy pear and tangy tropical fruit flavors.

2002 Adelsheim Vineyard Tocai Friulano,
Willamette Valley ★★★ $$
dry, full-bodied, no oak, medium acidity   **drink now–3 years**
This northern Italian grape shows its worth with spicy exotic fruit and almonds.

DIJON CLONES

Is a cabal of mad Oregon winemakers crossbreeding Chardonnay with Dijon mustard? You might think so from all the labels announcing "Dijon clones." However, when it comes to wine, a clone has little to do with the genetic engineering that went into creating Dolly the sheep—it just refers to a select cutting from a vine. When a vintner finds a vine that produces grapes of a special character, all he has to do is take a cutting from it and graft it onto rootstock. In the case of Chardonnay, the clones typically used in California didn't perform well in Oregon's cooler climate, and so many vintners sought out clones imported from a nursery in Dijon, Burgundy; thus, "Dijon clones."

2002 Anne Amie Hawks View Vineyard Pinot Gris, Willamette Valley ★★★ $$
dry, full-bodied, light oak, high acidity   drink now–8 years
The heavy bottle can barely contain this wine's seductive spiced fruit flavors.

2002 Chehalem Reserve Pinot Gris, Willamette Valley ★★★ $$
dry, full-bodied, light oak, high acidity   drink now–12 years
Luscious Pinot Gris, with indulgent spice, autumn fruit, and herb flavors.

2002 Domaine Drouhin Arthur Chardonnay, Oregon ★★★ $$
dry, medium-bodied, light oak, high acidity   drink now–10 years
A delicious explosion of apples, pears, and juicy citrus.

2002 Adelsheim Vineyard Chardonnay, Oregon ★★ $$
dry, medium-bodied, light oak, high acidity   drink now–3 years
This is buttery and tropical, yet mineral flavors keep it elegant.

2002 Amity Vineyards Dry Gewürztraminer, Oregon ★★ $
dry, medium-bodied, no oak, high acidity   drink now–3 years
Friendly wine, this Gewürz invites a taste with floral scents and spicy citrus.

2003 Bethel Heights Vineyard Estate Grown Pinot Blanc, Willamette Valley ★★ $
dry, medium-bodied, no oak, high acidity   drink now–3 years
A nice alternative to Chardonnay, this offers soft pear and lemon flavors.

2002 Foris Vineyards Winery Pinot Blanc, Rogue Valley ★★ $
dry, medium-bodied, no oak, high acidity   drink now–3 years
Whimsical wine, this skips between light pear, lemon chiffon, and soft spice.

2002 Oak Knoll Pinot Gris, Willamette Valley ★★ $
dry, medium-bodied, light oak, high acidity   drink now–3 years
Hazelnut tones add delicious richness to this Pinot Gris' baked apple flavors.

2002 The Eyrie Vineyards Pinot Blanc, Oregon ★★ $
dry, light-bodied, no oak, high acidity   drink now–3 years
Light lime and Granny Smith apple flavors add zip in a sea of minerals.

WINES WE WISH WE HAD MORE ROOM FOR
2001 Domaine Serene Etoile Vineyard Dijon Clones Chardonnay, Willamette Valley ★★★★ $$$ dry, medium-bodied, medium oak, high acidity, drink now–12 years; **2003 Amity Vineyards Wedding Dance Riesling, Willamette Valley** ★★ $ off-dry, medium-bodied, no oak, high acidity, drink now–3 years; **2003 Bethel Heights Vineyard Pinot Gris, Oregon** ★ $ dry, medium-bodied, no oak, high acidity, drink now–3 years

red wines

Given the press Oregon Pinot Noir has received over the years, one could be excused for thinking that it was the only game going. More graceful than most Pinots made in California, Oregon Pinot Noir comes closer to expressing the Burgundian ideal than any other Pinot outside of France. However, there are also some fine Cabernet- and Merlot-based wines from Oregon that fall in profile somewhere between California and Bordeaux. Smoky Syrah shows promise, too.

at the table
Salmon running up the Pacific coast need to swim fast as they head past Oregon lest all those Pinot lovers sweep them up as the wine's perfect accompaniment. Land-based Pinot lovers will find pleasure with a roast saddle of lamb or milk-fed veal. Bordeaux-style wines are delicious with heartier leg of lamb or sirloin steaks. Open an Oregon Syrah with venison or wild boar.

the bottom line Pinot Noir is always pricey. Expect to pay at least $15; most run $20 to $30, with exceptional single-vineyard wines reaching $50 to $75. Cabernet and Merlot begin at $10 for simple versions and run to $40 for fancier reserve bottlings and Bordeaux-style blends; Syrah averages about $25, though special bottles can cost much more.

what to buy PINOT NOIR

1999	2000	2001	2002	2003
★★★★	★★★★	★★★	★★★	★★

recommended pinot noir

2002 Domaine Serene Yamhill Cuvée,
Willamette Valley   ★★★★ $$$
dry, full-bodied, medium tannin, high acidity   **drink now–12 years**
Delicious in every way, from complex berry and cherry flavors, to palate-provoking mineral, smoke, and herbal notes.

2002 Adelsheim Vineyard, Oregon   ★★★ $$$
dry, medium-bodied, medium tannin, high acidity   **drink now–8 years**
Roasted meat, cherry, and spice flavors cry out for roast lamb.

2000 Amity Vineyards Winemakers Reserve,
Willamette Valley   ★★★ $$$
dry, medium-bodied, medium tannin, high acidity   **drink now–8 years**
Smooth from first to last sip, cherry and violet flavors show no rough edges.

2002 Anne Amie Deux Vert Vineyard, Willamette Valley ★★★ $$$
dry, medium-bodied, medium tannin, high acidity   **drink now–8 years**
Despite its name, there's nothing green in this mixed berry–flavored wine.

2001 Bethel Heights Vineyard Freedom Hill Vineyard,
Willamette Valley   ★★★ $$$
dry, medium-bodied, medium tannin, high acidity   **drink now–10 years**
Tart fruit and loads of smoke, stone, and herb.

2001 Cristom Louise Vineyard, Willamette Valley   ★★★ $$$
dry, medium-bodied, medium tannin, high acidity   **drink in 1–10 years**
Tart cherry and smoky herb flavors deserve some time to relax; this wine will reward with time.

2001 Domaine Drouhin, Willamette Valley   ★★★ $$$
dry, medium-bodied, medium tannin, high acidity   **drink now–8 years**
Toujours la finesse, Drouhin is as at home in Oregon as in Burgundy.

2001 Panther Creek Shea Vineyard, Willamette Valley ★★★ $$$
dry, medium-bodied, medium tannin, high acidity   **drink now–12 years**
Pinot as one always hopes for, this is elegant, full of cherry fruit, and sparked with mineral notes and light spice.

2001 De Ponte Cellars, Willamette Valley ★★★ $$
dry, medium-bodied, medium tannin, high acidity   drink now–8 years
With its first vintage, the new kid already looks like a star, with layers of smoke, mixed fruit, and herb flavors.

1998 Oak Knoll Vintage Reserve, Willamette Valley ★★★ $$
dry, medium-bodied, medium tannin, high acidity   drink now–6 years
At six years old, this Pinot is just hitting its stride, with smoky, leathery, wild mushroom and dried cherry flavors.

2001 The Eyrie Vineyards Estate, Willamette Valley ★★★ $$
dry, light-bodied, medium tannin, high acidity   drink now–8 years
David Lett's preference for elegance over power shows in this gossamer-textured wine with light cherry and spice notes.

2002 Amity Vineyards Eco-Wine, Oregon ★★ $$
dry, medium-bodied, medium tannin, high acidity   drink now–3 years
Fully organic and sulfite-free, this Pinot Noir is very earthy yet full of exuberant, spicy fruit.

2001 Chehalem 3 Vineyard, Willamette Valley ★★ $$
dry, medium-bodied, medium tannin, high acidity   drink now–6 years
Three vineyards contribute to this smoky, earthy, fruity Pinot Noir.

2002 Erath, Oregon ★★ $$
dry, medium-bodied, medium tannin, medium acidity   drink now–6 years
Cherries jubilee in a glass.

2002 Argyle, Willamette Valley ★ $$
dry, medium-bodied, medium tannin, high acidity   drink now–3 years
Unscrew the top for loads of peppery, mixed-berry goodness.

WINES WE WISH WE HAD MORE ROOM FOR
2001 Adelsheim Elizabeth's Reserve, Yamhill County ★★★ $$$ dry, medium-bodied, medium tannin, high acidity, drink now–12 years; **2001 Cristom Reserve, Willamette Valley** ★★★ $$$ dry, medium-bodied, medium tannin, high acidity, drink in 1–12 years; **2001 Domaine Serene Evenstad Reserve, Willamette Valley** ★★★ $$$ dry, medium-bodied, medium tannin, high acidity, drink in 1–12 years; **2001 Erath Estate Selection, Willamette Valley** ★★★ $$$ dry, medium-bodied, medium tannin, high acidity, drink now–10 years; **2002 Anne Amie, Willamette Valley** ★★★ $$ dry, full-bodied, medium tannin, high acidity, drink now–12 years; **2002 Bethel Heights Vineyard, Willamette Valley** ★★ $$ dry, medium-bodied, medium tannin, high acidity, drink now–6 years; **2001 Oak Knoll, Willamette Valley** ★★ $ dry, medium-bodied, medium tannin, high acidity, drink now–6 years

washington state

Washington earns its reputation for excellent wines from grapes grown in the arid, semi-desert valleys in the eastern part of the state rather than in the cool, humid regions near the coast. Bordeaux is the model here, though Merlot, Syrah, and Riesling are also winning esteem.

on the label

Washington wines, like those from California and Oregon, tend to be labeled by grape variety. Bordeaux blends are sometimes called *Meritage*, though wineries also use proprietary names, such as Sorella, a blend from Andrew Will Winery.

white wines

Washington's white wine scene is dominated by Chardonnay, made in a nervy, citrusy style or oak-aged to accentuate vine-ripened tropical fruit flavors. It's arguable, though, that Sauvignon Blanc and Semillon do better. Washington Sauvignon Blanc tends to be lemony with grassy undertones. Semillon is richer, with indulgent orange and peach flavors. Washington also makes some of the finest Rieslings in the U.S.

at the table

Though the state's wine industry is far from the coast, look west for culinary accompaniment. Briny oysters from Puget Sound will sing with Sauvignon Blanc. Oak-aged Chardonnay is wonderful with roasted Alaskan salmon; lighter versions will pep up a chicken Caesar salad. Pour Semillon with a seafood bisque or creamy clam chowder, and Riesling with smoked salmon or moderately spicy Asian dishes.

the bottom line

Washington's whites represent some of the country's best wine values. Most hover in the $8 to $12 range, with top-of-the-line wines rarely crossing $20 .

recommended wines

**2003 Chateau Ste. Michelle & Dr. Loosen Eroica Riesling,
Columbia Valley** ★★★★ $$
off-dry, medium-bodied, no oak, high acidity **drink now–8 years**
In collaboration with Germany's Ernst Loosen, Ste. Michelle puts out one of
the best Rieslings in the U.S. It sings with a chorus of vibrant citrus, herb, and
mineral flavors.

2002 Glen Fiona Viognier, Walla Walla Valley ★★★★ $$
dry, medium-bodied, light oak, high acidity **drink now–6 years**
One of Washington's best whites, full of floral and nut flavors.

2002 DeLille Cellars Chaleur Estate, Columbia Valley ★★★ $$$
dry, medium-bodied, medium oak, high acidity **drink now–8 years**
Inspired by the great wines of Graves, this Sauvignon Blanc-Semillon blend
has minerals, smoky oak, and baked quince flavors.

**2002 Woodward Canyon Winery Chardonnay,
Columbia Valley** ★★★ $$$
dry, medium-bodied, light oak, high acidity **drink now–6 years**
Citrus and minerals, perfectly proportioned.

2002 Abeja Chardonnay, Washington State ★★★ $$
dry, medium-bodied, light oak, high acidity **drink now–8 years**
Indulgent ripe pineapple and apple flavors are kept in line by stony notes.

**2002 Buty Roza Bergé Vineyard Chardonnay,
Yakima Valley** ★★★ $$
dry, medium-bodied, medium oak, high acidity **drink now–12 years**
A parade of marzipan and mineral flavors highlighted by citrusy acidity makes
for excellent Chardonnay.

2002 Forgeron Cellars Chardonnay, Columbia Valley ★★★ $$
dry, medium-bodied, medium oak, high acidity **drink now–8 years**
Tropical fruit and bright acidity make for a balanced Chardonnay.

**2002 L'Ecole No. 41 Seven Hills Vineyard Estate Semillon,
Walla Walla Valley** ★★★ $$
dry, medium-bodied, medium oak, high acidity **drink now–8 years**
Autumn in a glass, with baked fruit, roasted nuts, and sweet spice. Delicious.

2002 McCrea Roussanne, Red Mountain ★★★ $$
dry, medium-bodied, light oak, high acidity **drink now–8 years**
A fascinating Roussanne, with a waxy texture and late-summer floral flavors
that recall honeycomb, except it's dry.

2002 Serience White Wine, Columbia Valley ★★★ $$
dry, medium-bodied, no oak, high acidity drink now–6 years
Wonderful floral pear flavors suggest Viognier and Roussanne should come together more often.

2003 Whitman Cellars Viognier, Walla Walla Valley ★★★ $$
dry, medium-bodied, light oak, high acidity drink now–6 years
A spicy, peppery edge lends this peachy Viognier appreciated restraint.

2001 Chateau Ste. Michelle Cold Creek Vineyard Chardonnay, Columbia Valley ★★ $$$
dry, medium-bodied, medium oak, high acidity drink now–3 years
Straight-on Chardonnay, done well. Its citrus and oak flavors would be delicious with grilled salmon.

2003 Columbia Winery Cellarmaster's Riesling, Columbia Valley ★★ $
off-dry, medium-bodied, no oak, high acidity drink now–3 years
A sassy wine, a whip of limey acidity keeps the sweet pear flavors in line.

2002 Columbia Winery Pinot Gris, Yakima Valley ★★ $
dry, medium-bodied, no oak, high acidity drink now–3 years
This is as tasty as a frangipane-pear tart, with vibrant acidity to keep it fresh.

2003 Covey Run Gewürztraminer, Washington State ★★ $
off-dry, medium-bodied, no oak, high acidity drink now–3 years
Good, textbook Gewürz, fragrant with flowers, stones, and spice.

2003 Hedges Fumé-Chardonnay, Columbia Valley ★★ $
dry, medium-bodied, light oak, high acidity drink now–3 years
Sauvignon Blanc provides lemon and grass zip; Chardonnay provides the stuffing. A nice combo.

2002 Robert Karl Sauvignon Blanc, Columbia Valley ★★ $
dry, medium-bodied, no oak, high acidity drink now–3 years
Charmingly zesty lime and nut flavors keep going long after you've put your glass down.

2003 Thurston Wolfe PGV, Yakima Valley ★★ $
dry, medium-bodied, no oak, high acidity drink now–3 years
A blend of Pinot Grigio and Viognier, this offers fruit and spice flavors as fresh as springtime.

2002 Waterbrook Sauvignon Blanc, Columbia Valley ★★ $
dry, medium-bodied, no oak, high acidity drink now–2 years
Grapefruit flavors gain extra substance from earthy almond flavors.

2003 Hogue Pinot Grigio, Columbia Valley ★ $
dry, medium-bodied, no oak, high acidity drink now–3 years
This zippy Pinot Grigio will stand in for any Italian version.

2002 Hoodsport Madeleine Angevine, Puget Sound ★ $
dry, light-bodied, no oak, high acidity drink now
A charming example of a rare grape, with light floral and lime flavors.

2002 Snoqualmie Vineyards Chenin Blanc, Columbia Valley ★ $
off-dry, medium-bodied, no oak, medium acidity drink now–2 years
Light, sweet fruit flavors provide a good backdrop to spicy Asian dishes.

red wines

Washington State produces the country's best Merlot. Yes, California offers Merlots that rank among the best in the world, but for consistency, Washington smokes, offering wines with more finesse than their California counterparts. Cabernet Sauvignon and Cabernet Franc hold their own as well. Syrah becomes graceful yet powerful here; Sangiovese, soulful. Lemberger parallels California's Zinfandel with juicy blueberry flavors. The same grape as Austria's Blaufränkisch, Lemberger is sometimes called "Blue Franc."

at the table

Washington's full-bodied Bordeaux blends and varietal wines require hearty foods. Merlot is a good choice for pork loin or filet mignon; more tannic Cabernet Sauvignon has the grip to take on slow-roasted short ribs or dry-aged sirloin. Peppery Cabernet Franc was made for *steak au poivre,* but its leaner profile lends itself to grilled portobello mushrooms or the eggplant-based Turkish favorite *imam bayildi*. Serve Syrah with Provençal lamb stews or herb-stuffed veal chops. Pour Sangiovese with chicken cacciatore. Simpler Lemberger is great burger wine; more complex versions can handle roast game.

the bottom line Good-quality Bordeaux-variety reds can be found for $8 to $12, though they get more interesting at $18 to $30; $40 to $55 buys superb single-vineyard wines. There are some low-priced Syrah and Sangiovese, but quality jumps at $18 to $35. Lemberger runs about $8 to $15.

what to buy MERLOT & CABERNET SAUVIGNON

1999	2000	2001	2002	2003
★★★	★★★	★★★	★★★	★★★★

recommended bordeaux varietals & blends

2001 Andrew Will Ciel du Cheval Vineyard, Red Mountain ★★★★ $$$
dry, full-bodied, heavy tannin, high acidity — **drink now–15 years**
Sublime wine, fragrant and graceful with perfumed berry flavors structured by smoky mineral notes.

2001 Seven Hills Klipsun Vineyard Merlot, Columbia Valley ★★★★ $$$
dry, medium-bodied, medium tannin, high acidity — **drink now–10 years**
Fine red fruit, light, smoky spice, and highly polished mineral flavors make for a beautiful Merlot.

2001 Woodward Canyon Artist Series #10 Cabernet Sauvignon, Columbia Valley ★★★★ $$$
dry, full-bodied, medium tannin, high acidity — **drink now–12 years**
Stellar Cabernet Sauvignon from one of Washington's great vintners, with earth, animal, and fruit all at once.

2001 Cayuse Vineyards Camaspelo, Walla Walla Valley ★★★ $$$$
dry, full-bodied, heavy tannin, high acidity — **drink now–15 years**
Black currant, green and black pepper, earth, and oak flavors make this a baronial Cabernet blend.

2001 Andrew Will Cellars Sorella, Columbia Valley ★★★ $$$
dry, full-bodied, medium tannin, high acidity — **drink now–12 years**
This has the intensity and feel of many classified Bordeaux wines, but it's easier to enjoy young—and it's more affordable.

2002 Buty, Columbia Valley ★★★ $$$
dry, full-bodied, medium tannin, high acidity — **drink now–10 years**
The stylish label delivers its promise of stylish wine, fruity and sleek.

2001 Fort Walla Walla Cellars Merlot, Walla Walla Valley ★★★ $$$
dry, full-bodied, medium tannin, high acidity — **drink now–8 years**
Plush yet refined spicy berry flavors showcase Washington Merlot.

2001 L'Ecole No. 41 Cabernet Sauvignon,
Walla Walla Valley ★ ★ ★ $$$
dry, full-bodied, heavy tannin, high acidity   **drink now–12 years**
Consistently excellent, L'Ecole Cab shines with bright fruit and restrained, peppery spice.

2001 Nicholas Cole Cellars Claret, Columbia Valley ★ ★ ★ $$$
dry, full-bodied, medium tannin, high acidity   **drink in 2–12 years**
A robust "claret," full of dark fruit and minerals, yet refined, with a floral edge.

2001 Pepper Bridge Cabernet Sauvignon,
Walla Walla Valley ★ ★ ★ $$$
dry, full-bodied, heavy tannin, high acidity   **drink in 2–10 years**
Ripe berry flavors smooth out this Cabernet's peppery notes nicely.

2001 Three Rivers Winery Champoux Vineyard
Cabernet Sauvignon, Columbia Valley ★ ★ ★ $$$
dry, full-bodied, medium tannin, high acidity   **drink now–10 years**
One of Washington's best vineyards, Champoux lathers up minerals, dark fruit, and spice in a very fine Cabernet.

2002 Colvin Vineyards Carmenère, Walla Walla Valley ★ ★ ★ $$
dry, medium-bodied, medium tannin, high acidity   **drink now–6 years**
Bordeaux in origin, Carmenère is rare everywhere but Chile these days. This one from Walla Walla provides peppery, red berry elegance.

2001 Gordon Brothers Family Vineyards Cabernet Sauvignon,
Columbia Valley ★ ★ ★ $$
dry, full-bodied, medium tannin, high acidity   **drink now–8 years**
Deliciously pure black cherry flavors backed by earthy tobacco notes.

2001 Novelty Hill Merlot, Columbia Valley ★ ★ ★ $$
dry, medium-bodied, medium tannin, high acidity   **drink now–8 years**
A whisper of pepper adds pizzazz to this Merlot's abundance of ripe fruit.

2001 Forgeron Cellars Merlot, Columbia Valley ★ ★ $$
dry, full-bodied, medium tannin, high acidity   **drink now–8 years**
Here's a deliciously ferrous, lavender-scented, dark-fruited Merlot.

2000 Preston Reserve Merlot, Columbia Valley ★ ★ $$
dry, full-bodied, heavy tannin, high acidity   **drink now–6 years**
There's a lot of wood flavor in this wine, but with air and a steak, the berry flavors can handle it.

2001 Robert Karl Claret, Columbia Valley ★ ★ $$
dry, full-bodied, medium tannin, medium acidity   **drink now–4 years**
Gentle wine, with ripe berry flavors sweetened up with vanilla-toned oak.

washington reds pacific northwest

2001 Waterbrook Merlot, Red Mountain ★★ $$
dry, full-bodied, medium tannin, high acidity **drink now–8 years**
A dusty, mineral-laden Merlot with mountains of red fruit flavors.

2002 Hedges CMS, Columbia Valley ★★ $
dry, full-bodied, heavy tannin, high acidity **drink now–6 years**
Honest, fun drinking, full of juicy fruit flavors.

2000 Powers Merlot, Columbia Valley ★★ $
dry, full-bodied, medium tannin, high acidity **drink now–6 years**
Solid Merlot, with powerful berry and mineral flavors.

2001 Sagelands Vineyard Four Corners Cabernet Sauvignon,
Columbia Valley ★★ $
dry, full-bodied, medium tannin, high acidity **drink now–4 years**
Finding a good Cab for a low price is like tracking a lone sagebrush in the
desert, but Sagelands delivers.

2001 Sockeye Merlot, Washington State ★ $
dry, medium-bodied, medium tannin, high acidity **drink now–3 years**
Cherry, cherry, cherry.

WINES WE WISH WE HAD MORE ROOM FOR

2001 DeLille Cellars Chaleur Estate, Yakima Valley ★★★★ $$$$
dry, full-bodied, heavy tannin, high acidity, drink now–12 years; **2001 Seven
Hills Klipsun Vineyard Cabernet Sauvignon, Columbia Valley**
★★★★ $$$ dry, full-bodied, heavy tannin, high acidity, drink now–15
years; **2001 Hogue Reserve Cabernet Sauvignon, Columbia Valley**
★★★ $$$ dry, full-bodied, medium tannin, high acidity, drink now–8 years;
1999 Kestrel Cabernet Sauvignon, Yakima Valley ★★ $$$ dry, full-
bodied, medium tannin, high acidity, drink now–8 years; **2002 Saviah
Cellars Une Vallée, Walla Walla Valley** ★★ $$$ dry, full-bodied, heavy
tannin, high acidity, drink now–8 years; **2001 Snoqualmie Vineyards
Rosebud Vineyard Cabernet Sauvignon, Columbia Valley** ★★ $ dry,
full-bodied, heavy tannin, high acidity, drink now–4 years; **2001 Canoe
Ridge Vineyard Cabernet Sauvignon, Columbia Valley** ★ $$ dry,
full-bodied, medium tannin, high acidity, drink now–4 years

recommended other reds

2001 Cayuse Vineyards Cailloux Vineyard Syrah,
Walla Walla Valley ★★★ $$$$
dry, full-bodied, medium tannin, high acidity **drink now–12 years**
Super Syrah, full of dense, smoky mixed berry flavors and firm as stone.

2002 Dunham Cellars Frenchtown Vineyard Syrah, Walla Walla Valley ★★★ $$$$
dry, full-bodied, heavy tannin, high acidity   drink in 1–10 years

A delicious muddle of wild berries and citrus, with plenty of minerals and spice besides. Give it time to sort itself out.

2000 Columbia Winery Red Willow Vineyard Syrah, Yakima Valley ★★★ $$$
dry, full-bodied, heavy tannin, high acidity   drink now–10 years

Consistently one of Washington's better Syrahs, Red Willow shows its earthy side this year, with appealing red fruit.

2001 DeLille Cellars Doyenne, Yakima Valley ★★★ $$$
dry, full-bodied, medium tannin, high acidity   drink now–10 years

Commanding Syrah, with luscious dark berry, lanolin, and spice flavors.

2001 Glen Fiona Cuvée Lot 57, Walla Walla Valley ★★★ $$$
dry, medium-bodied, medium tannin, high acidity   drink now–6 years

This Rhône blend could be at home anywhere in the southern Rhône.

2002 McCrea Mourvèdre, Red Mountain ★★★ $$$
dry, full-bodied, medium tannin, high acidity   drink now–6 years

Fabulous Mourvèdre, with all the sappy, dark berry goodness of the grape.

2001 Glen Fiona Syrah, Walla Walla Valley ★★★ $$
dry, medium-bodied, medium tannin, high acidity   drink now–10 years

An excellent, St-Joseph-like Syrah.

2001 Three Rivers Winery Pepper Bridge Vineyard Sangiovese, Walla Walla Valley ★★ $$$
dry, medium-bodied, medium tannin, high acidity   drink now–6 years

With light, spiced strawberry flavors, this could stand in for Chianti.

2000 Hogue Genesis Syrah, Columbia Valley ★★ $$
dry, full-bodied, medium tannin, high acidity   drink now–6 years

In the beginning there was heaven and earth, and once there was light, Syrah could ripen, giving forth ripe berry and earthy minerals.

2002 Thurston Wolfe Sangiovese, Columbia Valley ★★ $$
dry, full-bodied, medium tannin, high acidity   drink now–6 years

These tart berry and herb oil flavors are ideal with lamb.

2001 Zefina Sangiovese, Columbia Valley ★★ $$
dry, medium-bodied, medium tannin, high acidity   drink now–5 years

Mediterranean breezes visit the Columbia Valley in this Sangiovese full of pomegranate and herb flavors.

2002 Badger Mountain Vintners Estate Syrah,
Columbia Valley ★ ★ $
dry, full-bodied, medium tannin, high acidity   drink now–3 years
An organic Syrah, this offers soft, spicy, earthy berry flavors.

2002 Thurston Wolfe Dr. Wolfe's Family Red,
Columbia Valley ★ ★ $
dry, medium-bodied, medium tannin, high acidity   drink now–3 years
Juicy, spicy, with lots of acidity, this unusual mix of grapes including
Lemberger can pair with a wide range of dishes.

BEYOND CALIFORNIA WINE

Today every state in the Union has a wine industry. Here
are some of the best from outside of California, Oregon,
Washington, and New York State:

**2001 Basignani Belfast Vineyard
Chardonnay,** Maryland: Stony Chardonnay with a twist
of Queen Anne cherries.

2002 Callaghan Vineyards Syrah, Arizona: A
Syrah full of lusty fruit, minerals, and spice.

2000 Chamard Estate Reserve Chardonnay,
Connecticut: A surprisingly Burgundian Chardonnay.

2001 Gruet Pinot Noir, New Mexico: A Pinot Noir
with berries, spice, and finesse.

2001 Horton Cellars Tannat, Virginia: A tender
Tannat, with dark berry and tobacco flavors.

**L. Mawby Blanc de Blanc Brut Sparkling
Wine,** Michigan: Tart apple-lemon flavors—a great way
to celebrate.

2000 Linden Glen Manor, Virginia: The Virginian
Bordeaux-style red Jefferson always wanted.

**2002 Spanish Valley Vineyards & Winery
Cabernet Sauvignon,** Utah: Vibrant dark berry flavors from high-elevation desert Cab.

2001 Ste. Chapelle Cabernet Sauvignon,
Idaho: Idaho makes steak lovers happy, supplying both
potatoes for the fries and this solid Cabernet Sauvignon at
an excellent price.

new york state

It's tough to tell from wine lists around the country, but the Empire State is the third largest producer of wine in the U.S. Much of it is sweet and rough, made from *Vitis lambrusca* grapes, but Long Island makes some great wines from Bordeaux varieties; the Hudson Valley, from "hybrid" varieties. And the Finger Lakes makes some of the finest Pinot Noir, Riesling, and Gewürztraminer in the U.S.

BUFFALO •
Lake Erie
Lake Erie

on the label

New Yorkers label according to grape variety, per California custom. A few blended wines are given proprietary names.

white & rosé wines

New York produces some of the best whites in the U.S. Chardonnay dominates, but New York's relatively cool climate yields lemon- and mineral-tinged wines that resemble Burgundy's versions more than California's. Long Island has fine Chardonnay, too, but it's Pinot Blanc that really excites folks with its pearlike flavors and unctuous texture. The island also makes delicious, spicy rosés. Upstate, the Hudson Valley offers enjoyable wines from hybrids (crosses between American and European grapes) such as Seyval Blanc and Vidal Blanc. In the Finger Lakes, Riesling and Gewürztraminer produce some of the best examples in the States, most of them dry.

80

at the table

Long Island's fishermen provide the perfect fare for New York whites. Unoaked Chardonnay or Pinot Blanc will draw out the sweetness from relatively mild fish like porgy or cod and add zing to clambakes. Enjoy oaked versions with crab cakes and monkfish or, for landlubbers, a free-range chicken. Riesling is a fine choice with sole meunière. Gewürz goes well with Thai-style snapper or other spicy, delicate foods. A glass of Seyval or Vidal Blanc will liven up a luncheon salad. Sip rosé as an aperitif, then finish off the bottle with duck or salmon.

the bottom line Finger Lakes Riesling and Gewürztraminer offer the best buys in American white wines. From bottom to top—$10 to $25—quality is high. Most Chardonnay and Pinot Blanc cost $10 to $20 with a handful nearing $30. Hybrid grape wines sell from $8 to $17.

what to buy WHITE WINES

2000	2001	2002	2003
★★★	★★★★	★★★	★

recommended wines

**2002 Hermann J. Wiemer Reserve Gewürztraminer,
Finger Lakes ☼** ★★★★ $$
off-dry medium-bodied, no oak, high acidity   drink now–10 years
A fantasy perfumed by rose water, orange blossoms, and wild strawberries,
yet subtle as if half-robed by a veil of gossamer silk.

2000 Wölffer Estate Selection Chardonnay, The Hamptons ☼★★★ $$$
dry, medium-bodied, medium oak, high acidity   drink now–8 years
An Atlantic sunrise of flavors, from sea breeze minerality to gold-hued fruit.

2003 Dr. Konstantin Frank Rkatsiteli, Finger Lakes ☼ ★★★ $$
dry, medium-bodied, no oak, high acidity   drink now–6 years
Rare in the U.S., Rkatsiteli stands proud with lime, herb, and stone flavors.

2002 Lieb Pinot Blanc, North Fork ☼ ★★★ $$
dry, medium-bodied, no oak, high acidity   drink now–3 years
Pinot Blanc is rarely so lusty, with juicy pear and marzipan flavors.

**2002 Millbrook Castle Hill Vineyard Chardonnay,
Hudson River Region ☼** ★★★ $$
dry, medium-bodied, medium oak, high acidity   drink now–6 years
Unexpectedly good Chardonnay, full of minerals and baked apple flavors.

2001 Pellegrini Vineyards Chardonnay, North Fork ☼ ★★★ $
dry, medium-bodied, medium oak, medium acidity   drink now–6 years
Beautifully crafted wine with melt-in-the-mouth fruit and custard flavors.

2003 Standing Stone Vineyards Riesling, Finger Lakes ☼ ★★★ $
off-dry, medium-bodied, no oak, high acidity   drink now–8 years
Tutti-frutti and spicy, this slightly off-dry wine would be great with banana leaf–
roasted fish and fruit salsa.

2003 Paumanok Chenin Blanc, North Fork ☼ ★★ $$
dry, medium-bodied, no oak, high acidity   drink now–2 years
This zesty wine could stand in for a squeeze of lemon on your fish.

2003 Macari Early Wine Chardonnay, North Fork ☼ ★★ $
dry, light-bodied, no oak, high acidity   drink now–1 year
A zippy kiwi- and lime-scented Chardonnay.

**2002 Martha Clara Vineyards Cabernet Franc Rosé,
North Fork ☼** ★★ $
dry, medium-bodied, high acidity   drink now–2 years
Light and pink, Cabernet Franc still shows its telltale pepper and berry flavors.

2003 Palmer Vineyards Pinot Blanc, North Fork ♥ ★★ $
dry, medium-bodied, no oak, medium acidity   drink now–3 years
With citrus and melon flavors, this wine would be wonderful with crab salad.

WINES WE WISH WE HAD MORE ROOM FOR
2002 Hermann J. Wiemer Dry Johannisberg Riesling, Finger Lakes
★★★★ $ dry, medium-bodied, no oak, high acidity drink now–10 years; **2003
Dr. Konstantin Frank Dry Riesling, Finger Lakes** ★★★ $ dry, medium-
bodied, no oak, high acidity, drink now–6 years; **2002 Hermann J. Wiemer
Semi Dry Riesling, Finger Lakes** ★★★ $ off-dry, medium-bodied, no oak,
high acidity, drink now–10 years; **2003 Paumanok Semi Dry Riesling, North
Fork** ★★ $$ off-dry, medium-bodied, no oak, high acidity, drink now–3 years;
2003 Palmer Vineyards Sauvignon Blanc, North Fork ★★ $ dry, medium-
bodied, no oak, high acidity, drink now–2 years

FREEDOM AND EMPIRE

Will the grapes finally be free? One by one, federal courts
are overturning state laws established after Prohibition
that ban out-of-state wine shipments to residents within.
In the past two years, several states have legalized the
practice—good news for those who live in wine-deprived
markets or who want a souvenir from their Napa vacation.
Yet, despite ranking second in per capita wine consump-
tion, New York remains the unattainable Holy Grail for
direct-shipping advocates. But within his proposed
2004–2005 budget, Governor George Pataki introduced
provisions to allow out-of-state wineries to ship wine
directly to New Yorkers, and for New York wineries to ship
their wine to out-of-state consumers. At the time of this
writing, the verdict was still out. Stay tuned.

red wines

Long Island reds come closer to Bordeaux than California's gen-
erally more robust analogues. Merlot makes juicy reds here, but
more exciting is the dark, peppery Cabernet Franc. Cabernet
Sauvignon adds oomph to some impressive Bordeaux blends
here, too. The Hudson Valley also puts out some good Cabernet
Franc, while Finger Lakes producers excel at Pinot Noir.

at the table

Serving Long Island duck with cherry sauce? Look upstate for a Finger Lakes Pinot Noir. Pull out a Long Island Merlot or Cabernet Franc for a New York Strip. Long Island Bordeaux blends are wonderful with venison—which is raised just up the Hudson Valley.

the bottom line Most Long Island Bordeaux-style wines sell for between $15 and $25, with some top Bordeaux blends scratching the $45 mark. Pinot Noirs average $13 to $25.

what to buy RED WINES

1999	2000	2001	2002	2003
★★	★★	★★★★	★★★	★★

recommended wines

2001 Macari Reserve Merlot, North Fork ★★★ $$$
dry, full-bodied, heavy tannin, high acidity drink now–10 years
Regality in a bottle, though sweet spice, mineral, and dry floral flavors make this more Emperor Augustus than Queen Elizabeth.

2000 Macari Bergen Road, North Fork ★★★ $$$
dry, full-bodied, medium tannin, high acidity drink now–12 years
Why did the wine geek cross Bergen Road? To get to all the lusty dark berry, tobacco, and spice flavors of this Bordeaux blend.

2001 Wölffer Cabernet Franc, The Hamptons ★★★ $$$
dry, full-bodied, medium tannin, high acidity drink now–8 years
Claret defined, this Cab Franc offers subtle yet substantial mixed berry, fine mineral, and spice flavors.

2002 Millbrook Pinot Noir, New York State ★★★ $$
dry, medium-bodied, medium tannin, high acidity drink now–4 years
The bright lights of Broadway may be a couple of hours away, but this shines with light fresh cherry and spice.

2001 Palmer Vineyards Proprietor's Reserve Cabernet Franc, North Fork ★★★ $$
dry, full-bodied, medium tannin, high acidity drink now–8 years
Complex stuff, this starts out with easy fruit, then turns immediately to minerals.

2002 Paumanok Cabernet Franc, North Fork ★★★ $$
dry, medium-bodied, medium tannin, high acidity   drink now–6 years
Steering away from the herbal side of Cab Franc, Paumanok goes for the cherry, glistening and luscious.

2000 Pellegrini Vineyards Cabernet Sauvignon, North Fork ★★★ $$
dry, full-bodied, medium tannin, high acidity   drink now–8 years
Pellegrini's long record of first-rate Long Island wines is preserved here with a refined wine laden with cassis and minerals.

2000 Schneider Cabernet Franc, North Fork ★★★ $$
dry, full-bodied, medium tannin, high acidity   drink now–8 years
Cab Franc done *à la bordelaise,* with lush berry flavors and peppery minerals.

2001 Standing Stone Vineyards Pinnacle, Finger Lakes ★★★ $$
dry, full-bodied, medium tannin, high acidity   drink now–8 years
At first this seems simple; then it grabs the tongue with an array of bramble berries, flowers, and minerals.

2001 Wölffer Reserve Merlot, The Hamptons ★★★ $$
dry, full-bodied, medium tannin, high acidity   drink now–8 years
Velvety smooth and elegant, this is terrific Merlot.

2000 Bedell Cellars Cupola, North Fork ★★ $$$
dry, full-bodied, medium tannin, high acidity   drink now–8 years
Fruit and animal flavors should get even better with a little more time to meld.

2001 Palmer Reserve Merlot, North Fork ★★ $$$
dry, full-bodied, medium tannin, high acidity   drink in 1–10 years
Here's a powerful Merlot, staunchly dry and structured by lots of minerals.

2001 Dr. Konstantin Frank Pinot Noir, Finger Lakes ★★ $$
dry, medium-bodied, medium tannin, high acidity   drink now–6 years
Cool-climate Pinot to a T, with elegant fruit and spice.

2002 Fox Run Vineyards Lemberger, Finger Lakes ★★ $$
dry, medium-bodied, medium tannin, high acidity   drink now–3 years
A Lemberger with loads of wild fruit and smoky, peppery flavors.

2002 Hermann J. Wiemer Pinot Noir, Finger Lakes ★★ $$
dry, light-bodied, medium tannin, high acidity   drink now–3 years
Light Pinot Noir, impressive for its refined raspberry and herb flavors.

2000 Potato Barn Red, North Fork ★★ $
dry, full-bodied, medium tannin, high acidity   drink now–2 years
Easy, juicy berry flavors are just the thing for lazy afternoon barbecues.

france

From the cool Champagne region, famed for its fine bubbly, to the end of Corsica, where grapes roast under the Mediterranean sun, French vintners make nearly every style of wine possible, in their own inimitable fashion.

grapes & styles

The French grow hundreds of grape varieties, and the country is home base for the so-called "international" varieties—Merlot, Cabernet Sauvignon, Chardonnay, Sauvignon Blanc, Syrah, and Pinot Noir—that vintners around the world now grow. Ironically, grape varieties do not get much billing in France. Centuries of experience have favored certain grape varieties over others in particular regions, and use of those superior varieties is often codified into law. White Burgundy, for instance, must be made from Chardonnay, though most bottles don't list the grape on the label; the place is information enough. To the French, *terroir* trumps everything. Loosely translated, terroir is the sense of a particular place in a wine, a flavor determined by a specific combination of minerals in the soil, the climate, the amount of sun, the plants growing nearby—everything that might affect the vine and its fruit. A wine with a taste of terroir is one whose flavor reflects the place from which it came. So when a French bistro lists wine by region instead of winery or grape, it does so on purpose: The French expect wines from a particular region to taste a certain way.

on the label

The French concept of terroir carries over to the country's wine labels. Except for wines from Alsace and some from the Languedoc, French wine labels usually omit grape names and play up the regional appellation. To be allowed a regional label, wines must be made according to regulation rules, including

Featured Wine-Growing Regions

REIMS
PARIS
Champagne
STRASBOURG
Alsace
ORLEANS
Loire Valley
NANTES
DIJON
Burgundy
Atlantic Ocean
LIMOGES
LYON
BORDEAUX
Bordeaux
Rhône Valley
Southwest
AVIGNON
NICE
NIMES
Provence
MARSEILLE
Languedoc-Roussillon
Mediterranean Sea

permitted grape varieties and particular viticultural practices. The system that governs regional regulations is known as the *Appellation d'Origine Contrôlée* (AOC) or, "controlled region of origin." The AOC hierarchy from top to bottom is:

AOC The majority of French wines imported to the U.S. are AOC wines, which means they have met the standards of their region. These standards differ from region to region, but typically define grape varieties, vinification practices, alcohol levels, and harvest size (overly large grape harvests are assumed to yield dilute wines). There are AOCs within AOCs in France, too. Generally speaking, the more specific the subregion, the more stringent the standards. For example, wines from Pauillac, a subregion of the Médoc, must meet greater standards than the wines of Médoc, a subregion of Bordeaux, which must meet stricter requirements than those labeled simply "Bordeaux."

Vin Délimité de Qualité Supérieure (VDQS) Best understood as the minor leagues for newly defined wine regions, VDQS standards are usually a tad lower than for those for AOC wines. If enough winemakers in a VDQS region produce wines at sufficiently high quality levels, the region might be promoted to AOC status.

Vin de Pays Literally "country wines," Vins de Pays meet lower standards than VDQS wines, but can list the name of their region and grape variety. The designation used to be a lowly one, but an increasing number of innovative winemakers who work beyond the strictures of AOC requirements are producing some impressive Vins de Pays.

Vin de Table Translated as "table wine," Vin de Table does not meet AOC board requirements. Vintners may not mention the wine's place of origin, its vintage, or the grapes from which it was made on the label. Most are coarse, but certain brave iconoclasts are making some stunning Vins de Table. American importers will often add a sticker to the bottle that provides the banned information.

alsace

French, yet twice part of Germany in the 20th century, Alsace has its own unique style. German names turn up frequently in places and cuisine, and its mostly white wines are made with grapes common to Germany. But just as Alsatians call sauerkraut *choucroute,* they put a distinct French twist on their wines. Highly aromatic with racy acidity, Alsatian wines are nearly always fermented dry, like their French compatriots.

grapes & styles

Given its history, it's little surprise that three of Alsace's most common grapes are German in origin: Riesling, Gewurztraminer, and Sylvaner. The first two are responsible for some of France's best whites. Pinot Blanc, Pinot Gris, and Pinot Auxerrois are also widely planted. Muscat has a presence, too, but is waning. Alsace also produces fabulous sweet wines labelled *Vendanges Tardives* (Late Harvest) and *Sélection de Grains Nobles* (Selected Noble Berry). See Fortified & Dessert Wines, p. 285, for more information. Alsatians also make a Champagne-style wine known as Crémant d'Alsace, covered on p. 272. Pinot Noir provides the only permitted red wine in Alsace.

on the label

Most wines from Alsace are labeled by grape variety, which by law must make up 100 percent of the bottle's contents. Some producers also blend grapes to make a wine commonly known as *Edelzwicker* or *Gentil*. Fifty vineyards in Alsace have achieved *Grand Cru* status and may label their wines as such. However, because of controversies surrounding the criteria for Grand Cru designations, some firms prefer to use the name of the vineyard alone, or their own proprietary terms like *Réserve Personnelle* or *Cuvée Particulière*. These have no legal meaning but are mostly applied to wines of superior quality.

what to buy ALSACE

1998	1999	2000	2001	2002	2003
★★	★★★	★★★	★★★	★★	★★

PINOT BLANC & PINOT GRIS

Though closely related, Pinots Blanc and Gris are quite different in taste. Pinot Blanc is flighty, with gentle lemon and nut flavors. Pinot Gris, also known here as Tokay Pinot Gris, is broader, weighted down by an embarrassment of thick apricot, smoky almond, and dry orange peel flavors—completely different from Italy's Pinot Grigio, though it's the same grape. Pinot Blanc is sometimes blended with another grape called Pinot Auxerrois.

at the table

Pinot Blanc's light, simple flavors are good with simple food: chicken salads, light fish like sand dabs, or pasta with fresh tomatoes and basil. Pour Pinot Gris with Alsatian specialties such as the pizzalike *tarte flambée, choucroute garnie* (sauerkraut baked with sausages), or roast goose. Heavier fish like pike also work well.

the bottom line
The weak dollar is doing lovers of French wines no favors. Producers and importers are trying to hold the line, but they'll have to give soon. Expect to pay $10 to $12 for a basic Pinot Blanc. Those labeled Pinot Auxerrois cost a few dollars more. Pinot Gris is unavoidably pricey, ranging from $16 to $65 for Reserve and Grand Cru bottlings.

recommended wines

**2002 Domaine Weinbach Clos des Capucins Cuvée
Ste. Catherine Tokay Pinot Gris** ★★★★ $$$$
off-dry, full-bodied, no oak, high acidity **drink now–20 years**
A wine dreams are made of—juicy, spicy, and soulful.

1999 Trimbach Réserve Personnelle Pinot Gris ★★★★ $$$
dry, medium-bodied, no oak, high acidity **drink now–15 years**
Spectacular wine, full of polished minerals and spice, baked apple, and pear.
Stash some away: it will mature beautifully over the next decade.

2002 Pierre Frick Cuvée Précieuse Pinot Blanc ★★★ $$
dry, medium-bodied, no oak, high acidity **drink now–3 years**
Lively Pinot Blanc, this brightens the palate with pure pear, lemon, and nut flavors.

**2002 Domaines Schlumberger Les Princes Abbés
Pinot Blanc** ★★★ $
dry, medium-bodied, no oak, high acidity **drink now–5 years**
The princely abbot's cup runneth over with almonds, pears, and stone.

2002 Dopff & Irion Pinot Blanc ★★★ $
dry, medium-bodied, no oak, high acidity **drink now–8 years**
Terrific Pinot Blanc, full of earthy truffle and juicy pineapple flavors.

2002 J.B. Adam Réserve Pinot Blanc ★★★ $
dry, medium-bodied, no oak, high acidity **drink now–6 years**
Sunny fruit shines on earthy mineral flavors, all wrapped in smoke.

2002 Haag Pinot Gris ★★ $$
dry, medium-bodied, no oak, high acidity **drink now–6 years**
Haag gets spicy, with lemons and pears.

2002 Josmeyer Mise du Printemps Pinot Blanc ★★ $$
dry, medium-bodied, no oak, high acidity **drink now–4 years**
An ode to spring, fragrant with fresh-picked wildflowers and Meyer lemon.

2002 Hugel Cuvée Les Amours Pinot Blanc ★★ $
dry, light-bodied, no oak, high acidity **drink now–3 years**
Hugel sets the standard for Alsace wines in America with this lemony, mineral-
filled wine.

2002 J.B. Adam Réserve Tokay Pinot Gris ★★ $
off-dry, medium-bodied, no oak, high acidity **drink now–4 years**
A tad of sweetness combined with fruit and spice make this great with grilled
shrimp with a sweet glaze.

2002 Willm Pinot Blanc ★ ★ $
dry, light-bodied, no oak, high acidity drink now–2 years
A savory little wine, with lemon flavors and earthy, slightly bitter spice.

2002 Pierre Sparr Pinot Gris ★ $
off-dry, medium-bodied, no oak, high acidity drink now–3 years
This offers the musky honeycomb flavors and slightly sweet fruit typical of Pinot Gris, at a low price.

RIESLING
& GEWURZTRAMINER

Riesling and Gewurztraminer are the ying and yang of Alsatian wine. Riesling shows subtlety and grace, even while loaded with mineral, citrus, and peach flavors. It is almost always medium-bodied and bone-dry. Fuller-bodied and also dry, Gewurztraminer is as subtle as a brass band, blaring flower and spice (*Gewürz* in German) flavors and scents without inhibition. Some wine lovers find Gewurztraminer (spelled without the umlaut in France) too much. For others, excess is no sin.

at the table

Alsatian Riesling goes as well with grilled snapper as it does with game birds. It has the acidity to cut through cream-based sauces and enough zest for sweet-and-sour Asian dishes. Gewurztraminer's bold flavors can stand up to full-flavored, pungent, or spicy foods. Cumin-sprinkled Muenster cheese is a classic accompaniment.

the bottom line Good Riesling can be found for $12, Gewurztraminer for about $14, but pay $18 to $25 for a tremendous improvement in quality, and up to $30 or more for sublime examples.

recommended wines

2001 Pierre Frick Steinert Grand Cru Gewurztraminer ★ ★ ★ ★ $$$
dry, medium-bodied, no oak, high acidity drink now–15 years
This Grand Cru Gewurztraminer is as subtle, elegant, and timelessly beautiful as a design by Valentino.

1999 Trimbach Cuvée des Seigneurs de Ribeaupierre
Gewurztraminer ★★★★ $$$
dry, medium-bodied, no oak, high acidity drink now–15 years
This is dry as stone and remarkable for its generous lime, sweet and savory spice, and orchid aromas and flavor.

2000 Domaines Schlumberger Kessler Grand Cru
Gewurztraminer ★★★ $$$
off-dry, full-bodied, no oak, medium acidity drink now–12 years
An indulgent Gewurz, fleshy and enticing with soft spice, lemon, and caramel-pear flavors.

1998 Dopff & Irion Schoenenbourg Grand Cru Riesling ★★★ $$$
dry, medium-bodied, no oak, high acidity drink now–10 years
Six years of age have brought out deeply petrol-like minerals from the lush yet dry pineapple and citrus base.

2002 Josmeyer Le Dragon Riesling ★★★ $$$
dry, medium-bodied, no oak, high acidity drink now–8 years
Highly polished mineral flavors tightly woven with almond, strawberry, and orange promise more deliciousness in years to come.

2001 Josmeyer Les Folastries Gewurztraminer ★★★ $$$
dry, medium-bodied, no oak, high acidity drink now–8 years
From Josmeyer's "Art Series," Les Folastries paints a smoky symboliste portrait of lime blossom, piquant spice, and stone.

2001 Dopff & Irion Domaines du Château de Riquewihr
Les Murailles Riesling ★★★ $$
dry, medium-bodied, no oak, high acidity drink now–8 years
A wall of mineral flavors holds up impressive amounts of savory orange and almond flavors.

2001 Bruno Hunold Gewurztraminer ★★★ $
dry, medium-bodied, no oak, high acidity drink now–8 years
A festival of mineral and lime flavors, with streamers of honeysuckle and rose.

2002 Hugel et Fils Gewurztraminer ★★ $$
dry, medium-bodied, no oak, high acidity drink now–5 years
Terrific starter Gewurz, this offers the grape's typical flowers, minerals, and spice encapsulated in soft pear flavors.

2002 Hugel et Fils Riesling ★★ $$
dry, light-bodied, no oak, high acidity drink now–6 years
Lovely, vibrant wine with light floral flavors and minerals—drinking this Riesling just feels healthy.

2001 Trimbach Gewurztraminer ★★ $$
dry, medium-bodied, no oak, high acidity drink now–6 years

Make a list: almonds, dry spice, minerals, lemon, and pear, and yet more almonds. Delish.

2002 Pierre Sparr Gewurztraminer ★ $
dry, medium-bodied, no oak, high acidity drink now–3 years

Dry floral and mineral pleasures are as modest in flavor as in price.

OTHER ALSATIAN WHITES

Some of Alsace's most charming wines are blends. Some vintners label them *Edelzwicker* or *Gentil*; others give blends a proprietary name. Simple examples often contain Chasselas or Sylvaner. Chasselas bottled on its own is often light and lemony. Sylvaner has more heft and an almond underside. Muscat is considered one of Alsace's noble grapes, and it makes wines with fresh citrus blossom and honeysuckle flavors.

recommended wines

2000 Domaine Marcel Deiss Burg ★★★★ $$$$
off-dry, medium-bodied, no oak, high acidity drink now–15 years

One of Alsace's quiet philosophers offers a blend that tastes of flowers, citrus zest, apples, and pears, profoundly set on a mineral base.

2002 Domaine Marcel Deiss Muscat ★★★★ $$$
dry, medium-bodied, no oak, high acidity drink now–3 years

If there were a perfect Muscat, this would be it, with a florist's range of aromas and a miner's depth of minerals, sweetened by lightly honeyed citrus.

2002 Domaine Ostertag Les Vieilles Vignes Sylvaner ★★ $
dry, light-bodied, no oak, high acidity drink now–2 years

Proof Sylvaner is no has-been, this is a crisp apple- and pear-scented treat.

2002 Domaines Schlumberger Les Princes Abbés Sylvaner ★★ $
dry, medium-bodied, no oak, high acidity drink now–3 years

A little gem, with zingy citrus and minerals and an indescribable something one gets from good Sylvaner.

2002 Hugel et Fils Gentil ★★ $
dry, medium-bodied, no oak, high acidity drink now–2 years

Gentil is an apt name: a sip is a like a gentle kiss of apples and fine minerals.

VITICULTURAL PRIMER

Words like "organic" and "biodynamic" don't often show up on wine labels, but they are tossed around among winemakers and wine lovers with more frequency these days. To make sense of some of the different viticultural practices, here's a primer.

Organic Like other organic foods, organic (*biologique* in French) wines are made from grapes grown without the aid of chemical pesticides, herbicides, or fertilizers. However, it is rare to see an organic wine, as U.S. law states that organic wines cannot contain any added sulfites, a commonly used preservative. Wineries that add even a small quantity of sulfites yet use organically grown grapes are allowed to state on the label "made with organic grapes." The great majority of wines commonly understood as organic fall in this category.

Biodynamics Perhaps best explained as organic with an alchemic and homeopathic twist, biodynamics (*biodynamie* in French) views the earth as a living organism that lives in symbiosis with the air and cosmos. Biodynamic practitioners eschew chemical pesticides, but also, for example, tend their vines, harvest their grapes, and bottle their wines according to phases of the moon. It might sound archaic, but its followers are prominent among the world's elite winemakers. Biodynamics' best known sanctioning body is the Demeter Society.

Sustainable agriculture What the French call *lutte raisonnée* (roughly meaning "rational control"), sustainable agriculture requires practitioners to tend their vines as organically as possible, using natural methods of pest control and encouraging biodiversity. Nonorganic pesticides are to be used only as a last resort.

Conventional It is an odd sign of modern society that the use of synthetic fertilizers and pesticides is considered "conventional." Still, the overwhelming majority of grape growers, eager to assure a good crop, apply these materials to ward off the blight of vine diseases, insects, weeds, and molds.

bordeaux

Elegant yet substantial, the great wines of Bordeaux have inspired imitators the world over—many to good effect, but none with the same results. Bordeaux wines find themselves in the cellars of some of the world's greatest restaurants, and they frequently fetch the world's highest prices. Yet, among the 700 million bottles produced in the region per year—the biggest production of any wine-growing region in France—there are plenty of quality wines sold at everyday prices. And since the region offers red, white, dry, and sweet wines, there are plenty of styles from which to choose.

lay of the land

Bordeaux is large; it traverses one estuary, the Gironde; two rivers, the Garonne and Dordogne; and broad expanses of land in between. The Médoc and its highly regarded subregion, the Haut-Médoc, occupy the west bank of the estuary. It's there that you'll find the famed communes of St-Julien, St-Estèphe, Margaux, and Pauillac, plus Listrac and Moulis. Farther south lie Graves and its prestigious subregion Pessac-Léognan, and yet farther south, Sauternes, famed for its luxurious, intense sweet wines (see p. 285). On the east bank—typically referred to as the Left Bank—are the regions of Bourg and Blaye; the celebrated villages of Pomerol and St-Émilion are a little farther south and east from there. Between the Garonne and Dordogne rivers is Entre-Deux-Mers ("between two seas"), where prodigious amounts of light whites and simple reds are made.

on the label

Bordeaux wines are labeled by region, and they confirm the adage that the more specific the region the higher the quality of the wine. This is because wine standards become more stringent as the region becomes more specific. For example, wines labeled Haut-Médoc are made to stricter standards than those labelled Bordeaux Supérieur, which meet stricter standards still than simple "Bordeaux." Wines may also bear a designation that corresponds to their placement within the *Cru Classé* system. This system was devised in 1855 by a consortium of Bordeaux merchants, who drew up a hierarchy of châteaux based on the price their wines fetched. Limited to châteaux in the Médoc, plus one in Graves, the finest wines were ranked by *cru* (growths), from *Premier Cru* (first growth) to *Deuxième Cru* (second growth), and so on down to fifth cru. Most châteaux ranked from second to fifth blur their rankings by simply announcing *Grand Cru Classé* on their labels; those that did not earn Grand Cru status were accorded the ranking *Cru Bourgeois*. In 1955, a similar system was developed to rank St-Émilion's wines, though this system is subject to revision every decade. The famed wines of Pomerol remain unranked.

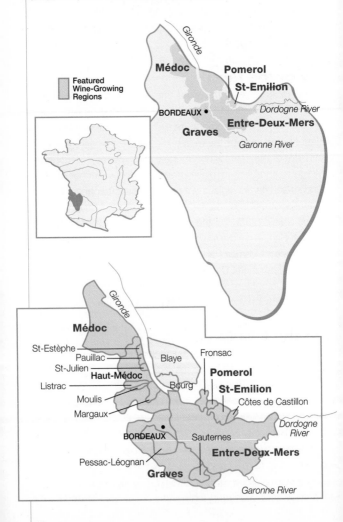

white wines

grapes & styles

Bordeaux white wines range from the light and lemony wines of Entre-Deux-Mers to the dry, mineral-rich treasures of Graves and Pessac-Léognan and the sweet nectars of Sauternes. Whatever the style, Bordeaux whites must be made from one or more of Sauvignon Blanc, Sémillon, or Muscadelle. Whites made in any other part of Bordeaux than these four regions must take the simple Bordeaux appellation.

at the table

Entre-Deux-Mers seems made for Bordeaux's local oysters, though it's a fine choice for any shellfish. The weightier whites of Graves and Pessac-Léognan are best served with more substantial seafood like lobster or monkfish, or full-flavored fowl.

the bottom line

Most simple whites labeled Bordeaux or Entre-Deux-Mers are, at less than $10, a skinflint's delight. You'll have to double that for decent Graves, and triple that for some of the better Pessac wines. A small number of Bordeaux whites from classified châteaux pass the $50 mark.

recommended wines

**2001 Château Smith Haut-Lafitte Grand Cru,
Pessac-Léognan** ★★★ $$$
dry, medium-bodied, medium oak, high acidity **drink in 1–12 years**
There's so much stony flavor here, it's a wonder there's room for all the concentrated peach and herb flavors.

2001 Château Carbonnieux Grand Cru, Pessac-Léognan ★★★ $$
dry, medium-bodied, light oak, high acidity **drink now–10 years**
A classic, *bien equilibré,* as they would say in France, full of peach and lime fruit and stony, savory flavor.

2002 Barons de Rothschild (Lafite) Réserve Spéciale, Bordeaux ★★ $
dry, medium-bodied, light oak, high acidity **drink now–3 years**
Smooth and round, this is nicely shaped with lightly spiced pear, lemon, and peach flavors.

2001 Château Brondelle, Graves ★ ★ $
dry, medium-bodied, light oak, high acidity **drink now–3 years**
Nicely priced white Graves, with smoky peach and light mineral flavors.

2002 Château Graville-Lacoste, Graves ★ ★ $
dry, medium-bodied, no oak, high acidity **drink now–3 years**
Unlike many Graves, this trades oak flavors for a zingy, mixed-citrus brightness.

2002 Château La Freynelle, Bordeaux ★ ★ $
dry, medium-bodied, light oak, high acidity **drink now–3 years**
Breezy apple blossom, honey, and lemon flavors at a bargain price.

2002 La Fleur du Roy, Bordeaux ★ $
dry, medium-bodied, no oak, high acidity **drink now–1 year**
Light grapefruit and almond flavors make this a nice wine for luncheon salads.

2002 Michel Lynch Sauvignon Blanc, Bordeaux ★ $
dry, light-bodied, no oak, high acidity **drink now**
These lemon and minerals flavors are built for oysters.

red wines

grapes & styles

Cabernet Sauvignon dominates the red wines made on Bordeaux's left bank, while Merlot dominates on the right. Most all, however, are blended with some proportion of Cabernet Sauvignon, Merlot, Cabernet Franc, Malbec, Petit Verdot, and/or Carmènere. Proportions differ among châteaux and depend on how well a particular variety does in a vintage. All red Bordeaux wines are typically fragrant and elegant with lean red fruit flavors; however, the Left Bank's Cabernet-based wines tend to be more tannic with pencil-lead scents, and the Merlot-based wines of Pomerol and St-Émilion more plush, with ripe plum and cedar flavors.

at the table

The commune of Pauillac, home of famed Châteaux Latour, Lafite, and Mouton-Rothschild, also stamps its name on some of the best lamb in France. No matter where it's from, roast lamb is great with red Bordeaux, as is roast duck, venison, or boar. Vegetarians can indulge in Bordeaux's graces with smoked and grilled tofu, or a slice of farmhouse Cheddar.

the bottom line With the combination of enormous production, a string of good vintages from 1998 to 2002, and fierce competitors near and far, it's possible to find many good basic Bordeaux and Médoc wines for $10 to $20. For cru-classified wines or their equivalents, prices have dropped by more than a third of the exorbitant $300 asked for bottles of the 2000 vintage. When buying Grand Cru wines, shop around: prices vary tremendously among retailers. Also, good deals can be found for $15 to $25 in less-famous appellations like Moulis and Listrac, as well as Côtes de Fronsac, Castillon, and Bourg.

what to buy BORDEAUX RIGHT BANK

1992	1993	1994	1995	1996	1997
★	★★	★★★	★★★	★★★★	★★

1998	1999	2000	2001	2002	2003
★★★★	★★★	★★★★	★★★	★★★	★★

what to buy BORDEAUX LEFT BANK, EXCLUDING GRAVES

1992	1993	1994	1995	1996	1997
★	★★	★★★	★★★★	★★★★	★★

1998	1999	2000	2001	2002	2003
★★★	★★★	★★★★	★★★	★★★	★★

what to buy RED GRAVES

1992	1993	1994	1995	1996	1997
★	★★★	★★★	★★★	★★★	★★★

1998	1999	2000	2001	2002	2003
★★	★★★	★★★★	★★	★★★	★★

recommended wines

2001 Château Pichon Longueville Comtesse de Lalande Grand Cru, Pauillac ★★★★ $$$$
dry, full-bodied, heavy tannin, high acidity   **drink in 4–15 years**
Graceful and elegant, this impresses quietly with fine fruit and minerals, though it lacks none of Pauillac's power.

SMASH THE GLASSES

Lots of effort (and marketing) has gone into creating glassware that will enhance the nuances of a particular wine, resulting in an array of glass shapes and styles that could make the head spin. While specialized glasses have their appeal—the tall and tulip-shaped Bordeaux glass or the fat, balloon-shaped Burgundy bowl—it's worth noting that restaurants all over France set their tables with two wine glasses, one large and one small. One for red, one for white? Nope. The large glass is for water, the small one for whatever wine you happen to order. In other words, take their cue and go with what you have.

2001 Château Angélus Premier Grand Cru, St-Émilion ★★★ $$$$
dry, full-bodied, heavy tannin, high acidity　　　drink now–15 years
Satin-smooth, with ripe berry and plum flavors and sleek minerality.

**2001 Château Canon-la-Gaffelière Grand Cru,
St-Émilion**　　　★★★ $$$$
dry, full-bodied, heavy tannin, high acidity　　　drink in 2–12 years
Black on black, this plays dark fruit flavors off of sultry smoke, stone, and roasted meat notes.

2001 Château Figeac Premier Grand Cru, St-Émilion ★★★ $$$$
dry, full-bodied, heavy tannin, high acidity　　　drink in 5–15 years
Lose this in your cellar for a few years so the tannin softens and the roast coffee, tobacco, and blackberry flavors have a chance to express themselves.

**2001 Château Pape Clément Grand Cru,
Pessac-Léognan**　　　★★★ $$$$
dry, full-bodied, heavy tannin, high acidity　　　drink in 3–15 years
Red fruit, cedar, and minerals make for a luxurious red.

2001 Carruades de Lafite, Pauillac　　　★★★ $$$
dry, full-bodied, medium tannin, high acidity　　　drink now–10 years
Drink this while waiting for its parent, Château Lafite, to age: its concentrated dark fruit, light floral, and soft mineral flavors will keep you plenty happy.

2001 Château Brane-Cantenac Grand Cru, Margaux　　　★★★ $$$
dry, full-bodied, heavy tannin, high acidity　　　drink in 2–12 years
Majestic Margaux, this shows the commune's often elusive elegance with violet and fresh berry flavors.

2001 Château Gazin, Pomerol ★ ★ ★ $$$
dry, full-bodied, heavy tannin, high acidity **drink in 2–12 years**
Wonderfully wild for proper Pomerol, this oozes animal and bramble berry flavors.

2001 Château Lafon-Rochet Grand Cru, St-Estèphe ★ ★ ★ $$$
dry, full-bodied, heavy tannin, high acidity **drink in 2–12 years**
A challenge to the idea that St-Estèphe's wines are staid, this is velvety with cassis flavors and playfully peppery.

2001 Château Lynch-Bages Grand Cru, Pauillac ★ ★ ★ $$$
dry, full-bodied, heavy tannin, high acidity **drink in 3–15 years**
As always, Lynch-Bages goes far beyond its classification with elegant, powerful fruit, laden with minerals.

2000 Château Lyonnat Réserve de la Famille, Lussac-St-Émilion ★ ★ ★ $$$
dry, full-bodied, heavy tannin, high acidity **drink now–8 years**
A smooth weave of dark fruit, light spice, and fine minerals. A beauty.

2001 Château Phélan Ségur, St-Estèphe ★ ★ ★ $$$
dry, full-bodied, heavy tannin, high acidity **drink in 3–15 years**
Phélan stands firm with black fruit, smoke, and roasted meat flavors.

2001 Château Prieuré-Lichine Grand Cru Classé, Margaux ★ ★ ★ $$$
dry, full-bodied, heavy tannin, high acidity **drink in 3–12 years**
Marvelous, minerally Margaux, rich with dark cherry, coffee, and tobacco notes.

2001 Château Talbot Grand Cru, St-Julien ★ ★ ★ $$$
dry, full-bodied, heavy tannin, high acidity **drink in 3–15 years**
A swirl of delicious flavors, from coffee to chocolate, flowers, smoke, and berries.

2001 Château Cantemerle Grand Cru, Haut-Médoc ★ ★ ★ $$
dry, full-bodied, heavy tannin, high acidity **drink in 3–12 years**
Blackbirds (*merles*) sing a ribald, rustic tune, full of earthy, musky herb and wild blackberry notes.

2000 Château de Parenchère Cuvée Raphael Gazaniol, Bordeaux Supérieur ★ ★ ★ $$
dry, full-bodied, heavy tannin, high acidity **drink in 1–15 years**
Smooth, smoky, and lush, this peppery Bordeaux would be a good alternative to Napa Cab.

2001 Château Lagrange Grand Cru, St-Julien ★ ★ ★ $$
dry, full-bodied, heavy tannin, high acidity **drink in 3–15 years**
Smooth with sultry berry and flirtatious floral flavors, Lagrange seems to get better with each passing year.

france **bordeaux reds**

2001 Château Renard Mondesir, Fronsac ★★★ $$
dry, full-bodied, heavy tannin, high acidity **drink in 2–10 years**
With ripe red fruit flavors and lots of minerals, this gives a good taste of
Fronsac wines: powerful, a little rustic, but ultimately graceful.

2001 Château Sergant, Lalande-de-Pomerol ★★★ $$
dry, medium-bodied, medium tannin, high acidity **drink now–10 years**
A wine that will roll across your tongue as elegantly as the name Lalande, full
of red fruit, light spice, and minerals.

2001 Château Beychevelle Grand Cru, St-Julien ★★ $$$
dry, full-bodied, heavy tannin, high acidity **drink in 3–12 years**
Beychevelle wins attention for its cassis, coffee, and bramble profile.

2001 Château de Pez, St-Estèphe ★★ $$$
dry, medium-bodied, medium tannin, high acidity **drink now–8 years**
Classic St-Estèphe: give de Pez some air to open up with stories of berries,
tobacco, and earth.

2001 Château La Lagune, Haut-Médoc ★★ $$$
dry, full-bodied, heavy tannin, high acidity **drink now–10 years**
Big and juicy, this is easy to enjoy at any time, yet still serious enough to serve
for grand occasions.

2001 Blason d'Issan, Margaux ★★ $$
dry, medium-bodied, medium tannin, high acidity **drink now–8 years**
Château d'Issan's second-tier wine is loaded with delicious, fresh cassis and
cherry flavor.

2001 Château Coufran Cru Bourgeois, Haut-Médoc ★★ $$
dry, full-bodied, heavy tannin, high acidity **drink now–6 years**
Thick and chunky dark fruit flavors make a darn good steak-house wine.

2000 Château Larose-Trintaudon Cru Bourgeois, Haut-Médoc ★★ $$
dry, full-bodied, heavy tannin, high acidity **drink now–5 years**
A widely available classified Bordeaux, this shows all the stuff Médoc's made
of: cassis, mineral, and hints of cedar.

2000 Château Pavillon, Canon-Fronsac ★★ $$
dry, full-bodied, heavy tannin, high acidity **drink in 2–12 years**
So smoky, one sip is like a stroll down tobacco road, lined with berry bushes.

2001 Château Puy Arnaud Maurèze, Côtes de Castillon ★★ $
dry, full-bodied, medium tannin, high acidity **drink now–8 years**
A well-regarded winemaker gives his fans a low-cost treat, full of black fruit
and sweet, spicy quince jam flavors.

2001 Château Recougne, Bordeaux Supérieur ★★ $
dry, full-bodied, medium tannin, high acidity drink now–6 years
Peppery dark fruit flavors make a terrific *steak frites* wine.

**2000 Baron Philippe de Rothschild Mouton Cadet Réserve,
Médoc** ★ $
dry, medium-bodied, medium tannin, high acidity drink now–5 years
Mouton Cadet consistently offers a taste of the Médoc's typical cassis, tobacco,
and stone flavors for a reasonable sum.

2001 Château La Grange de Grenet, Bordeaux ★ $
dry, medium-bodied, heavy tannin, high acidity drink now–6 years
Here's a basic claret from Cap de Merle with appealing fruit and smoke flavors.

WINES WE WISH WE HAD MORE ROOM FOR
2000 Château Boutisse Grand Cru, St-Émilion ★★★ $$$ dry, full-
bodied, medium tannin, high acidity, drink now–12 years; **2001 Pavillon
Rouge du Château Margaux, Margaux** ★★★ $$$ dry, full-bodied,
medium tannin, high acidity, drink now–10 years; **2001 Château Clarke,
Listrac-Médoc** ★★ $$$ dry, full-bodied, medium tannin, high acidity,
drink in 1–10 years; **2000 Baron Philippe de Rothschild, St-Émilion**
★★ $$ dry, medium-bodied, heavy tannin, high acidity, drink now–6 years;
2000 Château Preuillac Cru Bourgeois, Médoc ★ $$ dry, medium-
bodied, medium tannin, high acidity, drink now–4 years; **2001 Château
Greysac Cru Bourgeois, Médoc** ★ $ dry, full-bodied, heavy tannin, high
acidity, drink now–4 years

burgundy

At their best, Burgundies are the finest, most graceful wines in
the world, reflecting a perfect balance between sun-ripened
fruit, minerals, and heavenly smokiness. At their worst, they
remind that the one who captures hearts is often the one who
breaks them. Still, Burgundy lovers find the risk well worth taking.

lay of the land
Burgundy is, frankly, confusing. Vineyards can be owned by
dozens of people, some with only a few rows of vines. Grapes
from these vineyards may be used in the wines of dozens of dif-
ferent wineries. Some wineries make wines from their own
grapes; others purchase grapes, or purchase and blend wines
made by others, and bottle them under their own names.

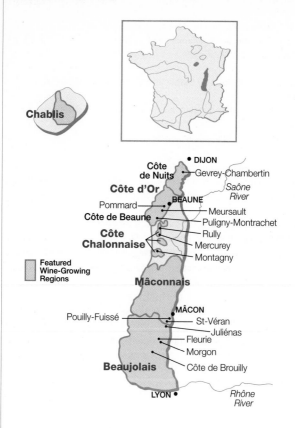

However, consider Burgundy by districts, and it's more manageable. In the northeast is the celebrated white wine district of Chablis. In the center sits the 35-mile long Côte d'Or ("golden slope"), which is divided into the Côte de Nuits, home of some of the world's most revered reds, and the Côte de Beaune. home to some of the world's most esteemed whites. To the south is the Côte Chalonnaise, an archipelago of well-regarded reds and whites. Farther south lies the Chardonnay-dominated Mâconnais, and below that sits Beaujolais, the center of good-time reds.

grapes & styles

Proof that there's some justice in the world, mastering Burgundy's grapes is a cinch. If a white wine doesn't list a grape variety on the label—and most don't—it's made from

Chardonnay. There are some Sauvignon Blanc wines from St-Bris, near Chablis, and parts of the Côte Chalonnaise are known for light, lemony Aligoté. In these instances, the grape will be identified on the label. All red Burgundies are made from Pinot Noir, except for those from Beaujolais, which use Gamay.

on the label

Burgundy wine labels list the place where the wine's grapes grew. As a general rule, the more specific the place, the better the wine. The established hierarchy, outlined here, is meaningful, but don't get too caught up in it. Great producers can make remarkable wines with grapes from modest areas, while shoddy producers turn gold into straw.

Region The most general appellation, *Bourgogne* ("Burgundy" in French) signifies a wine made from grapes grown anywhere within Burgundy.

District Wines made from grapes grown exclusively in one of Burgundy's districts: Chablis, for instance. District wines appended with the word *Villages* are from even more specific areas within the district.

Village Wines made from grapes grown within the boundaries of a particular village: Meursault, for example. The designation is helpful since the soil and climate are frequently consistent within a village's boundaries and produce wines with a particular terroir. However, since village boundaries are drawn for reasons other than geology, caution is in order.

Premier Cru Wines made from grapes grown in one of the less than 600 vineyards among Burgundy's 4,500 vineyards that have earned *Premier Cru* status. Wines from specific Premier Cru vineyards are allowed to mention the name of the vineyard along with the village and the ranking, such as Puligny-Montrachet Folatières Premier Cru. Wines made from grapes from different Premier Cru vineyards can take the village name, plus Premier Cru, like Pommard Premier Cru. Note: Premier Cru is secondary to Grand Cru in Burgundy, unlike in Bordeaux, where Premier Cru wines are superior.

Grand Cru Wines from *Grand Cru* vineyards, which represent less than one percent of the region's vineyards. Wines from these vineyards are usually the finest, most concentrated and complex, and often require several years of aging for their potential to emerge. Grand Cru wines are typically labeled only by the name of the vineyard, such as Montrachet, La Romanée, or Le Musigny. If the names don't ring "Grand Cru" in your ears, the prices certainly will.

However, be aware that several Grand Cru vineyards traverse the borders of more than one village. Some village councils, eager to attach their name to glory, have appended the name of the great vineyard to their village's name; Chassagne-Montrachet, for instance. It may share part of the great Montrachet vineyard, but it isn't Montrachet.

at the table

Chablis' mineral flavors match perfectly the briny qualities of oysters and add complexity to pan-fried trout. A simple Mâcon white is good for hors d'oeuvres or grilled chicken breasts. More substantial Premier Cru and Grand Cru white wines need full-flavored fish like striped bass, sturgeon, or salmon. They can also handle roast pork loin.

Burgundy's red wines offer great flexibility. Lighter versions can be served with most fish, heavier versions with roast lamb or venison. Most red Burgundy falls somewhere in between and makes an excellent choice when people have ordered very different dishes in a restaurant. Beaujolais is a definitive bistro wine, the simplest ones for burgers, the more complex versions for lamb stews, boeuf bourguignon, roasted chicken.

the bottom line Despite Burgundy's renown, total production is relatively small, one-tenth that of Bordeaux. Still, its prices are often less than those asked for many Bordeaux. Simple Mâcon whites start at $10; Bourgogne Blancs at $11, with many hovering in the low $20s. Village wine prices start around $20, Premier Cru wines in the high $20s. A smattering of Grand Crus can be found in the $40s, but prices accelerate to over $200.

Red Burgundies cost a few dollars more in each category. Modest Bourgogne reds start at $12; quality Premier Cru wines begin at $35. Grand Crus can be acquired in the mid-$40s, but the great stuff will cost multiples of that. Going the other direction the simplest Beaujolais can be picked up for $8; superior Cru Beaujolais can be found for $11 to $20.

chablis

If imitation is the greatest compliment, Chablis has it in spades. Unfortunately many of Chablis' imitators have stolen its good name for insipid wines that bear no resemblance to the real thing. Chablis' distinction is due to the combination of cool climate, which keeps acid levels high, and the region's chalky soil, which gives its wines an unmistakable mineral edge. Basic Chablis, which is rarely aged in oak barrels, sings with fresh citrus and apple flavors. Premier Cru and Grand Cru wines usually spend time in oak barrels, which contribute a smoky complexity to their powerful fruit and mineral flavors. Petit Chablis is made from grapes grown in vineyards near Chablis that are not considered as fine.

what to buy CHABLIS

1998	1999	2000	2001	2002	2003
★★★	★★★	★★	★★	★★★	★★★

recommended wines

2001 Domaine William Fèvre Grand Cru Valmur   ★★★★ $$$$
dry, full-bodied, light oak, high acidity   **drink now–10 years**
With a complex array of flavors ranging from herbs to beeswax, apple, citrus, passion fruit, peach, and mineral, this is a wine to contemplate with each sip.

2002 Domaine Laroche Grand Cru Les Blanchots   ★★★★ $$$
dry, full-bodied, light oak, high acidity   **drink now–15 years**
Truffles and minerals share the stage with ripe pear and citrus flavors in a never-ending passion play of flavor.

2002 Corinne et Jean-Pierre Grossot Premier Cru
Les Fourneaux   ★★★ $$$
dry, medium-bodied, no oak, high acidity   **drink now–8 years**
Citrus flavors infused with stone make for a terrific Chablis.

2002 Joseph Drouhin Premier Cru Montmains   ★★★ $$$
dry, full-bodied, no oak, high acidity   **drink now–6 years**
Four seasons of flavor, from spring blossoms, to summer and autumn fruit, to wintery mineral austerity.

2002 Domaine Servin Première Cuvée Les Pargues ★★★ $$
dry, medium-bodied, no oak, high acidity drink now–8 years
A Chablis redolent of almond, lemon confit, and apple, all lined with minerals.

2002 Domaine Christian Moreau Père et Fils ★★ $$
dry, medium-bodied, no oak, high acidity drink now–3 years
Classic Chablis, full of citrus, pear, and fine mineral flavors.

2002 Domaine Laroche Saint Martin ★★ $$
dry, medium-bodied, no oak, high acidity drink now–6 years
This is surprisingly affordable for a Chablis that sports truffley mineral flavors along with its citrus fruits.

2002 Jean-Marc Brocard Domaine Ste-Claire Vieilles Vignes ★★ $$
dry, medium-bodied, no oak, high acidity drink now–4 years
Hints of olive oil join Chablis's classic chalk and citrus notes.

2002 Laurent Tribut ★★ $$
dry, medium-bodied, no oak, high acidity drink now–6 years
Solid Chablis, with baked apple and chalky mineral flavors.

côte d'or

For many an enophile, *le* Côte d'Or, the "golden slope," could not have been better named. It is from here that come the crown jewels of the wine world. Its northern half, called the Côte de Nuits, is revered for its smoky, mineral, cherry-scented Pinot Noir from celebrated villages like Gevry-Chambertin, Fixin, and Vosne-Romanée. Its southern half, the Côte de Beaune, is heralded for its superb Chardonnay villages, Meursault, Chassagne-Montrachet, and Santenay. Superb red wines are also made in district villages, including the powerful Pommard, velvety Volnay, and the commanding Aloxe-Corton.

what to buy CÔTE D'OR WHITE WINES

1998	1999	2000	2001	2002	2003
★★	★★★	★★	★★	★★★	★★★

what to buy CÔTE D'OR RED WINES

1998	1999	2000	2001	2002	2003
★★	★★★	★	★★	★★★★	★★★★

recommended white wines

2001 Bonneau du Martray Grand Cru,
Corton-Charlemagne ★★★★ $$$$
dry, full-bodied, medium oak, high acidity **drink now–15 years**
This is expensive, but it offers an emperor's ransom of gleaming minerals,
rare exotic fruits, precious spice, and luscious sweetmeats in flavor.

2001 Domaine Amiot Guy et Fils Les Caillerets Premier Cru,
Chassagne-Montrachet ★★★★ $$$$
dry, medium-bodied, light oak, high acidity **drink now–12 years**
Silky as the fabrics they used to weave down the road in Lyon, with nutty
grapefruit and spice flavors.

2002 Vincent Girardin Les Combettes Premier Cru,
Puligny-Montrachet ★★★★ $$$$
dry, medium-bodied, light oak, high acidity **drink now–12 years**
Premier Cru going for the Grand, this is full of beautifully concentrated apple
and almond tart flavors lightened by lemon and dusted with minerals.

2002 Bernard Moreau Les Vergers Premier Cru,
Chassagne-Montrachet ★★★ $$$$
dry, medium-bodied, medium oak, high acidity **drink now–12 years**
More Montrachet than Chassagne, this gives an intense reading of citrus,
smoke, minerals, licorice, and mint.

2001 Domaine Bouchard Père & Fils Premier Cru Genevrières,
Meursault ★★★ $$$$
dry, medium-bodied, medium oak, high acidity **drink now–8 years**
Junipers (*genévriers*) give way to nuts and oranges in this highly aromatic,
nutty, delicious wine.

2001 Etienne Sauzet Champ-Canet Premier Cru,
Puligny-Montrachet ★★★ $$$$
dry, medium-bodied, medium oak, high acidity **drink now–6 years**
Toasty, nutty Chardonnay, this would be splendid with hazelnut-crusted monkfish or cod.

2002 Domaine Vincent Girardin Les Narvaux, Meursault ★★★ $$$
dry, medium-bodied, light oak, high acidity **drink now–12 years**
Seamless wine, this Meursault offers fruit, oak, and minerals smoothed and
polished to a satiny sheen.

2002 Hubert Lamy La Princée, St-Aubin ★★★ $$$
dry, medium-bodied, medium oak, high acidity **drink now–10 years**
A sophisticate, bred on smoke and minerals.

TEN FAVORITE WINE BOOKS

1. Wine by Hugh Johnson. Somewhat out of date, but for a gentle, informative, well-written overview of wine, there's no better.

2. The Oxford Companion to Wine edited by Jancis Robinson. From abboccato to zymase, it's all here in this essential reference book.

3. Wine Snobbery: An Insider's Guide to the Booze Business by Andrew Barr. An iconoclastic approach to the good, the bad, and the ugly of the wine world by a cheeky Brit.

4. Henry IV by Shakespeare. One of the greatest tributes to Sherry ever written.

5. The Wine Song in Classical Arabic Poetry: Abu Nuwas and the Literary Tradition by Philip F. Kennedy. Among the best collections and commentaries on Arab bacchic poetry in English.

6. Ancient Wine: The Search for the Origins of Viniculture by Patrick E. McGovern. A fascinating exploration through science, history, and anthropology that takes you back to where it all began.

7. Wine from Sky to Earth: Growing and Appreciating Biodynamic Wine by Nicolas Joly. A passionate journey into the world of biodynamics from the famed Loire Valley winemaker.

8. Napa Wine: A History from Mission Days to Present by Charles L. Sullivan. A detailed account of the ups and downs of California's greatest wine region, illustrated by fine sepia prints.

9. The New Sotheby's Wine Encyclopedia by Tom Stevenson. Comprehensive and full of useful, full-color illustrations of everything from grape varieties to wine labels.

10. Bordeaux and Its Wines 15th Edition, by Marc-Henry Lemay. A tome in the tradition of France's great *encyclopédistes*, for the Bordeaux fanatic.

2002 Joseph Drouhin, Puligny-Montrachet ★★★ $$$
dry, medium-bodied, light oak, high acidity drink now–6 years
Toasty oak quickly gives way to vibrant tangerine and salty mineral flavors.

2001 Michel Colin-Deléger & Fils Combe Bazin, St-Romain ★★★ $$$
dry, medium-bodied, light oak, high acidity drink now–8 years
Aromatic with apple, citrus, nuts, and spice, this offers Premier Cru quality.

2002 Olivier Leflaive, Puligny-Montrachet ★★★ $$$
dry, medium-bodied, light oak, high acidity drink now–8 years
Definitive Puligny, balanced and laden with mineral and apple flavors.

2001 Louis Jadot, Chassagne-Montrachet ★★ $$$
dry, medium-bodied, medium oak, high acidity drink now–6 years
With rich citrus, mineral, and smoky highlights, this shows what makes Chassagne special.

2001 Domaine Caillot Les Herbeux, Bourgogne ★★ $$
dry, medium-bodied, light oak, high acidity drink now–3 years
Full of mineral and citrus flavors, this offers great value at less than $20.

2002 Verget Terroirs de Côte d'Or, Bourgogne ★★ $$
dry, medium-bodied, light oak, high acidity drink now–3 years
Fragrant as fresh flowers and crisp with minerality, this offers an elegance that goes far beyond its price.

2002 Vincent Girardin Emotion de Terroirs, Bourgogne ★★ $$
dry, medium-bodied, light oak, high acidity drink now–3 years
Creamy yet vibrant citrus and mineral notes bring this wine to life.

2002 Olivier Leflaive Les Sétilles, Bourgogne ★★ $
dry, medium-bodied, light oak, high acidity drink now–3 years
A taste of Burgundy for a very good price.

2001 Faiveley Georges Faiveley Chardonnay, Bourgogne ★ $
dry, medium-bodied, light oak, high acidity drink now–2 years
Light strawberry aromas and citrus flavors make this more than simple Chard.

recommended red wines

2001 Domaine Jacques Prieur Grand Cru, Musigny ★★★★ $$$$
dry, full-bodied, medium tannin, high acidity drink now–15 years
Complex flavors of fresh berries, dried apricots, fine minerals, and more put the grand in Grand Cru.

2001 Bouchard Père & Fils Vigne de l'Enfant Jésus
Premier Cru Grèves, Beaune ★★★ $$$$
dry, medium-bodied, heavy tannin, high acidity   **drink in 2–10 years**
Inspired Beaune, chewy with tannin, minerals, and concentrated fruit flavors.

2000 J.M. Boillot Premier Cru Volnay-Pitures,
Volnay ★★★ $$$$
dry, medium-bodied, medium tannin, high acidity   **drink now–8 years**
Polished minerals, smoothed tannin, and beautifully tamed fruit.

2001 Vincent Girardin Premier Cru Les Suchots,
Vosne-Romanée ★★★ $$$$
dry, medium-bodied, medium tannin, high acidity   **drink now–10 years**
A vampish wine, this entices with voluptuous fruit, caresses of spice, and exciting promises for the future.

2001 Domaine de Courcel Premier Cru Grand Clos des Épenots,
Pommard ★★★ $$$
dry, medium-bodied, heavy tannin, high acidity   **drink in 1–10 years**
Heavy-duty Pommard, rich in minerality wrapped by layers of thick fruit.

2001 Domaine Tollot-Beaut Premier Cru Clos-du-Roi,
Beaune ★★★ $$$
dry, medium-bodied, medium tannin, high acidity   **drink now–8 years**
In a challenging year, Tollot manages to provide irresistibly ripe fruit flavors.

2002 Lignier-Michelot Morey St-Denis En la Rue de Vergy,
Morey St-Denis ★★★ $$$
dry, full-bodied, medium tannin, high acidity   **drink now–12 years**
Pure animal, with wild fruit, herb, tar, and smoke.

2001 Bernard Morey et Fils Vieilles Vignes, Santenay ★★★ $$
dry, medium-bodied, medium tannin, high acidity   **drink now–8 years**
Slow rotations of ripe fruit are punctuated by rhythms of smoke and mineral.

2000 Domaine Charles Audoin Les Longeroies, Marsannay ★★★ $$
dry, medium-bodied, medium tannin, high acidity   **drink now–10 years**
Satiny smooth, this seduces with velvety cherry flavors scented by violets.

2002 Nicolas Potel Maison Dieu Vieilles Vignes,
Bourgogne ★★★ $$
dry, medium-bodied, medium tannin, high acidity   **drink now–6 years**
A Bourgogne with earthy fruit and smoky meat flavors make Potel a rising star.

2001 Domaine Chandon de Briailles, Savigny-Les-Beaune ★★ $$$
dry, light-bodied, medium tannin, high acidity   **drink now–4 years**
Light but lovely, this Savigny charms with diaphanous fruit and spice.

2001 Bernard Morey et Fils Vieilles Vignes,
Chassagne-Montrachet   ★★ $$
dry, medium-bodied, heavy tannin, high acidity   drink in 1–8 years
Chunky Chassagne, chew this well to let up the earthy fruit and minerals, or
cellar it for some years.

2001 Catherine & Claude Maréchal Cuvée Gravel,
Bourgogne   ★★ $$
dry, medium-bodied, medium tannin, high acidity   drink now–5 years
Supple, smoky, and suave.

2001 Joseph Drouhin Laforet Pinot Noir, Bourgogne   ★ $
dry, light-bodied, medium tannin, high acidity   drink now–3 years
Simple, tart berry flavors for salmon sandwiches, at an affordable price.

WINES WE WISH WE HAD MORE ROOM FOR
2001 Louis Jadot, Pommard ★★★ $$$ dry, medium-bodied, heavy
tannin, high acidity, drink now–8 years; **2001 Bouchard Père & Fils,**
Gevrey-Chambertin ★★ $$$ dry, medium-bodied, medium tannin, high
acidity, drink now–8 years; **2001 Bernard Morey et Fils La Fussière**
Premier Cru, Maranges ★★ $$ dry, medium-bodied, medium tannin,
high acidity, drink in 1–6 years; **2002 Joseph Drouhin, Côte de Beaune**
★★ $$ dry, medium-bodied, medium tannin, high acidity, drink now–6 years

côte chalonnaise

Burgundy lovers with more sense than cash have long known
that some of the region's best bargains can be found in the quiet
Côte Chalonnaise. Except for the acclaimed reds of Mercurey
and Givry, villages such as Rully and Montagny are often overlooked and less pricey, although they grow Chardonnay as fine
as most villages to the north. Look also for Aligoté, Burgundy's
other white grape, especially from the village of Bouzeron.
Aligoté wines will bear the name of the grape on the label.

recommended white wines

2002 J.M. Boillot Premier Cru Meix Cadot, Rully   ★★★ $$$
dry, medium-bodied, light oak, high acidity   drink now–8 years
All about freshness, from fresh-cut herbs to just-squeezed grapefruit
smoothed by the richness of butter straight out of the churn.

2002 J.M. Boillot Premier Cru, Montagny ★ ★ ★ $$
dry, medium-bodied, medium oak, high acidity drink now–8 years
Citrus melts into smooth, light, nutty minerality, fresh and clean.

2002 Paul Jacqueson Premier Cru La Pucelle, Rully ★ ★ ★ $$
dry, medium-bodied, light oak, high acidity drink now–8 years
Aromatic wine, this offers exotic notes ranging from fennel to orange peel to
white pepper, all tethered by firm minerality.

2002 Chofflet-Valdenaire Les Galaffres, Givry ★ ★ $$
dry, medium-bodied, light oak, high acidity drink now–4 years
Givry Blanc is rare, but the song of minerals, smoke, and ripe fruit in this one
makes it worth hunting down.

2002 Joseph Drouhin, Rully ★ ★ $$
dry, medium-bodied, light oak, high acidity drink now–5 years
Almond and citrus flavors roll together for a light and easy Chardonnay.

recommended red wines

**2002 Château Génot-Boulanger Les Saumonts Premier Cru,
Mercurey** ★ ★ $$
dry, medium-bodied, heavy tannin, high acidity drink in 1–8 years
Behind the considerable tannins there's plenty of dark, mineral-laden fruit:
give it some time to emerge.

2002 Chofflet-Valdenaire, Givry ★ ★ $$
dry, medium-bodied, heavy tannin, high acidity drink now–4 years
Great bistro wine, this is chewy with tannin and ripe berry flavors.

2001 Faiveley Domaine de la Croix Jacquelet, Mercurey ★ ★ $$
dry, light-bodied, medium tannin, high acidity drink now–4 years
Fun wine with a serious edge, this offers light, lively berry flavors grounded
with minerality.

mâconnais

Most Mâconnais wines are flighty numbers with zippy lemon
flavors, but growing numbers of ambitious winemakers and
négociants are focusing on quality over quantity and making
juicy wines with a cornucopia of fruit flavors. Pouilly-Fuissé is the

area's most highly regarded—and expensive—appellation. St-Véran offers similar quality for a few dollars less. For terrific value, look for wines with a village name appended to the Mâcon designation, such as Mâcon-Viré.

what to buy MÂCONNAIS

1999	2000	2001	2002	2003
★★★★	★★	★★★	★★	★★★★

recommended wines

2002 Château Fuissé, Pouilly-Fuissé ★★★ $$$
dry, medium-bodied, light oak, high acidity drink now–8 years
A sleeper of a wine, showing fruit, mineral, and nut flavors that awaken with some time and air.

2002 Château de la Greffière Vieilles Vignes, Mâcon La Roche-Vineuse ★★★ $$
dry, medium-bodied, no oak, high acidity drink now–4 years
Pine and herb notes add extra interest to snappy lemon and lime flavors.

2002 Domaine Chataigneraie-Laborier Bélemnites, Pouilly-Fuissé ★★★ $$
dry, medium-bodied, light oak, high acidity drink now–10 years
A fine line of vanilla runs through satin-textured citrus and mineral flavors, vibrant and elegant.

2000 Jean Thévenet Domaine de la Bongran Cuvée Tradition, Mâcon-Villages ★★ $$$
dry, medium-bodied, light oak, high acidity drink now–6 years
Sweet strawberry, floral, and orange flavors surprise when they end dry.

2002 Domaine Thomas, St-Véran ★★ $$
dry, medium-bodied, no oak, high acidity drink now–2 years
Vivacious St-Véran, full of zingy citrus and almond flavors.

2002 Domaine Jean Touzot Vieilles Vignes, Mâcon-Villages ★★ $
dry, medium-bodied, medium oak, high acidity drink now–3 years
Flinty, juicy grapefruit and lemon flavors make this lipsmacking.

2002 Louis Jadot Domaine de la Chapelle aux Loups, St-Véran ★★ $
dry, medium-bodied, light oak, high acidity drink now–4 years
From fruits to nuts, fresh lemon, and quince.

2002 Verget Les Vallons de Lamartine, Mâcon-Villages   ★ ★ $
dry, medium-bodied, no oak, high acidity   **drink now–3 years**
Minerals joined by apple and spice make this an outstanding Mâcon.

2002 Cave de Lugny Les Charmes, Mâcon-Lugny   ★ $
dry, medium-bodied, light oak, high acidity   **drink now–2 years**
Simple almond and citrus flavors offer a good option for a lunch wine.

beaujolais

Beaujolais produces rivers of easy-to-drink, affordable wines, but it also offers complex wines that can satisfy the cravings of a light-pocketed Burgundy lover. There are differences, however. Instead of Pinot Noir, Gamay rules the land. A little Chardonnay is also grown. Also, Beaujolais has its own ranking system:

Beaujolais Nouveau Made directly after harvest and released on the third Thursday of November—just in time for Thanksgiving—Beaujolais Nouveau is as simple as wine gets. It is usually inexpensive.

Beaujolais Made from grapes grown anywhere in Beaujolais, these wines have a bit more weight than Beaujolais Nouveau.

Beaujolais Villages Wines made from grapes grown in thirty-nine villages that occupy the rolling, granite-laden hills in the center of Beaujolais are entitled to this ranking. Most offer more fresh fruit and complex mineral flavors than basic Beaujolais.

Cru Beaujolais Ten hillside villages are home to Beaujolais' best, most serious wines. They tend to offer concentrated dark berry flavors, smoky minerality, and noticeable tannin—qualities that allow some to age well. "Beaujolais" is almost never found on a Cru label. Instead, look for the village names: Brouilly, Chénas, Chiroubles, Côte de Brouilly, Fleurie, Juliénas, Morgon, Moulin-à-Vent, Régnié, and St-Amour.

at the table
Folks in Beaujolais usually put a slight chill on their reds. The simplest Beaujolais makes good party wine. More complex wines can fill in for other red Burgundy, though they're most at home with bistro standards like *coq au vin* or *steak frites*.

recommended wines

2002 Louis Jadot Château des Jacques, Moulin-à-Vent ★ ★ ★ ★ $$
dry, full-bodied, medium tannin, high acidity   drink now–10 years
As good as Beaujolais gets, with concentrated fruit and minerals presented with Beaujolais' hallmark ease and verve.

2002 André Rampon, Régnié ★ ★ ★ $$
dry, medium-bodied, medium tannin, high acidity   drink now–3 years
Rampon's biodynamic practices bring the earthly pleasures to this wine's spicy berry flavors.

2002 Clos de la Roilette, Fleurie ★ ★ ★ $$
dry, medium-bodied, medium tannin, high acidity   drink now–5 years
Worthy of a triple crown for wild berry, flowery herb, and mineral notes.

2002 Domaine de Robert La Chapelle, Fleurie ★ ★ ★ $$
dry, medium-bodied, medium tannin, high acidity   drink now–6 years
This is fully Gamay, yet its rich, firm flavors could pass for a village Burgundy.

2002 Michel Tete Domaine du Clos du Fief, Juliénas ★ ★ ★ $$
dry, medium-bodied, medium tannin, high acidity   drink now–6 years
A cinnamon-scented, berry-rich wine.

2002 Potel-Aviron Château Gaillard Vieilles Vignes, Morgon ★ ★ ★ $$
dry, medium-bodied, medium tannin, high acidity   drink now–8 years
Magical Morgon, loaded with fine herbs, stone, and velvety berry flavors.

2002 Jean-Paul Brun Terres Dorées L'Ancien Vieilles Vignes, Beaujolais ★ ★ ★ $
dry, medium-bodied, medium tannin, high acidity   drink now–5 years
This basic Beaujolais goes far beyond its pedigree, with profound minerality and intense fruit.

2002 Château des Péthières, Beaujolais ★ ★ $
dry, light-bodied, medium tannin, high acidity   drink now–2 years
All you can ask from easy-drinking Beaujolais: light, juicy fruit with an herbal edge, fresh and fun.

2002 Georges Duboeuf Domaine Desmures, Chiroubles ★ ★ $
dry, medium-bodied, medium tannin, high acidity   drink now–3 years
More peppery blueberry flavors than blackberry (*mûre*), but darn good.

2002 Joseph Drouhin, Morgon ★ ★ $
dry, medium-bodied, medium tannin, high acidity   drink now–4 years
Thoroughly enjoyable, with juicy, herbal, cherry flavors.

loire valley

Over a stretch of 250 miles, from the oyster-rich estuaries that feed the Atlantic, past the magnificent châteaux of dukes and dauphins, to the rich farmlands of central France, the wine regions that line the Loire River offer some of the country's most fascinating wines, from white to red, dry to sweet, and sparkling to still. Yet, save for Sancerre and Pouilly-Fumé, Loire Valley wines are terribly underappreciated in the U.S.—which keeps prices low.

grapes & styles

Five grapes dominate the Loire Valley, each with its own sphere of influence. In the eastern end, it is Sauvignon Blanc for whites, Pinot Noir for reds. In the center, Chenin Blanc reigns for whites, and Cabernet Franc for reds. The white grape Melon de Bourgogne has the Atlantic edge of the region to itself, making up the wines of Muscadet.

on the label

Loire Valley wines are labeled by appellation, and since vintners rarely blend grape varieties, the appellation name alone will tell you what's in the bottle. In the few cases in which a wine is made from grape varieties different than the norm, the variety will be appended to the region's name: for example, Sauvignon de Touraine.

white wines

at the table

Light and crisp, Muscadet is the *ne plus ultra* match for oysters. Sauvignon Blanc pairs well with light vegetarian dishes, freshwater fish, or herb-stuffed roast chicken. Grassy, mineral-laden Sancerre seems designed especially for chalky chèvre. Chenin Blanc from Anjou, especially Savennières, has enough personality to stand up to roast pork loin or wild turkey, but try it also with full-flavored freshwater fish like pike. More modest Chenin Blancs make a pleasant aperitif. Off-dry versions work well with Thai and other moderately spicy Asian cuisines. Pull out a sweet (*moelleux*) Vouvray for foie gras.

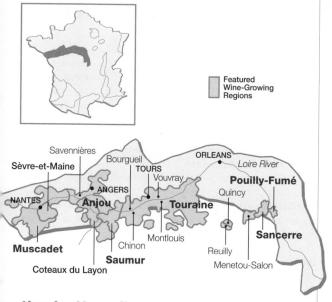

Featured
Wine-Growing
Regions

Savennières
Bourgueil
ORLEANS
Loire River
Sèvre-et-Maine
TOURS
Vouvray
Pouilly-Fumé
ANGERS
Quincy
NANTES
Anjou
Touraine
Muscadet
Chinon
Montlouis
Reuilly
Sancerre
Saumur
Menetou-Salon
Coteaux du Layon

the bottom line Quality Muscadet can be found for
less than $10. For Chenin Blanc wines, excellent Savennières
sells for $14 to $22; good Vouvray for $15 to $25; and
Montlouis from $9 to $15. Good Sauvignon Blanc from
Sancerre and Pouilly-Fumé tends to range from $15 to $25. The
appellations of Quincy, Menetou-Salon, and Reuilly provide
Sauvignon relief for around $14.

CHENIN BLANC

Painfully ordinary when grown elsewhere, Chenin Blanc in the
Loire Valley can be flowery, nutty, honeyed, mineral, or all those
at once. Styles range from bone-dry to luxuriously sweet, always
with high acidity. Vouvray is the most famous Chenin appellation. With significant exceptions, most of its wines are dull, as
are those of its cross-river neighbor Montlouis. Savennières, on
the other hand, can leave self-proclaimed red-wine-only people
speechless. Most are enjoyed young, but many age beautifully.

what to buy DRY CHENIN BLANC

1999	2000	2001	2002	2003
★★	★★	★★★	★★★	★★★

recommended wines

2001 Nicolas Joly Clos de la Coulée de Serrant, Savennières ★★★★ $$$$
dry, full-bodied, light oak, high acidity drink now–20 years
From the high priest of biodynamics comes a Chenin Blanc that captures flavors of baked fruit, truffle, nut, and smoke, not to mention plenty of minerality. Try Becherelle, too, for a taste of Joly's magic for less.

2002 Domaine de la Haute Borne Sec, Vouvray ★★★ $$
off-dry, medium-bodied, no oak, high acidity drink now–8 years
Wish all Vouvray were this full of citrus, pear, and berry flavors lifted by acidity.

2001 Domaine des Baumard Clos du Papillon, Savennières ★★★ $$
dry, full-bodied, no oak, high acidity drink now–12 years
Profound minerals and vibrant acidity provide backing for baked fruit flavors.

2002 Domaine du Closel La Jalousie, Savennières ★★★ $$
dry, full-bodied, no oak, high acidity drink now–8 years
If this peppery, spicy, baked fruit–scented wine is the most basic of Closel's range, imagine what the rest of the portfolio has to offer.

2002 François Chidaine Clos Habert, Montlouis ★★★ $$
off-dry, medium-bodied, no oak, high acidity drink now–10 years
This is soft but exuberant with spicy quince jam and mineral flavors.

2001 Olga Raffault Champ-Chenin, Chinon ★★★ $$
dry, medium-bodied, no oak, high acidity drink now–6 years
A rare Chenin from the Cabernet Franc–heavy town of Chinon, this very dry, lemony, mineral-laden wine puts forth a good case for planting more.

2001 Domaine Langlois-Château, Saumur ★★★ $
dry, medium-bodied, no oak, high acidity drink now–8 years
Mushrooms, minerals, and orange flavors make for exotic drinking.

2002 François Pinon Cuvée Tradition, Vouvray ★★ $$
off-dry, medium-bodied, no oak, high acidity drink now–6 years
With sweet pear fruit scented with flowers and spice, this is beautiful stuff.

2002 Château de la Guimonière Sec, Anjou ★★ $
dry, medium-bodied, no oak, high acidity drink now–6 years
These pineapple and lemon flavors are prodigiously packed with minerals.

2002 Clos Le Vigneau, Vouvray ★★ $
off-dry, medium-bodied, no oak, high acidity drink now–8 years
A firm case for Vouvray, with vibrant, floral, quince and lemon flavors.

TOP 10 PARTY WINES

What's the ideal party wine? One that's tasty, inexpensive, and easy to access so that you can enjoy your guests, not pull corks all night long. The solution? Bottles that are at least one liter in size, or the ultimate convenience: bag-in-a-box. Below are some favorite bargain-priced big bottles, reliable from one vintage to the next, from light whites to dark, juicy reds.

1. E. & M. Berger Grüner Veltliner, Kremstal, Austria $/1L

2. Torresella Pinot Grigio, Veneto, Italy $$/1.5L

3. La Vieille Ferme Blanc, Côtes du Luberon, France $/1.5L

4. Fetzer Sauvignon Blanc, California $/1.5L

5. Black Box Wines Chardonnay, Monterey County, California $$/3L

6. Straccali, Chianti, Italy $/1.5L

7. Citra, Montepulciano d'Abruzzo, Italy $/1.5L

8. Concha y Toro Frontera Cabernet Sauvignon-Merlot, Central Valley, Chile $/1.5L

9. Three Thieves Zinfandel, California $/1L

10. Lindemans Bin 50 Shiraz, Australia $/1.5L

2001 Domaine du Vieux Pressoir, Saumur　　　　　　★ ★ $
dry, medium-bodied, no oak, high acidity　　　　**drink now–3 years**
Loire Chenin's typical mushroom and pineapple flavors for a low price.

MELON DE BOURGOGNE

It is said that it took a very brave man to eat the first oyster. His courage might well have been found in a bottle of Muscadet. Made from the Melon de Bourgogne grape, Muscadet provides all the sharp lemon, prickly mineral, and light, yeasty flavors needed to complement an oyster's briny freshness. Look for Muscadets labeled *sur lie* ("on lees"): these have more complex flavors from spending extra time in contact with the yeasty sediment (lees) left after fermentation. Wines from the subregion Sèvre-et-Maine tend to be the best.

recommended wines

2002 Domaine Les Hautes Noëlles Muscadet sur Lie,
Côtes de Grandlieu ★★★★ $
dry, medium-bodied, no oak, high acidity   drink now–3 years
With all the minerals of the sea, plus vibrant citrus and a pinch of cinnamon, this is definitely four-star Muscadet.

2001 Comte de Laudonnière Muscadet sur Lie,
Sèvre-et-Maine ★★★ $
dry, medium-bodied, no oak, high acidity   drink now–3 years
With aromas and flavors recalling ripe mangos and limes, this is atypical Muscadet but impressive.

2002 La Pepière Cuvée Eden Muscadet sur Lie,
Sèvre-et-Maine ★★★ $
dry, medium-bodied, no oak, high acidity   drink now–10 years
Muscadet that can age, with honeyed marzipan, citrus, and pear confit flavors, and lots of minerality.

2002 Pierre Luneau-Papin Les Pierres Blanches Vieilles Vignes
Muscadet sur Lie, Sèvre-et-Maine ★★★ $
dry, medium-bodied, no oak, high acidity   drink now–8 years
Vines that have been around since World War II tell salty tales of apples, citrus, and spice in this fine Muscadet.

2002 Château de la Ragotière Muscadet sur Lie,
Sèvre-et-Maine ★★ $
dry, medium-bodied, no oak, high acidity   drink now–2 years
This Muscadet delivers minerals and grapefruit flavors, straightforward, refreshing, and well done.

SAUVIGNON BLANC

The eastern Loire Valley produces iconic Sauvignon Blanc. Sancerre and Pouilly-Fumé make the most famous wines, but neighboring Quincy, Menetou-Salon, and Reuilly offer tough competition at lower prices. Herbs, grass, grapefruit, and gooseberry flavors lively with refreshing acidity are typical in Sauvignons throughout the region. In addition, Sancerre offers a distinctly smoky, "gun-flint" flavor. Pouilly-Fumé owes its name (*fumé* means "smoked") as much to the frequent fog in its vineyards as to the supposedly smoky qualities it acquires from the area's flinty soil.

recommended wines

2002 Domaine des Berthiers, Pouilly-Fumé ★★★ $$
dry, medium-bodied, no oak, high acidity drink now–8 years
Savory wine, this is full of spice, truffle, and stone flavors against a backdrop
of ripe citrus. Delicious.

2002 Domaine Vincent Delaporte, Sancerre ★★★ $$
dry, medium-bodied, no oak, high acidity drink now–4 years
Fun, fruit-loopy Sancerre, this might seem frivolous at first taste but it has a
firm grounding of minerals.

2002 La Poussie, Sancerre ★★★ $$
dry, medium-bodied, no oak, high acidity drink now–3 years
Quality Sancerre, with lime, grass, peach, and mineral flavors that seem to
grow more intense with every sip.

2002 Michel Thomas La Chaume, Sancerre ★★★ $$
dry, medium-bodied, no oak, high acidity drink now–3 years
Fresh-chopped herb, lemon, and asparagus-like flavors provide the perfect fit
for asparagus.

2001 Pascal Jolivet Château du Nozay, Sancerre ★★★ $$
dry, medium-bodied, no oak, high acidity drink now–6 years
A taste of the tropics from the center of France, this offers pineapple-rich fla-
vors with wildflower honey sparked by smoky flintiness.

2001 Serge Laloue Cuvée Réservée, Sancerre ★★★ $$
dry, medium-bodied, no oak, high acidity drink now–6 years
This is so flinty it could start a fire, but loads of orange and peach flavors cool
things off.

2002 Domaine de Chatenoy, Menetou-Salon ★★ $$
dry, medium-bodied, no oak, high acidity drink now–3 years
A tropical delight, full of ripe mango, key lime, and herb flavors.

2003 Domaine du Tremblay, Quincy ★★ $$
dry, medium-bodied, no oak, high acidity drink now–3 years
One taste and zing!—a flood of lime, herb, and spice notes come tumbling
from this crisp, lively Quincy.

2002 Patient Cottat, Vin de Pays du Jardin de la France ★★ $
dry, medium-bodied, no oak, high acidity drink now–3 years
Sancerre specialist Cottat applies his expertise to affordable Sauvignon Blanc,
producing a wonderfully simple wine full of springtime blossoms and stones.

red wines

Cabernet Franc is more at home in the Loire than anywhere else. There are two styles: light, fruity, peppery wines to drink young, and weighty wines with concentrated fruit, peppercorn, and smoky mineral flavors suitable for long aging. Those from Chinon and Saumur-Champigny are especially good. Pinot Noir grows in the eastern Loire, especially in Sancerre and Menetou-Salon, making light, cherry-scented wines with high acidity.

at the table

Medium-bodied and high in acidity, Loire Valley reds make a fine complement to a range of dishes. Serve lighter Cabernet Franc with pâté or sausages. Weightier versions have the power to take on game; try one with a venison and mushroom stew. Red Sancerre can fill in for simple red Burgundies.

the bottom line Loire reds are a bargain. Few of the best sell for more than $30. Most cost $14 to $24.

what to buy CABERNET FRANC

1999	2000	2001	2002	2003
★★	★★★	★★	★★★	★★★

recommended wines

2002 Bernard Baudry Les Grézeaux, Chinon　　★★★★ $$$
dry, full-bodied, heavy tannin, high acidity　　**drink now–12 years**
Smoke, earth, and animal notes add a wild streak to this wine's ripe fruit. Enjoy it now, or let time tame it a bit.

2001 Domaine St-Vincent Léa, Saumur-Champigny　　★★★ $$
dry, full-bodied, heavy tannin, high acidity　　**drink now–8 years**
Wonderful Saumur, full of cherries and Cabernet Franc's telltale pepper note.

2001 Jean-Maurice Raffault Clos des Capucins, Chinon　★★★ $$
dry, full-bodied, heavy tannin, high acidity　　**drink now–12 years**
Roasted coffee and light vanilla notes add richness to this surprisingly full-bodied Cabernet Franc.

1999 Olga Raffault Les Picasses, Chinon ★★★ $$
dry, full-bodied, heavy tannin, high acidity   drink now–10 years
Big, lusty, and black, this is addictive in taste as well as price.

2001 Philippe Alliet Vieilles Vignes, Chinon ★★★ $$
dry, full-bodied, medium tannin, high acidity   drink now–12 years
Wine built for aging, this old-vine Chinon is full of peppery, brambly berry goodness and lots of minerals.

2002 Domaine des Roches Neuves, Saumur-Champigny ★★★ $
dry, medium-bodied, medium tannin, high acidity   drink now–3 years
Great value, this offers loads of cherry fruit flavor, piquant spice, and minerality for a surprisingly low cost.

2002 Catherine & Pierre Breton Les Galichets, Bourgueil ★★ $$
dry, medium-bodied, medium tannin, high acidity   drink now–3 years
Berry, herbs, and minerals, all in dynamic harmony.

2002 Clos Roche Blanche Côt, Touraine ★★ $$
dry, medium-bodied, heavy tannin, high acidity   drink now–4 years
Rambunctious, peppery berry flavors match this rare Côt to braised brisket.

2000 Domaine de Chatenoy, Menetou-Salon ★★ $$
dry, medium-bodied, medium tannin, high acidity   drink now–4 years
With smoke and delicious dry cherry flavors, here's a Pinot Noir that could substitute for Burgundy.

2002 Philippe Alliet, Chinon ★★ $$
dry, full-bodied, medium tannin, high acidity   drink now–4 years
Juicy and readily enjoyable, this is perfect to drink while waiting for Alliet's Vieilles Vignes bottling to come around.

2001 Château de la Guimonière La Haie Fruitière, Anjou ★★ $
dry, medium-bodied, medium tannin, high acidity   drink now–3 years
Smoky maple flavors add a complex note to this fruity red.

the midi

Until the 1970s, France's Mediterranean hinterland, known as the Midi, produced vast quantities of indifferent wine. However, in the last couple of decades, vintners have improved their vineyards and winemaking techniques to produce some of the country's most soulful wines.

lay of the land

The Midi can be broken down into three regions: Provence to the east, extending from Nice to Arles; Languedoc, from Arles curving around the Mediterranean coast and spreading inland; and Roussillon, a rugged Catalan-flavored region contiguous to Languedoc that runs to the Spanish border. Languedoc and Roussillon are commonly hyphenated into one region.

languedoc-roussillon

Today, vintners in Languedoc-Roussillon (shortened often to "Languedoc") are France's most energetic. Some are reviving the fortunes of formerly disregarded subregions; others are using the Vin de Pays and Vin de Table categories to experiment with grape varieties and techniques they would otherwise be denied. The result is a variety of unique and delicious wines.

grapes & styles

There's been a revolution of grape varieties and styles in today's Languedoc. Red grapes dominate as they did in the past, but fresh consideration has been given to local whites such as Grenache Blanc, Maccabèo, Muscat, Picpoul, and Viognier. International variety Sauvignon Blanc now appears, as does Chardonnay, which does especially well around the area of Limoux. Carignan is the region's most widely grown red wine grape, offering delicious, spicy flavors when treated well. Those from Corbières are often the best. Syrah, Grenache, and Mourvèdre are commonly blended with Carignan for the full-bodied wines of Minervois and Fitou. Grenache dominates the Rhône-style Vins de Pays de l'Hérault at Languedoc's eastern edge, as well as inky Collioure on Roussillon's southern border. Cabernet and Merlot also appear, occasionally to excellent effect. The Languedoc is also famed for its red and white dessert wines (see Fortified & Dessert Wines, p. 278).

on the label

Most Languedoc-Roussillon wine is designated Vin de Pays d'Oc, meaning it can be made with grapes grown anywhere within the region. Pays d'Oc wines typically list the grape used to make the wine on the label, and they are usually inexpensive. Vin de Pays wines that include the name of a place, such as Vin de Pays de l'Hérault, come from specific areas within the Languedoc, and adhere to stricter regulations regarding allowed grapes and farming techniques than generic Vin de Pays. There are also several AOC and VDQS wines in the region that are subject to even more stringent regulations. Appellations Coteaux du Languedoc and Coteaux du Roussillon are umbrellas for smaller ones. As elsewhere, the more specific the place name, the higher the standards. Wines from small appellations such as Montpeyroux, Pic St-Loup, Faugères, and Corbières often show distinct local characteristics, or *terroir*.

at the table

White wines from Languedoc-Roussillon are terrific with fried or grilled calamari, or lean fish like red snapper. Pour a Limoux Chardonnay with jumbo grilled shrimp. The region's robust, often rustic reds from appellations such as Collioure, Pic St-Loup, Minervois, or Coteaux du Languedoc inspire cravings for braised meats such as short ribs or lamb shanks. Gentler reds like Corbières and Fitou are best served with milder dishes, like lamb loin chops or a tender filet mignon.

the bottom line You'll find some indifferent Vins de Pays d'Oc reds and whites for $7, but a couple of dollars more will buy much better. Fashionable appellations such as Collioure or Pic St-Loup may cost $20 to $30. Few rise above that.

what to buy LANGUEDOC-ROUSSILLON REDS

1999	2000	2001	2002	2003
★★★★	★★★	★★★	★	★★

recommended
white & rosé wines

2000 Toques et Clochers Autan, Limoux ♥　　　　★★★ $$
dry, medium-bodied, medium oak, high acidity　　　**drink now–8 years**
Proof positive that Chardonnay can grow well in regions other than Burgundy, this impresses with restrained fruit and lots of minerals.

**2002 Novellum Chardonnay,
Vin de Pays des Coteaux de Fontcaude** 🍷 ★★★ $
dry, full-bodied, no oak, high acidity **drink now–6 years**
The good life in southern France reflected in a bottle, with luscious ripe fruit and a taste of the earth.

2002 Gérard Bertrand Viognier, Vin de Pays d'Oc 🍷 ★★ $
dry, medium-bodied, no oak, high acidity **drink now–3 years**
Here's a Languedoc Viognier that actually tastes like Viognier, fragrant with peach, peach blossom, and orange flavors.

**2002 Hugues Beaulieu Picpoul de Pinet,
Coteaux du Languedoc** 🍷 ★★ $
dry, light-bodied, no oak, high acidity **drink now–1 year**
A perfect summer wine: zippy, loaded with green apples, and affordable.

2003 La Noble Chardonnay, Vin de Pays de l'Aude 🍷 ★★ $
dry, medium-bodied, no oak, high acidity **drink now–2 years**
Citrus, herbs, and bright acidity make this a good pour for anytime.

2003 Les Clos de Paulilles Rosé, Collioure 🍷 ★★ $
dry, medium-bodied, high acidity **drink now–2 years**
An easy-to-love rosé, with clear cherry flavors and refreshing acidity.

2003 Val d'Orbieu Les Deux Rives, Corbières 🍷 ★★ $
dry, medium-bodied, no oak, medium acidity **drink now–2 years**
Soft pear and apple flavors, just right for lazy summer evenings.

2003 Fortant White Merlot, Vin de Pays d'Oc 🍷 ★ $
dry, medium-bodied, high acidity **drink now–2 years**
Give this pink wine a good chill and enjoy the tutti-frutti flavors.

recommended red wines

**2001 Prieuré de St-Jean de Bébian,
Coteaux du Languedoc** ★★★★ $$$
dry, full-bodied, heavy tannin, high acidity **drink in 2–12 years**
One of Languedoc's most ambitious producers offers a titan of black fruit, bitter herb, sweet spice, and minerals. Give this time.

**2001 Guilhem Dardé Mas des Chimères,
Coteaux du Languedoc** ★★★★ $$
dry, full-bodied, heavy tannin, high acidity **drink in 1–12 years**
This smoky, earthy, dark-berried red can compete with wines from Châteauneuf-du-Pape, yet it's a fraction of the price.

1999 Canet Valette Le Vin Maghani, St-Chinian ★★★ $$$
dry, full-bodied, medium tannin, high acidity   drink now–12 years
Fun wine, full of sweetly spiced ripe berry flavors with a lick of tar.

2001 Château de Lancyre Grande Cuvée, Pic St-Loup ★★★ $$
dry, full-bodied, heavy tannin, high acidity   drink in 2–10 years
All this grand black fruit, spice, smoke, and tannin will become even more impressive with time.

2002 Domaine de la Casa Blanca, Collioure ★★★ $$
dry, full-bodied, heavy tannin, high acidity   drink in 2–12 years
Century-old vines pull out an impressive depth of thick cherry, berry, and lavender flavors in this Collioure.

2001 Domaine du Champ des Soeurs, Fitou ★★★ $$
dry, full-bodied, heavy tannin, high acidity   drink in 2–12 years
Funky Fitou, this wine's stony, smoky mineral flavor is saturated with wild blackberry and blueberry fruit.

**2001 Massamier la Mignarde Expression Carignan,
Vin de Pays des Coteaux de Peyriac** ★★★ $$
dry, full-bodied, medium tannin, high acidity   drink in 1–12 years
Cedar and fine tobacco scents give this berried Carignan extra class.

2000 Château de Caraguilhes, Corbières ★★★ $
dry, medium-bodied, medium tannin, high acidity   drink now–6 years
An elegant Corbières, with exotic spice woven through tart red berry flavors.

**2002 Château d'Oupia Les Hérétiques,
Vin de Pays de l'Hérault** ★★★ $
dry, full-bodied, medium tannin, high acidity   drink now–3 years
Super value, with big, fat fruit flavors garnished by smoke and minerality.

2002 Domaine de la Brune, Coteaux du Languedoc ★★★ $
dry, full-bodied, medium tannin, high acidity   drink now–10 years
Remarkable wine, heavy on the Syrah, this could fill in for Côte-Rôtie without breaking your budget.

**2002 Domaine des Schistes Tradition,
Côtes du Roussillon Villages** ★★★ $
dry, full-bodied, heavy tannin, high acidity   drink now–6 years
The schist in the name shows up in the wine, with lots of stone flavor graciously softened by ripe, earthy berry and wild herb notes.

2001 Domaine du Roc Expression, Minervois ★★★ $
dry, full-bodied, medium tannin, high acidity   drink now–8 years
Violets and berries framed in stone.

france languedoc reds

2001 Château Belot L'Argilière, St-Chinian ★★ $$
dry, full-bodied, medium tannin, high acidity drink now–5 years
Chocolate and coconut notes enrich already dense, juicy berry flavors for a lush, mouthfilling red.

2001 Les Clos de Paulilles, Collioure ★★ $$
dry, full-bodied, heavy tannin, high acidity drink in 1–10 years
The *sauvage* flavors of the south come together in this smooth, dark wine, rich with berry, wild sage, and lavender flavors.

2001 Arauris, Vin de Pays de l'Hérault ★★ $
dry, medium-bodied, medium tannin, high acidity drink now–2 years
Succulent strawberry and earthy herb flavors, simple and mouthwatering.

2001 Château de Pena, Côtes du Roussillon Villages ★★ $
dry, full-bodied, heavy tannin, high acidity drink now–6 years
Wild herb, berry, and lanolin flavors, rustic and refined at once.

**2002 Domaine de Clairac Cuvée des Cinq Filles,
Vin de Pays de l'Hérault** ★★ $
dry, medium-bodied, heavy tannin, high acidity drink now–8 years
These meaty red berry and laurel leaf flavors are made for lamb stew or other hearty food.

2001 Domaine Louise-Fabry Malacoste, Corbières ★★ $
dry, full-bodied, heavy tannin, high acidity drink now–5 years
Tobacco and salty licorice flavors add intriguing detail to this wine's dark, dense, tannic flavors.

2002 Château de Jau, Côtes du Roussillon Villages ★ $
dry, full-bodied, heavy tannin, high acidity drink now–4 years
This Rhône-like wine offers smoky red berry flavors for a very fair price.

2001 Michel Laroche Syrah, Vin de Pays d'Oc ★ $
dry, medium-bodied, medium tannin, high acidity drink now–3 years
Spicy Syrah for a Sunday, or any day there's a barbecue on.

WINES WE WISH WE HAD MORE ROOM FOR

2000 Gérard Bertrand Le Viala, Minervois La Livinière ★★★ $$ dry, full-bodied, heavy tannin, high acidity, drink in 1–12 years; **2000 Toques et Clochers Occurus, Vin de Pays de la Haute Vallée de l'Aude** ★★★ $$ dry, full-bodied, medium tannin, high acidity, drink now–8 years; **2000 Ermitage du Pic St-Loup, Pic St-Loup** ★★ $ dry, full-bodied, heavy tannin, high acidity, drink now–8 years; **2003 Val d'Orbieu Les Deux Rives, Corbières** ★ $ dry, full-bodied, medium tannin, high acidity, drink now–4 years

provence

Provence wines aren't all frivolous rosés sipped in St-Tropez. Look harder and you'll find powerful, elegant reds, intelligent rosés, and serious, aromatic whites, too.

grapes & styles

Bandol, Provence's best-known wine region, is the only appellation in France where the Mourvèdre grape dominates. It makes dark wines full of blackberry, leather, and truffle flavors, redolent with scents of the region's stony soils and wild, herb-covered hillsides. Dark and tannic, most benefit from five years or more of bottle-aging. Grenache, Cinsault, Carignan, Syrah, and, increasingly, Cabernet Sauvignon, are also planted in Provence. These also turn out full-bodied wines loaded with berry and herb flavors. The most familiar of these come from Les Baux de Provence and Coteaux d'Aix en Provence. Rosés are made mostly from Cinsault, Grenache, and Mourvèdre and are almost invariably dry. Some evolve beautifully with age, but most should be enjoyed within a year of purchase. The region's best-known white wines come from the appellation of Cassis, named for a small seaside town, not black currants. Light and sometimes a little spritzy, they're made with differing blends of local grapes. Heavier, mineral-rich whites come from Bandol.

at the table

The flighty whites of Cassis are best with simple baked or fried fish. Pour a heavier Bandol white for bouillabaisse or lobster. Provençal rosés are wonderful with pepper-crusted seared tuna. The accent on rosemary, garlic, tomato, and olives in Provençal cuisine marries beautifully with the region's bold reds. Throw some garlic-and-rosemary-marinated lamb chops on the grill, open a bottle of Bandol, and indulge in a Provençal fantasy.

the bottom line
Simple Provençal whites can be found for about $10; superior examples break the $20 mark. Rosés start, too, at $10, but a few of the best run $35 or more. Good reds from Les Baux start at $10 and run up to $45 for superb Cabernet blends. Bandol reds start at $18; $45 or so will buy examples that count as some of France's best wines.

what to buy PROVENCE REDS

1999	2000	2001	2002	2003
★★★	★★★	★★★	★	★★

recommended
white & rosé wines

2003 Château de Roquefort Corail Rosé, Côtes de Provence 🍷 ★★ $
dry, medium-bodied, high acidity   drink now–2 years
Like summer in Provence, this offers orange-hued flavors of peach, mango,
and tangerine to drink against blue skies.

2003 Commanderie de la Bargemone Rosé,
Coteaux d'Aix-en-Provence 🍷   ★★ $
dry, medium-bodied, high acidity   drink now–1 year
Strawberry fields, plus a few minerals and smoke.

2002 Domaine de Triennes Ste-Fleur Viognier,
Vin de Pays du Var 🍷   ★★ $
dry, medium-bodied, no oak, high acidity   drink now–3 years
Glazed lemon and almond flavors lined with minerals make delightful sipping.

2002 Domaine La Courtade L'Alycastre Blanc,
Côtes de Provence 🍷   ★★ $
dry, light-bodied, no oak, high acidity   drink now–2 years
A head-turner, this Côtes de Provence white is loaded with attention-grabbing
lime and fresh pine flavors.

2002 Jean-Luc Colombo Pioche et Cabanon Côte Bleue Rosé,
Coteaux d'Aix-en-Provence 🍷   ★★ $
dry, medium-bodied, high acidity   drink now–2 years
A dry, tropical fruit–laden wine from a master of northern Rhône wines.

recommended red wines

2000 Château Ste-Anne Collection Vieilles Vignes,
Bandol   ★★★★ $$$
dry, full-bodied, heavy tannin, high acidity   drink in 3–15 years
This is a black monster of a wine, with tannic, dense berry and mineral flavors
tamed a bit by surprising florality.

1999 Château Pradeaux, Bandol ★ ★ ★ $$$
dry, full-bodied, heavy tannin, high acidity **drink in 1–10 years**
Wild yet elegant, this tastes of berry, earth, and aromatic *garrigue*.

2000 Jean-Luc Colombo Les Pins Couchés Côte Bleue,
Coteaux d'Aix-en-Provence ★ ★ ★ $$
dry, full-bodied, medium tannin, high acidity **drink now–6 years**
Velvety wild berry and mineral flavors make this a wine for sultry nights.

2003 Château de Roquefort Les Mûres, Côtes de Provence ★ ★ $$
dry, full-bodied, heavy tannin, high acidity **drink now–8 years**
Indulgent, rustic wine, full of blackberry and earth flavors.

2000 Domaine Terres Blanches, Les Baux de Provence ★ ★ $$
dry, full-bodied, medium tannin, high acidity **drink now–6 years**
The reward for being good to the earth? Ripe fruit and sweet spice flavors.

2001 Le Galantin, Bandol ★ ★ $$
dry, full-bodied, heavy tannin, high acidity **drink in 1–8 years**
Black as the Mediterranean is blue, this wine's tarry, dark fruit flavors offer
great value in Bandol.

1999 Domaine de Triennes St-Auguste, Vin de Pays du Var ★ ★ $
dry, full-bodied, medium tannin, high acidity **drink now–6 years**
Two great Burgundy winemakers, some Bordeaux grape varieties, and
Provençal sunshine make for a peppery, brightly berried, elegant red.

VARIETAL OAK

French oak, American oak, Slovenian oak? Vintners and
the folks who love them bandy these terms around like
golf enthusiasts speaking of putters. That's because dif-
ferent species of oaks have different effects on wine.
Generally speaking, French oak barrels come from
species with tightly grained wood, and they give wines
subtle vanilla and spice flavors. American barrels are
mostly from oaks grown in Missouri and Kentucky, which-
have a wider grain and impart robust vanilla, coconut, and
sweet spice flavors. Although American oak is integral to
some wines (think Rioja and Australian Shiraz), French oak
is more coveted. Unfortunately, it's double the price. Those
who remain seduced by French wood are seeking similar,
lower-priced oaks from Russia, Hungary, and even China.

rhône valley

Blame it on a river. If not for the Rhône's softly winding path from Switzerland to the Mediterranean, the steep hillsides and rolling plains of the northern Rhône Valley and the herb-blanketed slopes and stony, moonscape plateaus of the southern Rhône would surely be considered different regions. Despite different grape varieties and *terroir*, they weren't. Both are part of the Côtes-du-Rhône appellation.

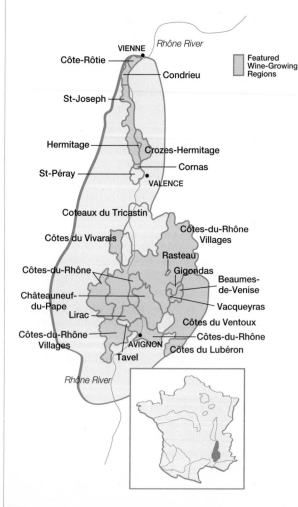

northern rhône

The northern Rhône shares both the cool temperatures of more northerly regions like Burgundy, and the south's long hours of warm sun. Its reds from famed appellations such as Hermitage, Cornas, and Côte-Rôtie, and whites from esteemed Condrieu and Hermitage (again), share something of each area, too: the lean structure of Burgundy energized by the power of Provence.

grapes & styles

Three grape varieties, alone, or in combination, go into northern Rhône whites. Marsanne and Roussanne are typically blended for the full-bodied, nutty, apricot-scented whites of Hermitage, Crozes-Hermitage, St-Péray, and the southern part of St-Joseph. Condrieu is home base for Viognier, a grape whose peachy, flowery charm has accelerated its popularity throughout the world. No others, however, reach the same depth of flavor as Condrieu. Some Viognier also finds its way into St-Joseph. Most Condrieu is dry, but there are some spectacular sweet versions, too.

Sultry, smoky Syrah is the only red grape permitted in the appellations of the northern Rhône, though most allow an addition of the floral white wine grape Viognier. Of the appellation wines, St-Joseph tends to be the lightest and least tannic, followed by Crozes-Hermitage, Côte-Rôtie, Hermitage, and, finally, Cornas, where traditionally styled wines can be so tannic and dark they require fifteen years or more of aging.

at the table

The rich, dry whites of the northern Rhône deserve rich foods like baked sturgeon or Arctic char. Smoky, tannic, and hearty, northern Rhône reds demand foods that won't get lost in contrast, like Cajun-style smoked meat or venison. Simpler Crozes-Hermitage and St-Joseph wines make a good pour with kebabs.

the bottom line Relatively simple wines from St-Péray, Crozes-Hermitage, and St-Joseph are available for $15, but prices jump by $10 for better versions. Good Condrieu starts at about $25; white Hermitage around $35. A few exceptional bottles of each ask more than $200.

france**northern rhône whites**

The same laws of supply and demand also apply to reds, especially in Hermitage, Cornas, and Côte-Rôtie. Expect to pay no less than $35 for any of these wines, up to $75 for Cornas, double that for Hermitage, and over triple for a few Côte-Rôties. Stunned? Take comfort in the fact that passable Crozes-Hermitage can be found for $14, better ones for $18 and the best for $65. St-Joseph starts for $16, up to $75.

what to buy NORTHERN RHÔNE WHITES

1998	1999	2000	2001	2002	2003
★★★	★★★★	★★★	★★★★	★	★★

what to buy NORTHERN RHÔNE REDS

1998	1999	2000	2001	2002	2003
★★★	★★★★	★★★	★★★	★	★★

recommended white wines

2001 Château Grillet, Château Grillet ★★★★ $$$$
dry, medium-bodied, light oak, high acidity drink in 3–25 years
One the great wines of the world, with intense tropical fruit, pear, and sparkling mineral flavors in a rich, almond-toned base.

2001 M. Chapoutier Chante-Alouette, Hermitage ★★★★ $$$$
dry, medium-bodied, medium oak, high acidity drink in 3–15 years
These mineral, nut, and white fruit flavors might seem subtle now, but they will become explosive with time.

2001 E. Guigal, Hermitage ★★★ $$$
dry, medium-bodied, medium oak, high acidity drink in 1–12 years
These stony almond flavors are delicious, but wait: there's more to come.

2002 Jean-Michel Gerin, Condrieu ★★★ $$$
dry, medium-bodied, light oak, high acidity drink now–10 years
Peppery orange notes add interest to a Viognier that's peachy enough to become Georgia's state wine.

2002 Domaine Louis Cheze Cuvée Ro-Rée, St-Joseph ★★★ $$
dry, medium-bodied, light oak, high acidity drink now–8 years
So much like honey, this tastes like it was aged in a beehive. Remarkably, it's also austere. Fascinating.

**2001 François Villard Les Contours de DePoncins Viognier,
Vin de Pays des Collines Rhodaniennes** ★ ★ ★ $$
dry, medium-bodied, light oak, high acidity drink now–6 years
This fresh, peachy Viognier could stand in for Condrieu at one-third the price.

2002 Domaine Les Chenêts, Crozes-Hermitage ★ ★ $
dry, medium-bodied, no oak, high acidity drink now–4 years
Gentle pear and mineral flavors offer simple deliciousness at a low price.

recommended red wines

2000 Jean-Luc Colombo Terres Brûlées, Cornas ★ ★ ★ ★ $$$$
dry, full-bodied, medium tannin, high acidity drink now–15 years
Dense and rich, this has floral, spicy black fruit flavors that are approachable
now, but it'll only be better in another decade or so.

2001 M. Chapoutier La Sizeranne, Hermitage ★ ★ ★ ★ $$$$
dry, full-bodied, heavy tannin, high acidity drink in 3–20 years
A red to age, this sports an armor of dark minerals that encases its muscular
blackberry fruit and sinews of spice.

2002 Jean-Michel Gerin La Landonne, Côte-Rôtie ★ ★ ★ $$$$
dry, full-bodied, heavy tannin, high acidity drink in 3–12 years
Dark berry flavors meld with smoke and minerals, powerful and graceful.

2001 Patrick & Christophe Bonnefond, Côte-Rôtie ★ ★ ★ $$$$
dry, full-bodied, heavy tannin, high acidity drink in 2–15 years
Robust wild berry flavors take on delicacy in a lacy veil of floral scents.

2001 Domaine Louis Cheze Cuvée des Anges, St-Joseph ★ ★ ★ $$$
dry, full-bodied, heavy tannin, high acidity drink in 3–12 years
A bruiser of a red, with black fruit, coffee, and feral flavors. Put it away, and
then drink it with steak or other hearty food.

2001 E. Guigal, St-Joseph ★ ★ ★ $$$
dry, full-bodied, medium tannin, high acidity drink now–8 years
Seductive St-Joseph, this entices with light, smoky herbs and minerals
embroidered into velvety red berry flavors.

**2001 Paul Jaboulet Aîné Domaine de Thalabert,
Crozes-Hermitage** ★ ★ ★ $$$
dry, full-bodied, medium tannin, high acidity drink now–8 years
Robust wild red berry flavors jump out, then recede into the background with
the emergence of spice.

2001 E. Guigal, Crozes-Hermitage ★ ★ $$
dry, medium-bodied, medium tannin, high acidity   drink now–6 years
Crozes with attitude, this has red fruit flavors that feel nervous, with fidgets of pepper and smoke.

2000 Domaine Les Chenêts, Crozes-Hermitage ★ ★ $
dry, full-bodied, medium tannin, high acidity   drink now–4 years
Affordable wine to have on hand all winter, this offers berry and spice flavors that would be delicious with a hearty stew.

southern rhône

With sunshine and warm temperatures, the southern Rhône produces 95 percent of the entire region's wines. Second only to Bordeaux in terms of volume of AOC wine produced, the southern Rhône is a great place to find wines that are sublime (and expensive), as well as good (and cheap).

grapes & styles

Grenache is the basis of most southern Rhône reds, but it shares the stage with many others. Châteauneuf-du-Pape, the region's most famous appellation, allows up to thirteen varieties—both red and white—in its wines, including Mourvèdre, Syrah, Cinsault, Grenache, Roussanne, and Bourboulenc. Appellations such as Gigondas, Vacqueyras, and Lirac follow similar rules. The region's few white wines are typically blended from local varieties Grenache Blanc, Marsanne, Roussanne, and Viognier. Dry rosés, most notably from Tavel, are made from blends similar to reds.

on the label

Rhône wines are labeled by appellation. The basic designation Côtes-du-Rhône can be taken by wines from anywhere in the Rhône Valley, though most of these come from the south. Wines labeled Côtes-du-Rhône Villages come from within dozens of designated villages that satisfy requirements for low yields and high alcohol levels. Consistently high quality has earned sixteen villages the right to add their name to the label, such as Côtes-du-Rhône Villages Rasteau. The best villages—Châteauneuf-du-Pape, Gigondas, Vacqueyras, Tavel, and Lirac—are allowed to use the village name alone.

at the table

Basic Côtes-du-Rhône wines are this writer's consistent choice for outdoor cookouts and casual get-togethers. They're just as good with burgers as they are with charred steaks or a North African stew. Fuller-bodied Châteauneuf-du-Pape, Gigondas, and Vacqueyras were made for garlic-studded leg of lamb, though any roasted or braised meat will do. The region's dry, rich white wines are perfect for saffron-scented bouillabaisse or Thai spice–rubbed chicken. Dry, spicy Tavel rosés do well with pork, veal, or salmon.

the bottom line Prices of southern Rhône reds are relatively low, but an unusually weak dollar and small harvest in 2003 will likely cause prices to rise. Côtes-du-Rhône starts at $9, but spend a couple of dollars more for a Villages wine, especially one with a named village. Rasteau and Cairanne offer terrific value for under $15. Châteauneuf-du-Pape starts at $18, but the best quality is in the high-$20s. Some exceptional examples cross the $75 mark. Gigondas starts at about $16, but reaches parity with Châteauneuf in the mid-range. Vacqueyras offers solid wines at $15 to $20. Most whites can be found for $9 to $16, though those from Châteauneuf-du-Pape are priced similarly to reds. Rosés from Tavel command $13 to $20.

what to buy SOUTHERN RHÔNE REDS

1999	2000	2001	2002	2003
★★★	★★★★	★★★	★	★★

recommended
white & rosé wines

2002 M. Chapoutier La Bernardine, ▼
Châteauneuf-du-Pape   ★★★ $$$
dry, medium-bodied, light oak, high acidity   **drink now–8 years**
This is so mineral it's as if it were built from stone, cemented by nuts and glazed fruit flavors.

2002 Domaine de l'Oratoire St-Martin, Côtes-du-Rhône ▼ ★★★ $
dry, medium-bodied, no oak, high acidity   **drink now–3 years**
Fabulous wine, full of fresh pear, juicy orange, floral, and mineral flavors.

2002 Perrin Réserve, Côtes-du-Rhône ♥ ★ ★ ★ $
dry, medium-bodied, no oak, high acidity   drink now–4 years
Here's an impressive display from the south of France, with wildflowers and thyme rising from the citrusy background.

2001 Delas Frères St-Esprit, Côtes-du-Rhône ♥ ★ ★ $
dry, medium-bodied, light oak, high acidity   drink now–3 years
Sweet summertime, with airs of melons and peaches.

2003 Domaine de la Janasse Rosé, Côtes-du-Rhône ♥ ★ ★ $
dry, medium-bodied, no oak, high acidity   drink now–2 years
Gentle, joyful wine, with a happy display of watermelon and mineral flavors.

2002 Domaine Pélaquié, Côtes-du-Rhône Villages Laudun ♥ ★ ★ $
dry, light-bodied, no oak, high acidity   drink now–2 years
Snappy stuff, full of the flavors of green apples drizzled with honey and citrus.

2002 E. Guigal, Côtes-du-Rhône ♥ ★ ★ $
dry, medium-bodied, light oak, high acidity   drink now–2 years
Sleek wine, smooth with soft lemon and pear flavors.

2003 Mas St-Joseph Rosé,
Vin de Pays des Coteaux du Pont du Gard ♥ ★ ★ $
dry, medium-bodied, high acidity   drink now–2 years
Sprightly light quince and strawberry flavors are as lovely as the pale pink hue.

2002 Nôtre Dame de Cousignac, Côtes du Vivarais ♥ ★ ★ $
dry, medium-bodied, no oak, high acidity   drink now–3 years
A bouquet of floral and apple flavors evokes springtime in Provence.

2002 La Vieille Ferme Grenache-Cinsault, Côtes du Ventoux ♥ ★ $
dry, medium-bodied, high acidity   drink now
Pretty in pink and lovely in the glass, this offers enjoyable tart berry flavors.

recommended red wines

2001 Domaine du Banneret, Châteauneuf-du-Pape ★ ★ ★ ★ $$$
dry, full-bodied, heavy tannin, high acidity   drink in 3–15 years
From a small winery comes a treasure chest of smoky, earthy, animal flavors.

2001 Féraud-Brunel, Gigondas ★ ★ ★ ★ $$$
dry, full-bodied, heavy tannin, high acidity   drink now–10 years
This captures the soul of Gigondas, from the sun down to the earth and its fragrant *garrigue*.

2000 Jean-Luc Colombo Les Bartavelles,
Châteauneuf-du-Pape ★★★★ $$$
dry, full-bodied, medium tannin, high acidity drink now–12 years
Blackberries aren't among the permitted grape varieties in Châteauneuf, but
this stunner makes you wonder.

2000 Domaine de Valori, Châteauneuf-du-Pape ★★★ $$$
dry, full-bodied, medium tannin, high acidity drink now–10 years
Elegant and earthy, Valori paints with light flowers and spice, in broad strokes
of minerals and mulberry.

2001 Patrick Lesec Chasse Temps,
Châteauneuf-du-Pape ★★★ $$$
dry, full-bodied, heavy tannin, high acidity drink in 2–15 years
A dark, brooding wine, loaded with blackberries, lanolin, and spice.

2001 Perrin & Fils Les Sinards, Châteauneuf-du-Pape ★★★ $$$
dry, full-bodied, medium tannin, high acidity drink now–12 years
The Perrin family's second Châteauneuf after revered Beaucastel, this shows
a family resemblance for a lower price.

2001 Domaine Bressy-Masson,
Côtes-du-Rhône Villages Rasteau ★★★ $$
dry, full-bodied, medium tannin, high acidity drink now–6 years
Heady wine, fragrant with ripe berry flavors and floral scents.

2001 Domaine d'Andezon, Côtes-du-Rhône Villages ★★★ $$
dry, full-bodied, heavy tannin, high acidity drink now–6 years
Powerful as the bull on the label suggests, this is full of spice and meaty, minty
berry flavors.

2002 Domaine de l'Oratoire St-Martin Réserve des Seigneurs,
Côtes-du-Rhône Villages Cairanne ★★★ $$
dry, full-bodied, heavy tannin, high acidity drink now–8 years
Berry, spice, and tangy mineral flavors come off as suave and jaunty at once.

2001 Domaine La Soumade Cuvée Prestige,
Côtes-du-Rhône Villages Rasteau ★★★ $$
dry, full-bodied, heavy tannin, high acidity drink in 1–12 years
If there were more wines like this indulgently spicy and mineral-laden wine,
the repute of Rasteau would skyrocket.

2000 Domaine Viret Cosmic,
Côtes-du-Rhône Villages St-Maurice ★★★ $$
dry, full-bodied, heavy tannin, high acidity drink now–8 years
This swirl of dense berry fruit, currylike spice, and walnuts will take you to
another dimension.

2001 Jean-Luc Colombo Les Forots Vieilles Vignes,
Côtes-du-Rhône   ★★★ $$
dry, full-bodied, medium tannin, high acidity   drink now–12 years
Nearly as dark as Colombo's Cornas, this artful Côtes-du-Rhône explodes with
berry flavors yet maintains subtlety and finesse.

2001 Mas St-Joseph Cuvée Aventure, Costières de Nîmes ★★★ $$
dry, full-bodied, heavy tannin, high acidity   drink now–8 years
Ripe and rich, these smoky anise, black olive, and berry flavors are as wild as
they are soul-satisfying.

2001 Domaine Duseigneur, Lirac   ★★★ $
dry, full-bodied, medium tannin, high acidity   drink now–6 years
Much like a Persian miniature, painted with pigments derived from spice, har-
monized in detail and color.

2001 Nôtre Dame de Cousignac Parcelle Sûd,
Côtes-du-Rhône   ★★★ $
dry, full-bodied, heavy tannin, high acidity   drink now–6 years
Minty black fruit and smoky minerals are a steal at just over ten bucks.

2001 Château Val Joanis Vigne du Chanoine Trouillet,
Côtes du Luberon   ★★ $$$
dry, full-bodied, medium tannin, high acidity   drink now–5 years
These smoky, oaky, dark berry flavors seem made for barbecue.

2002 Domaine de la Crillone, Côtes du Ventoux   ★★ $$
dry, full-bodied, medium tannin, high acidity   drink in 1–8 years
Complex, intriguing wine, this offers flavors ranging from white pepper to
berries and orange.

2002 Saint Cosme Les Deux Albion, Côtes-du-Rhône ★★ $$
dry, full-bodied, heavy tannin, high acidity   drink now–6 years
Smooth and lovely, this is full of dark fruit and spice, plus loads of mineral fla-
vors from the limestone-rich vineyard in which the grapes were grown.

2002 Château de Ségriès, Côtes-du-Rhône   ★★ $
dry, medium-bodied, medium tannin, high acidity drink now–4 years
Positively wild red fruit, balsam, and herb-oil flavors make this a perfect pour
for grilled lamb sausages.

2002 Château Mourgues du Grès Les Galets Rouges,
Costières de Nîmes   ★★ $
dry, medium-bodied, medium tannin, high acidity drink now–4 years
Marvelous Syrah from the south, this gracefully combines earthy, smoky notes
with piquant fruit.

2002 Delas Frères, Côtes du Ventoux ★★ $
dry, medium-bodied, medium tannin, high acidity   drink now–2 years
This might be a little rough-and-ready, but that's part of its brambly red berry appeal, especially at a cookout.

2002 Domaine de Mourchon,
Côtes-du-Rhône Villages Séguret ★★ $
dry, full-bodied, medium tannin, medium acidity   drink now–3 years
From a winery to watch in the coming years, here's a red filled with spicy and sultry flavors.

2002 Domaine Paul Autard, Côtes-du-Rhône ★★ $
dry, medium-bodied, medium tannin, high acidity   drink now–4 years
Despite the challenges of the rainy 2002 vintage, Autard turned out a cherry and spice gem.

2002 F. et F. Alary Le P'tit Martin, Côtes-du-Rhône ★★ $
dry, medium-bodied, medium tannin, high acidity   drink now–2 years
Peppery berry flavors, as easy as they are delicious.

2002 Les Vignerons d'Estézargues Terra Vitis,
Côtes-du-Rhône ★★ $
dry, medium-bodied, medium tannin, high acidity   drink now–3 years
Mouth-watering acidity enlivens this wine, wild with berry and spice.

2001 Marc Kreydenweiss Domaine des Perrières,
Costières de Nîmes ★★ $
dry, full-bodied, medium tannin, high acidity   drink now–6 years
The master of Alsatian subtlety flexes Rhône power in this smoky wine, chewy with roasted meat and berry flavors.

2002 Cave de Cairanne Le Pas de la Beaume,
Côtes-du-Rhône ★ $
dry, light-bodied, light tannin, medium acidity   drink now
Flowery fruit flavors, heavy on the cherry and light on the spice.

2002 M. Chapoutier Belleruche, Côtes-du-Rhône ★ $
dry, light-bodied, medium tannin, high acidity   drink now–2 years
Belleruche is an easy-to-find choice for easy-to-enjoy, tart fruit flavors.

WINES WE WISH WE HAD MORE ROOM FOR
2001 E. Guigal, Châteauneuf-du-Pape ★★★ $$$ dry, full-bodied, medium tannin, high acidity, drink now–12 years; **2000 Domaine des Grands Devers, Côtes-du-Rhône Villages Valréas** ★★★ $$ dry, full-bodied, medium tannin, high acidity, drink now–8 years; **2001 Domaine Rabasse-Charavin, Côtes-du-Rhône Villages Cairanne** ★★★ $$

dry, full-bodied, heavy tannin, high acidity, drink in 2–8 years; **2001 Perrin & Fils Les Christins, Vacqueyras** ★★★ $$ dry, full-bodied, heavy tannin, high acidity, drink in 1–8 years; **2001 Domaine Ste-Anne Cuvée Nôtre Dame des Cellettes, Côtes-du-Rhône Villages** ★★ $$ dry, full-bodied, heavy tannin, high acidity, drink now–8 years; **2001 E. Guigal, Côtes-du-Rhône** ★★ $ dry, full-bodied, medium tannin, high acidity, drink now–3 years; **2001 Barton & Guestier, Côtes-du-Rhône** ★ $ dry, medium-bodied, medium tannin, high acidity, drink now–2 years; **2000 J. Vidal Fleury, Côtes-du-Rhône** ★ $ dry, full-bodied, medium tannin, medium acidity, drink now–3 years

southwest

A land that nurtured the romance of Cyrano de Bergerac and the swashbuckling brashness of the Three Musketeers could only make wines filled with personality. From the southernmost edge of Bordeaux down to the Pyrenees Basque country, the wines of *le Sud-Ouest* certainly deliver: they are brash and bold, with a bit of nobility thrown in for good measure. Some of France's heartiest reds, black and tannic, are found here, as well as wines elegant enough to be confused for some Bordeaux. A few white wines are made, too.

grapes & styles

The Southwest is one of France's most diverse wine regions. Bergerac, southeast of Bordeaux, and Buzet to the south, make reds and whites that closely resemble basic Bordeaux wines in style and grape variety. Further south, Cahors has become famous for intense, inky black wines from the Auxerrois grape (called Malbec in Bordeaux and Argentina, and Côt elsewhere in France). Madiran is even blacker, and, as one might expect given the name of its base grape, "Tannat," more tannic. Basque country wines, made from indigenous grapes whose names puzzle all but a few red-nosed linguists, are hard and hearty.

Though reds dominate, there are a few white wines worth checking out. Gascogne produces light- to medium-bodied whites from international varieties and grapes like Ugni Blanc that are usually distilled into brandy. Jurançon is known for its full-bodied, spicy whites, and Bergerac makes some smooth, light whites from Sauvignon Blanc blended with local varieties.

at the table

Use Bergerac, both white and red, as you would Bordeaux. Cahors' deep reds are ideal with the region's duck breasts, *magret de canard*. Madiran's powerful flavors fare especially well with lamb shoulder braised with Agen prunes, the region's stick-to-your-ribs *cassoulet*, or a simple hangar steak. Jurançon's dry whites are good for chunky country patés and dry, piquant sheep's milk cheeses. Sweet Jurançon is the local's choice with their superb foie gras.

the bottom line Overlooked even in France, Southwest wines can be a terrific bargain. Gascogne whites can be found for under $10; Jurançon whites typically run $12 to $18. White and red wines from Buzet and Bergerac usually cost less than $16. Hearty red Cahors and Madiran can be picked up for less than $12, though it's worth spending a little more for an older vintage if you plan to drink the wine right away. Some excellent special cuvées run $40.

recommended white wines

2001 Tirecul La Gravière, Vin de Pays du Périgord ★★★★ $$
dry, medium-bodied, light oak, high acidity   drink now–6 years
Citrus and minerals slice across the palate like a well-honed blade, leaving behind a flurry of exotic fruit.

2002 Clos Lapeyre, Jurançon Sec ★★★ $
dry, full-bodied, light oak, high acidity   drink now–8 years
Beautifully exotic, this oozes pineapple and baked quince flavors with seductive hints of spice.

**2002 Château Tour des Gendres Cuvée des Conti,
Bergerac Sec** ★★ $$
dry, medium-bodied, light oak, high acidity   drink now–3 years
Waxy flavors of lemon confit, herbs, and minerals make for fine sipping on their own or with light food.

2003 Caves Plaimont Colombelle, Côtes de Gascogne ★★ $
dry, medium-bodied, no oak, high acidity   drink now–1 year
Lime, grapefruit, herbs, and minerals at a very low price make this a perfect summer standard.

recommended red wines

2001 Château Montus, Madiran ★★★★ $$
dry, full-bodied, heavy tannin, high acidity drink in 3–12 years
Dark, tannic, and intense, here's a wine of heroic proportions, made for musketeers, noblemen, and rebels. Even they, however, will need to approach it with a double-thick steak or other hearty food if they don't cellar it for a few years before opening.

2001 Château du Cèdre Le Prestige, Cahors ★★★ $$
dry, full-bodied, medium tannin, high acidity drink now–12 years
Dark fruit and minerals give this prime position in this vintage's array of Cahors wines.

2001 Château Tour des Gendres Cuvée La Gloire de Mon Père, Côtes de Bergerac ★★★ $$
dry, full-bodied, medium tannin, high acidity drink now–10 years
A velvety Cabernet-Merlot blend, this is so full of berry, plum, violet, and mineral flavors that it's approachable now, though it certainly has the stuffing to get better over the coming decade.

2001 Mouthes Le Bihan Viellefont, Côtes-de-Duras ★★★ $$
dry, full-bodied, medium tannin, high acidity drink now–6 years
Peppery cassis flavors with a touch of cinnamon spice make this a bargain alternative to good Bordeaux.

2000 Le Roc Cuvée Don Quichotte, Côtes du Frontonnais ★★★ $
dry, full-bodied, medium tannin, high acidity drink now–5 years
No chasing windmills here, just delicious, smoky wine from southern varieties Negrette and Syrah.

2001 Heart of Darkness, Madiran ★★ $$
dry, full-bodied, heavy tannin, high acidity drink in 2–10 years
Deep minerals and wild fruit plunge into the deepest recesses of the palate to delicious effect.

2000 Baron d'Ardeuil Vieilles Vignes, Buzet ★★ $
dry, medium-bodied, medium tannin, high acidity drink now–10 years
With a silken texture and red berry and slight animal flavors, this stands out as a fine alternative to basic Bordeaux.

2001 Caves Plaimont Chevalier d'Antras, Madiran ★★ $
dry, full-bodied, heavy tannin, high acidity drink in 2–10 years
This is as brooding as Madiran ought to be, loaded with black fruit and smoky tobacco flavors barbed with black tannin.

TEN FAVORITE OBSCURE WINES

1. Bobal A funky, dark grape grown in the hinterlands of Valencia, Spain. Handled with care, it can make great reds.

2. Fondillón Now almost forgotten, this unfortified tawny made from Monastrell grapes from Alicante in Spain was once counted among the great strong wines like Sherry, Port, and Madeira.

3. Freisa The underling red grape of Piedmont, Freisa can be flighty and lightly sparkling, or dark, pleasantly bitter, and brooding.

4. Petite Arvine Found in Italy's Valle d'Aosta and Switzerland, this makes aromatic, lightly floral, and completely charming wines.

5. Pineau d'Aunis This grape makes a peppery, earthy, tart red berry–flavored wine from the Loire Valley.

6. Rkatsiteli A great white grape from the Republic of Georgia, Rkatsiteli is widely grown in the world, but rarely seen in the U.S.

7. Roter Veltliner Now that Austria's Grüner Veltliner is every sommelier's favorite white, it's time to check out the red Veltliner and its fleshy, spicy wines.

8. Scheurebe A grape grown in Germany's Pfalz and Franken regions that makes delightfully funky whites.

9. Tazzelenghe Any grape that means "tongue cutter" has got to be attention-grabbing. It lives up to its name in the high-acid red wines it makes in Italy.

10. Xinomavro Not obscure in Greece, this Macedonian red grape makes wines resembling Barbaresco for a fraction of the cost.

2000 Domaine du Théron, Cahors ★★ $
dry, full-bodied, heavy tannin, high acidity drink now–8 years
Earthy, tannic dark cherry flavors prove that Cahors's famed "black wines" of yore aren't quite history.

2001 Domaine Lapeyre, Béarn ★★ $
dry, full-bodied, heavy tannin, high acidity drink in 1–10 years
Dark fruit and minerals get a spicy, floral twist.

italy

With twenty wine regions and some two thousand grape varieties, Italy offers a nearly endless selection of wines. From crisp, seafood-friendly whites to big, brooding reds, there's a wine here for every occasion. No wonder it's the land of *la dolce vita*.

on the label

Italian wine labeling protocols are as diverse as the country's wines. Most all mention the region in which the wine was grown; some also include grape variety and an indication of style.

Italy also uses a system like France's AOC system to distinguish quality wines, called the *Denominazione di Origine Controllata* (DOC). DOC wines must be made in defined areas and meet specific standards. *Denominazione di Origine Controllata e Garantita* (DOCG) wines are theoretically a step up, but in most places, the "G" doesn't offer much more of a guarantee. Wines can also carry an *Indicazione Geografica Tipica* (IGT) which includes wines made in specified regions but with grape varieties considered untraditional to the area.

Many Italian regions use *Classico* to designate wines that come from subdistricts of a defined region. For example, a Chianti Classico indicates a wine made from grapes grown in a particular part of Chianti. *Riserva* or *Superiore* may be used when a wine meets more stringent quality and aging requirements than are normally demanded for a region's wines.

northern italy

Framed by France, Switzerland, Austria, and Slovenia, the regions of northern Italy create some of the country's most fascinating wines, reflecting both the influences of their neighbors and their own distinctive personalities.

trentino-alto adige & fruili-venezia giulia

Sharing the Tyrolean Alps with Austria, Trentino-Alto Adige (also called Südtirol) is infused with Germanic influences, even in its favored grapes: Riesling, Gewürztraminer, and Müller-Thurgau. Many of Friuli's wines are made from local varieties Tocai Friulano, Ribolla Gialla, and Refosco, though, as a cosmopolitan crossroads from empires past, Friuli has been home to several "international" varieties for centuries.

white wines

The balance of sunshine and cool alpine breezes gives Trentino-Alto Adige whites plenty of vivacious fruit and vibrant acidity. Pinot Grigio and Chardonnay thrive here, but more interesting are the region's Traminer, Riesling, and Müller-Thurgau. Fruili's crisp Pinot Grigio is worthy of note, especially from Colli Orientali. Pinot Bianco, aromatic Tocai Friulano, meaty Ribolla Gialla, and grassy Sauvignon Blanc deserve attention, too.

at the table

Light-bodied, high in acidity, and full of citrus and herb flavors, Pinot Grigio and Sauvignon Blanc are ideal with spaghetti *alle vongole* or fried calamari. Ribolla Gialla's almost creamy texture makes it perfect with seafood risotto or braised veal loin. Tocai Friulano provides a wonderful counterpoint to sweet, seared scallops, or it can be paired with pork. Light, aromatic, and dry, the region's Riesling is terrific with island-inspired seafood and tropical fruit salads. Traminer and Müller-Thurgau are good choices with chicken paprikash.

the bottom line

Whites from Italy's northeast can run as low as $8, though quality is more assured around $12 to $16. Exceptional wines cost over $20, or even over $40 for rarer wines like Ribolla Gialla and Tocai from top producers.

THE FRUGAL MR. CHIPS

Oak barrels cost a lot—from $300 up to $1,400. And, like tea bags, they can be used only a limited number of times before they lose their flavor. So how can a thrifty vintner make an oaked wine that costs less than $10? Use pieces of oak—chips, staves, sawdust—and stir them into a tank of wine. However, the technique has been outlawed within the European Union and is therefore available only to vintners living outside Europe. To right this competitive disadvantage, E.U. lawmakers have proposed a ban on the sale in Europe of wines made with oak-barrel alternatives. At presstime, negotiations were still ongoing and the outcome uncertain.

---

recommended wines

2001 Damijan Ribolla Gialla, Collio
★ ★ ★ ★ $$$
dry, full-bodied, no oak, high acidity   drink now–12 years
Positively thrilling drinking, this masterful wine offers a cornucopia of bitter almond, mineral, and baked fruit flavors.

2002 Jermann Vintage Tunina, Venezia Giulia
★ ★ ★ $$$$
dry, medium-bodied, no oak, high acidity   drink now–12 years
One of Venezia's star wines, Vintage Tunina hints at summer fruits and sweet spice, but it needs patience to expose itself fully.

2002 Villa Russiz Sauvignon de la Tour, Collio
★ ★ ★ $$$
dry, medium-bodied, no oak, high acidity   drink now–10 years
No simple summer sipper here, this is a complex lot of minerals, cassis, and citrus, built to age.

2001 Bastianich Vespa Bianco, Friuli
★ ★ ★ $$
dry, full-bodied, light oak, high acidity   drink now–4 years
Stylish but substantial, this is full of baked quince, minerals, and nuts.

2002 Bottega Vinaia Pinot Grigio, Trentino
★ ★ ★ $$
dry, medium-bodied, no oak, high acidity   drink now–6 years
Honey, nut, and dry fruit flavors make this a Pinot Grigio with guts.

2002 Colutta Tocai Friulano, Colli Orientali del Friuli
★ ★ ★ $$
dry, medium-bodied, no oak, high acidity   drink now–8 years
Fascinating, aromatic Tocai, this showcases the grape's unique flavors through mango, exotic nut, and mineral flavors.

2002 Doro Princic Tocai Friulano, Collio
★ ★ ★ $$
dry, full-bodied, no oak, high acidity   drink now–6 years
Muscular Tocai, this is rich with nutty pear flavors, a citrus note adding zing.

2002 Santa Margherita Pinot Bianco, Alto Adige
★ ★ $$
dry, medium-bodied, no oak, high acidity   drink now–2 years
Sibling to Santa Margherita's Pinot Grigio, this shows a family resemblance for clean, balanced fruit.

2002 Alois Lageder Pinot Grigio, Alto Adige
★ ★ $
dry, medium-bodied, no oak, high acidity   drink now–3 years
Straightforward, well-made Pinot Grigio, with refreshing citrus flavors.

2002 Gradis'ciutta Ribolla Gialla, Collio
★ ★ $
dry, medium-bodied, no oak, high acidity   drink now–4 years
Bold lemon and nut flavors make for striking wine.

2002 Kris Pinot Grigio, Venezia ★ ★ $
dry, medium-bodied, no oak, high acidity drink now–2 years
There's a refreshing alpine breeziness to this fragrant wine, backed by zingy lime.

2002 La Vis Chardonnay, Trentino ★ ★ $
dry, medium-bodied, no oak, high acidity drink now–1 year
Good, honest Chardonnay, with fine fruit, light spice, and a touch of minerals, this is an excellent choice for a house Chardonnay.

2002 Peter Zemmer Pinot Grigio, Alto Adige ★ ★ $
dry, light-bodied, no oak, high acidity drink now–2 years
A Lamborghini of a Pinot Grigio, this offers racy acidity powered by intense minerality—at a Kia price.

WINES WE WISH WE HAD MORE ROOM FOR
2002 Schiopetto Mario Schiopetto Bianco, Collio ★ ★ ★ $$$$ dry, medium-bodied, light oak, high acidity, drink now–5 years; **2001 Livio Felluga Terre Alte, Colli Orientali del Friuli** ★ ★ ★ $$$ dry, medium-bodied, medium oak, high acidity, drink in 1–10 years; **2002 Alois Lageder Pinot Bianco, Alto Adige** ★ ★ $ dry, medium-bodied, no oak, high acidity, drink now–3 years; **2002 Bortoluzzi Chardonnay, Isonzo del Friuli** ★ ★ $ dry, medium-bodied, no oak, high acidity, drink now–2 years; **2003 Pighin Pinot Grigio, Grave del Friuli** ★ ★ $ dry, medium-bodied, no oak, high acidity, drink now; **2003 Tiefenbrunner Pinot Grigio, Venezia** ★ ★ $ dry, medium-bodied, no oak, high acidity, drink now–3 years

red wines

Unlike in the rest of Italy, red wines are second to whites in cool Trentino-Alto Adige and Friuli. Given proper attention, Merlot and Cabernet Franc (which might in fact be another Bordeaux grape, Carmenère) provide a suitable backdrop for northeast Italy's game- and pork-rich culinary cultures. Far more interesting are local grapes Refosco, Pignolo, Schioppettino, Teroldego Rotaliano, and Tazzelenghe.

at the table

Bold, sometimes even funky (in a good way) Refosco, Schioppettino, and Teroldego Rotaliano demand bold-flavored meats like venison, wild boar, or grass-fed beef. Drink Merlot or Pignolo with roast rack of lamb; Cabernet Franc with pepper-crusted pork loin.

the bottom line Well-made Merlot and Cabernet Franc from northern Italy start at $12. Refosco starts at $11, Teroldego at $13; both reach $45. Pignolo and Schioppettino run $20 to $35, with a few reaching more than double that.

recommended wines

2002 Borgo di Fradis Troi dal Tas Schioppettino, Colli Orientali del Friuli ★ ★ ★ $$$
dry, full-bodied, medium tannin, high acidity drink now–8 years
Peppery herbs balance florid red berry flavors.

2001 Franz Haas Lagrein, Alto Adige ★ ★ ★ $$$
dry, full-bodied, medium tannin, high acidity drink now–12 years
Dark cherry, roasted meat, dark chocolate, minerals, and spice make this a delicious mouthful.

2000 Cantina Terlan Gries Lagrein, Alto Adige ★ ★ ★ $$
dry, full-bodied, medium tannin, high acidity drink now–12 years
Lagrein tamed and whipped into dark cherry, bitter chocolate, and smoke.

2000 Conti Brandolini d'Adda Vistorta Merlot, Friuli ★ ★ ★ $$
dry, full-bodied, medium tannin, high acidity drink now–10 years
Straying far from the brackish depths of most Friuli Merlot, this impresses with sappy blackberry and pepper flavors.

2001 Foradori Teroldego Rotaliano, Trentino ★ ★ ★ $$
dry, full-bodied, medium tannin, high acidity drink now–8 years
Funky, *animale* flavors frolic with wild, smoky berries in this fascinating wine.

2001 Battistotti Marzemino, Trentino ★ ★ $$
dry, medium-bodied, medium tannin, high acidity drink now–6 years
A smoky, brightly acidic red, the perfect wine for sipping by the hearth over a hunter's stew.

2001 Borgo Conventi Merlot, Collio ★ ★ $
dry, medium-bodied, medium tannin, high acidity drink now–3 years
Bright berry flavors lined by violet aromas make nice drinking, especially at the very reasonable price.

2002 La Vis Pinot Nero, Trentino ★ ★ $
dry, medium-bodied, medium tannin, high acidity drink now–3 years
Good, inexpensive Pinot Noir at the right price.

2002 Muri Gries Lagrein, Alto Adige ★ ★ $
dry, medium-bodied, medium tannin, high acidity   drink now–4 years
A terrific introduction to Lagrein, spot on with smoky mineral and peppery light berry flavors.

WINES WE WISH WE HAD MORE ROOM FOR
2002 Cantina Rotaliana Teroldego Rotaliano, Trentino ★ ★ $ dry, full-bodied, heavy tannin, high acidity, drink now–8 years; **2001 Kris Heart, Alto Adige** ★ ★ $ dry, medium-bodied, medium tannin, high acidity, drink now–3 years

piedmont

Piedmont (*Piemonte* in Italian) makes many wines, not least of which are Barolo and Barbaresco, two of the alliterative quintet of the world's greatest red wines (Bordeaux, Burgundy, and Brunello are the others). Conveniently, they also offer the perfect accompaniment to the region's other gastronomic treasure, the white truffles of Alba.

white wines

Gavi di Gavi, a wine from the Cortese grape, is popular for its lithe lime and mineral flavors. Arneis from Roero is often more interesting, with peppery floral and apple flavors. Chardonnay appears, too, sometimes as ripe and tropical as California Chardonnay, but with more acidity. Piedmont's most charming white is the light, flowery, off-dry sparkler, Moscato d'Asti.

at the table

Gavi goes well with stuffed mussels, grilled anchovies, or angel-hair pasta dressed with pesto. The weightier Arneis can handle pesto, too, as well as breaded chicken or veal *alla milanese*. Piedmont Chardonnay is a good match with monkfish or veal.

the bottom line Good Gavi and Arneis tend to run $12 to $20, with a few rising to the mid-$40s. Chardonnay starts at $18 and can ask double that.

recommended wines

2002 Cogno Nas-cetta, Langhe ★★★★ $$
dry, medium-bodied, no oak, high acidity   drink now–2 years

Now a rarity in its native land, Nascetta's enchanting acacia, green apple, mineral, and fresh-snipped herb flavors cry for a comeback.

2001 Pio Cesare Piodilei Chardonnay, Langhe ★★★ $$$$
dry, medium-bodied, medium oak, high acidity   drink now–8 years

Stony, smoky flavor makes a good excuse for Chardonnay among all the indigenous whites in Piedmont.

2001 Bruno Broglia, Gavi di Gavi ★★★ $$$
dry, medium-bodied, light oak, high acidity   drink now–6 years

Gavi gone serious, with golden apple, orange confit, and stone flavors.

2002 Almondo Giovanni Bricco delle Ciliegie Arneis, Roero ★★★ $$
dry, medium-bodied, no oak, high acidity   drink now–2 years

Possibly the finest Arneis around, this earns its distinction through a parade of stone, lime, floral, and pine notes.

2002 Coppo La Rocca, Gavi ★★ $$
dry, medium-bodied, no oak, high acidity   drink now–2 years

Floral flavors need a few minutes before they begin to emerge from the stone wall of minerality here.

2002 Villadoria Arneis, Roero ★★ $
dry, light-bodied, no oak, high acidity   drink now–2 years

Lovely Arneis, this is fragrant with citrus, herb notes, and apple blossoms.

red wines

Nebbiolo is king in Piedmont. It makes both the majestic wines of Barolo and Barbaresco, as well as the wines of Gattinara, Ghemme, and Nebbiolo di Langhe. It's sometimes called Spanna locally. Wines from Barbera and Dolcetto grapes tend to be full-bodied and easy to drink, though some vintners coax out surprisingly concentrated, tannic versions, too. Another local grape, Freisa, offers many of the same charms as a light Beaujolais. Cabernet, Merlot, and Syrah also appear in the region, alone and blended, and often to good effect.

at the table

There is no better match for a well-aged Barolo or Barbaresco than *risotto alla piemontese* showered with shaved white truffles. Mushroom pasta is also marvelous, especially if you can get porcinis. Decant wines that are less than five years old for a few hours before serving and then serve them with a thick porterhouse. Simple Barbera or Dolcetto are delicious with grilled sausages or meatloaf. Open heavier versions with braised oxtails or a truffled pecorino cheese.

the bottom line Simple Barbera and Dolcetto wines start at about $9; more substantial examples cost $15 to $35, and the most exalted up to $85. Nebbiolo from less-prestigious DOCs like Langhe or Roero can offer terrific value at $16; Barolo and Barbaresco start at about $30, average about $50, and soar over $200. It's worth spending more for older vintages if you plan on drinking the wine soon instead of cellaring it.

BAROLO & BARBARESCO

A leisurely, if hilly, bike ride could get you from Barolo to Barbaresco in less than an hour. The wines from each place are made from Nebbiolo, and both are powerful, tannic, and long-aging, revealing flavors of black cherry, leather, truffle, and smoke. Barolo is the more powerful, tannic, and long-lived of the pair, and requires three years of age, two in barrel, before it leaves the winery. Riservas are required to be aged an extra year. Barbaresco tends to be a little softer and so it requires only two years aging, one in barrel, before it's sold. In times past, it took at least a decade before either wine was ready to drink. But innovative techniques have made wines that can be enjoyed sooner. Even then, patience is a virtue: these wines develop wonderfully complex flavors with age. Names of prestigious vineyards such as Cannubi and Brunate are noted on labels.

what to buy BAROLO & BARBARESCO

1994	1995	1996	1997	1998
★★	★★★	★★★★	★★★★	★★★

1999	2000	2001	2002	2003
★★★	★★★★	★★★	★	★★

recommended wines

1999 Pio Cesare Ornato, Barolo
★ ★ ★ ★ $$$$

dry, full-bodied, heavy tannin, high acidity   drink in 5–20 years

Top of the mountain in Pio Boffa's domaine, Ornato's coal-like mineral, sweet cherry, and leather flavors promise ample rewards with time.

1998 Camerano Cannubi San Lorenzo, Barolo
★ ★ ★ ★ $$$

dry, full-bodied, heavy tannin, high acidity   drink in 4–20 years

Camerano wraps a garland of herbs around berries and dark minerals.

1999 Giuseppe Cortese Rabajà, Barbaresco
★ ★ ★ ★ $$$

dry, full-bodied, heavy tannin, high acidity   drink in 3–20 years

Rabajà is a tribute to taut savory flavors that will take years to loosen up.

1998 Renato Ratti Marcenasco, Barolo
★ ★ ★ ★ $$$

dry, full-bodied, heavy tannin, high acidity   drink in 4–20 years

Subtle flavors weave through this powerful wine, hinting at the complexity to come in another decade.

1998 Anselmi Vigna Rionda, Barolo
★ ★ ★ $$$$

dry, full-bodied, heavy tannin, high acidity   drink in 3–12 years

Beefy, mushroomy flavors aren't everyone's cup of tea, but for those who love savory reds, this is worth a toast.

1999 Bruno Giacosa, Barbaresco
★ ★ ★ $$$$

dry, full-bodied, heavy tannin, high acidity   drink in 3–15 years

All the grace of Barbaresco emerges with quiet power from the mineral-studded purple berry flavors of this wine.

2000 Michele Chiarlo Cerequio, Barolo
★ ★ ★ $$$$

dry, full-bodied, heavy tannin, high acidity   drink in 4–15 years

A tannic yet juicy wine, this is perfect for pork spit-roasted over a fire fueled by fragrant dried herbs.

1997 Produttori del Barbaresco Pora Riserva, Barbaresco
★ ★ ★ $$$$

dry, medium-bodied, medium tannin, high acidity   drink now–12 years

From a cooperative that makes no compromises, this soulful beauty offers fragrances of roses and tastes of dried cherries with fine minerality.

1998 Castiglione Falletto Marchesi Fioravanti, Barolo
★ ★ ★ $$$

dry, medium-bodied, heavy tannin, high acidity   drink in 2–15 years

Barolo's kinship with Burgundy is apparent in this powerful, highly perfumed, wonderfully elegant wine.

1999 Ceretto Zonchera, Barolo ★★★ $$$
dry, full-bodied, heavy tannin, high acidity drink in 5–12 years

First step in Ceretto's lineup, and a delicious one at that, with fresh, juicy fruit and charming floral aromas.

1999 Prunotto, Barolo ★★★ $$$
dry, full-bodied, medium tannin, high acidity drink in 4–15 years

A classic, with multiple layers of mineral, smoke, and dry fruit flavors with a chocolate richness.

1999 Musso Bricco Rio Sordo, Barbaresco ★★ $$$
dry, medium-bodied, heavy tannin, high acidity drink in 2–12 years

Classy Barbaresco at a relatively low price, this offers mixed fruit flavors with a pleasantly bitter mineral edge.

BARBERA & DOLCETTO

Dolcetto or Barbera from Asti or Alba will almost guarantee a wine with luscious fresh berry flavors. Barbera tends to be the fuller-bodied and longer-aging of the two, though Dolcetto from Dogliano can be deeply smoky and full of minerals. Barbera grown in Monferrato is similar if heavier. The best Barbera can fill in for Barbaresco at a lower cost and with fewer years of age.

what to buy BARBERA & DOLCETTO

1994	1995	1996	1997	1998
★★	★★★★	★★★★	★★★★	★★★

1999	2000	2001	2002	2003
★★★	★★★★	★★★	★★	★★★

recommended wines

2001 Pira Vigna Landes, Dolcetto di Dogliani ★★★★ $$
dry, full-bodied, heavy tannin, high acidity drink now–10 years

A beauty in black: black fruit, black smoke, and black, bitter minerals.

2001 Michele Chiarlo La Court Nizza, Barbera d'Asti ★★★ $$$
dry, full-bodied, medium tannin, high acidity drink now–8 years

Somewhere between smokehouse and spice shop, with a fruit cart between them, this is delicious wine.

2001 Cascina Luisin Maggiur, Barbera d'Alba ★★★ $$
dry, full-bodied, heavy tannin, high acidity drink now–8 years
Proof that Barbera can be elegant, with fine fruit and minerals that feel like lace.

2001 Mossio, Dolcetto d'Alba ★★★ $$
dry, full-bodied, medium tannin, high acidity drink now–3 years
Dolcetto's luscious side shows in this deep berry- and cherry-scented wine.

2002 Pico Maccario Lavignone, Barbera d'Asti ★★★ $$
dry, medium-bodied, medium tannin, high acidity drink now–5 years
Ambrosial Barbera—red berry flavors surprise with a pleasant, fragrant note of honeysuckle.

2001 Poderi Alasia Rive, Barbera d'Asti ★★★ $$
dry, full-bodied, heavy tannin, high acidity drink now–10 years
Raging rapids of dark fruit flavors roll over massive stones and eddies of spice in this delicious Barbera.

2000 Nuova Cappelletta Minola, Barbera del Monferrato ★★ $$
dry, full-bodied, medium tannin, high acidity drink now–5 years
Barbera takes a nod toward Barbaresco in this earthy, dry berry-and-spice wine.

2001 Giuseppe Cortese Trifolera, Dolcetto d'Alba ★★ $
dry, medium-bodied, medium tannin, high acidity drink now–3 years
Lean, muscled Dolcetto, this is savory with cherry flavors bound in minerals.

2002 Prunotto Fiulot, Barbera d'Asti ★★ $
dry, medium-bodied, medium tannin, high acidity drink now–2 years
Fresh, juicy berries and a lot of sass.

2002 Renato Ratti, Barbera d'Alba ★★ $
dry, full-bodied, medium tannin, high acidity drink now–6 years
Stalwart wine, built of brambly berries, earthy minerals, and thick streams of berry and spice.

2002 Vigne Regali L'Ardì, Dolcetto d'Acqui ★★ $
dry, light-bodied, medium tannin, high acidity drink now–3 years
Put a light chill on this red, start up the grill, and enjoy the wine's tart cherry and spice flavors with burgers.

WINES WE WISH WE HAD MORE ROOM FOR
2002 Pio Cesare, Dolcetto d'Alba ★★ $$$ dry, medium-bodied, medium tannin, high acidity, drink now–4 years; **2001 Bruno Porro Barbera, Piedmont** ★★ $ dry, medium-bodied, medium tannin, high acidity, drink now–4 years; **2001 Grasso Fratelli Grasso, Dolcetto d'Alba** ★★ $ dry, medium-bodied, medium tannin, high acidity, drink now–4 years

OTHER PIEDMONT REDS

Considering that Piedmont is closer to France than to most of the Italian boot, it isn't surprising that classic French varieties Cabernet, Merlot, and Syrah are being blended—to impressive effect—with indigenous grapes. Wines made from Freisa can be charming, with a hint of sweetness and effervescence. Barolo lovers ought to take note of the Nebbiolo wines grown in other parts of Piedmont, such as Gattinara, Ghemme, and sometimes the Langhe hills outside of Barolo, which often offer very good quality at a lower price.

recommended wines

NV Tenuta La Tenaglia Paradiso, Italy ★★★★ $$$
dry, full-bodied, medium tannin, high acidity drink now–10 years
Unrecognized as an "official grape" until 1999, when this was made, this Italian Syrah takes a distinctly French accent—Hermitage, to be precise. Simply superb.

1999 Ceretto Monsordo, Langhe ★★★ $$$
dry, full-bodied, heavy tannin, high acidity drink in 1–10 years
Nebbiolo's animal qualities are juiced up by Cabernet and Merlot for a definitive Super-Piemontese.

1999 Mauro Sebaste Centobricchi, Langhe ★★★ $$$
dry, full-bodied, heavy tannin, high acidity drink now–12 years
A smoldering combination of tar, minerals, ripe cherry, and spice.

1999 Almondo Giovanni Bric Valdiana, Roero ★★★ $$
dry, full-bodied, heavy tannin, high acidity drink now–8 years
Known mostly for its flowery Arneis, Roero shows it can do Nebbiolo, too, with this smoky, dark-berried example.

2001 Giuseppe E. Figlio Mascarello Toetto Freisa, Langhe ★★ $$
dry, medium-bodied, medium tannin, high acidity drink now–3 years
Juicy wild strawberry flavors underlined by herbs make this Freisa a treat worth tracking down.

2000 Bricco Magno, Piedmont ★★ $
dry, medium-bodied, medium tannin, high acidity drink now–5 years
Nebbiolo takes a softer turn, with dried red berry flavors, light minerals, and an appealing nuttiness.

veneto

One of Italy's most productive areas in terms of industry and agriculture, the Veneto is arguably a victim of its own success. The industrial mentality that brought prosperity to the region tarnished both the quality and reputation of its best-known wines, Valpolicella and Soave. Fortunately some great vintners have turned their backs on factory winemaking and are making inspired wines that remind one why these regions became famous in the first place.

white wines

Veneto's most famous white, Soave, is a mostly insipid affair. But a band of winemakers in the hilly Classico zones outside of Verona are plumbing Garganega, the base grape of Soave, for all it's worth, creating wines with a generosity of lemon, apple, almond, and stone flavors. Outside of Soave, Sauvignon Blanc, Tocai, and Pinots Grigio and Bianco are made into crisp, enjoyable wines. Prosecco, a white grape that goes into the fun fizzer of the same name (see Champagne and Other Sparkling Wines, p. 268), is also widely grown.

at the table

If you're stuck with an industrial Soave, consider using it to make punch or a spritzer. Otherwise, save your money for the good stuff. Quality Soave was made for lemony, buttery scampi or sea bass; single-vineyard examples have the richness for seafood risotto. Pour Sauvignon Blanc and simple Pinots Grigio and Bianco as an aperitif; try pricier versions with chicken piccata. Nutty Tocai is great on its own or with veal scallopine.

the bottom line Simple Soave should not cost more than $8. Soaves from the Classico zone run a few dollars more; single-vineyard wines from superior producers cost $20 to $30 and are worth it. Decent Sauvignon Blanc, Pinot Grigio, and Pinot Bianco cost $8 to $15. Tocai and a few blends start under $10, but run up to $50 for superior wines.

recommended wines

2002 Pieropan Calvarino, Soave ★★★ $$$
dry, medium-bodied, no oak, high acidity drink now–3 years
An excellent example of what Soave can be, full of weighty mixed fruit flavors, almonds, and an almost salty minerality.

2002 Inama Vigneto du Lot, Soave Classico Superiore ★★★ $$
dry, medium-bodied, no oak, high acidity drink now–4 years
This is so aromatic you might forget to sip, but do—the tangerine and lime flavors underlined by minerals are delicious.

2002 Costaripa, Lugana ★★ $$
dry, medium-bodied, no oak, high acidity drink now–3 years
Few Trebbianos show the graceful peach blossom and spice of this example.

2003 Anselmi San Vicenzo, Veneto ★★ $
dry, light-bodied, no oak, high acidity drink now–2 years
Light, lively, lemony fruit and crisp acidity make one fine aperitif.

2003 Maculan Pino & Toi, Veneto ★★ $
dry, medium-bodied, no oak, high acidity drink now–3 years
Pinots Grigio and Bianco make this Tocai Friulano swing to a beat of citrus, berries, and light minerals.

2002 Suavia, Soave Classico ★★ $
dry, light-bodied, no oak, high acidity drink now–3 years
Suave Soave, its richness brightened by grapefruit flavors and floral notes.

2002 Torresella Sauvignon, Veneto ★ $
dry, light-bodied, no oak, high acidity drink now–2 years
This lemony, slightly mineral, lightly grassy Sauvignon is a terrific summer thirst quencher.

red wines

Valpolicella, made from the fragrant Corvina grape blended with Rondinella and Molinara, can be juicy and delicious when made with care; better Valpolicella comes from the Classico zone. Superiore wines are indeed superior, having more concentration and spending more time in barrels. Amarone is Valpolicella made from grapes that have been partially dried before pressing to give them increased intensity, then fermented dry. Ripasso is frugality in action, made by infusing Valpolicella wine with the must (the leftover pressed grapes) of Amarone wine. Recioto is the sweet version of Amarone (see Fortified & Dessert Wines, p. 278). Bardolino makes very light reds that are loosing ground to international varieties, particularly Merlot.

at the table

Simple Valpolicella and Bardolino are best with simple foods like burgers and grilled sausages. Classico versions are good matches for lasagna, with or without meat. Intense Superiore or Amarone wines demand rich fare such as short ribs braised with sweet spices or a Moroccan lamb tagine. They're also superb with aged Gouda, Parmesan, or farmhouse Cheddar.

the bottom line Basic Valpolicella costs less than $10 but a few dollars more will buy far better Classico and Superiore wines. You might come across some Amarone for under $20, but it begins to show its stuff at $25 to $55. Those costing over $100 are sublime. Merlot-based wines run from a modest $10 to a pricey $70.

recommended wines

2000 Novaia, Amarone della Valpolicella Classico ★★★★ $$$$
dry, full-bodied, heavy tannin, high acidity   **drink now–20 years**
Elegant and aromatic, these spiced mulberry flavors and dry flower scents offer delights only Amarone can provide.

1998 Cesari Il Bosco, Amarone della Valpolicella ★★★ $$$$
dry, full-bodied, heavy tannin, high acidity   **drink now–15 years**
Espresso-thick, this holds an abundance of blackberry and violet flavors.

2000 Zenato, Amarone della Valpolicella Classico ★★★ $$$$
dry, full-bodied, medium tannin, high acidity   **drink now–12 years**
Mixed berry flavors sparked with spice are as smooth as velour.

2000 Domìni Veneti, Amarone della Valpolicella Classico ★★★ $$$
dry, full-bodied, medium tannin, high acidity   **drink in 2–12 years**
Summer peach and raspberry flavors are loaded with spice and lined with Amarone's telltale, appealing bitterness.

1999 Remo Farina, Amarone della Valpolicella Classico ★★★ $$$
dry, full-bodied, medium tannin, high acidity   drink now–12 years
Flowers and spice add delicacy to unusually intense fruit. Cellar this: it will last.

2000 Sartori di Verona,
Amarone della Valpolicella Classico   ★★★ $$$
dry, full-bodied, medium tannin, high acidity   drink now–10 years
Seductive Amarone, full of sweet and savory spice, flowers, and mocha.

1999 Speri Sant'Urbano, Valpolicella Classico Superiore ★★★ $$$
dry, medium-bodied, medium tannin, high acidity   drink now–8 years
This Valpolicella seems more like Amarone undercover, a powerhouse of flowers, spice, cedar, and dark fruit.

2000 Christiaan Barnard Foundation, Garda Classico   ★★★ $$
dry, medium-bodied, medium tannin, high acidity   drink now–6 years
Dedicated to a South African medical charity, this wine is also good to its drinkers, with mixed fruit, light coffee, bitter herb, and mineral flavors.

2000 Allegrini Palazzo della Torre, Verona   ★★ $$
dry, full-bodied, medium tannin, high acidity   drink now–6 years
Red wine with a dash of curry for spicy food—its sweet spice, vanilla, and ripe berry flavors can go where other wines fail.

2001 Secco-Bertani Ripasso, Valpolicella Valpantena   ★★ $$
dry, medium-bodied, medium tannin, high acidity   drink now–6 years
The breezy charms of Vapolicella take on a spicy gravity in this Ripasso. A good choice with *bollito misto*.

2002 Tedeschi Capitel Lucchine, Valpolicella Classico   ★★ $
dry, full-bodied, medium tannin, high acidity   drink now–3 years
Easy-to-enjoy violet-scented berry flavors get extra weight from minerality.

2001 Santi Solane Ripasso, Valpolicella Classico Superiore ★ $
dry, full-bodied, heavy tannin, high acidity   drink now–6 years
Old-school Ripasso, this offers up an abundance of bittersweet spice and fruit.

2001 Torresella Cabernet, Veneto   ★ $
dry, medium-bodied, medium tannin, high acidity   drink now–3 years
Peppery red berry flavors brightened with vibrant acidity make this a good basic to have around.

WINES WE WISH WE HAD MORE ROOM FOR
2002 Costaripa Mazane, Garda ★★ $$ dry, medium-bodied, medium tannin, high acidity, drink now–3 years; **2002 Stella Merlot, Veneto** ★ $ dry, medium-bodied, medium tannin, high acidity, drink now–2 years

central italy

Just as it would be hard to imagine Italy without the Renaissance glories of Florence and Rome, it would be impossible to appreciate the gastronomic treasures of Emilia-Romagna, the Tuscan hillsides, and the Lazio plain without the famed central Italian wines of Chianti, Montalcino, Orvieto, and Frascati.

tuscany

Developments in the Tuscan wine industry over the last twenty years have been more exciting and innovative than at any time in its history. From nutty white wines like Vernaccia to elegant red Chianti, from baronial Brunello to super-charged Super Tuscans, the days of cheap, astringent wines in straw-covered *fiaschi* are but a fading memory.

white wines

Tuscany's most widely planted white grape, Trebbiano, typically produces little more than something with which to wash down fish on Friday. More noteworthy is Vernaccia di San Gimignano, which offers vibrant citrus and subtle marzipan aromas balanced by good acidity. Older styles show appealingly nutty, oxidized flavors. Chardonnay and Pinot Grigio make predictable appearances, too.

at the table

Light, fresh styles of Vernaccia di San Gimignano are delicious with spaghetti with grilled, marinated vegetables and grated pecorino cheese. Drink old-fashioned Vernaccia di San Gimignano with a spit-roasted free-range chicken or with traditional Tuscan bean soup. Pour cool Trebbiano with a spinach and goat cheese salad, or with Friday's fried fish. Chardonnay and Pinot Grigio are good with halibut baked with herbs and lemon, and make easy aperitifs.

the bottom line Indigenous varieties like Vernaccia and Trebbiano are bargains at less than $12; a few reach $15. Excellent Riserva versions cost about $20. The few Tuscan Chardonnays worth buying cost $25. Blends, some quite appealing, run between $10 and $20.

recommended wines

2002 Cima Candia Alto, Candia dei Colli Apuani ★★★★ $$
dry, full-bodied, no oak, high acidity drink now–5 years
Vermentino rarely shows this much personality: intense minerality reflects the area's marble quarries; ripe quince and almond fill the mineral flavors out.

2000 Fossi Renano Riesling, Toscana ★★★ $$$
dry, full-bodied, no oak, high acidity drink now–10 years
A terrific Riesling, concentrated and waxy, brightened by minerals and acidity.

2001 Marchesi de' Frescobaldi Benefizio, Pomino ★★★ $$$
dry, medium-bodied, light oak, high acidity drink now–4 years
A Tuscan classic full of citrusy verve, perfumed by citrus and hazelnuts.

2002 Teruzzi & Puthod Terre di Tufi, Toscana ★★★ $$
dry, full-bodied, medium oak, high acidity drink now–8 years
Quince, honeysuckle, sesame, and sweet spice flavors are wrapped in smoke.

2003 Castello Banfi San Angelo Pinot Grigio, Toscana ★★ $$
dry, light-bodied, no oak, high acidity drink now
Here's Banfi's light-hearted, grassy antidote to its brooding Brunello.

2002 Ca' del Vispo, Vernaccia di San Gimignano ★★ $
dry, medium-bodied, no oak, high acidity drink now–2 years
Sweet summertime in a bottle, with flowers, limeade, and hints of cherries.

2002 San Quirico, Vernaccia di San Gimignano ★★ $
dry, medium-bodied, no oak, high acidity drink now–2 years
Benchmark Vernaccia, with crisp apple flavors softened by hints of almond and a pleasant bitter edge.

2001 Tenimenti Angelini Tenuta Trerose Renaio Chardonnay, Toscana ★★ $
dry, medium-bodied, no oak, high acidity drink now–4 years
Tuscan Chardonnay? With light tropical and pear flavors and an appealing nuttiness, why not?

red wines

Sangiovese means the "blood of Jove," and indeed the region would be lifeless without it. Sangiovese wines can be light-bodied and astringent or indulgent and bold, but either way, Sangiovese wines are high in acidity with vibrant cherry and herb flavors. Vintners have traditionally blended the grape with others, both red and white, but 100 percent Sangiovese wines are increasingly common. French varieties Cabernet Sauvignon and Merlot are establishing themselves with success, especially on the Mediterranean coastal area of Bolgheri. Wines that do not adhere to DOC standards are often labeled "Toscana." Wine lovers around the world know them as "Super Tuscans"—an appropriate moniker given their full-bodied, muscular profile.

CHIANTI

Chianti is Italy's largest classified winegrowing region. The expanse is divided into seven subdistricts. The most famous is Chianti Classico, between Florence and Siena. Chianti Rùfina, Chianti Colli Senesi, and Chianti Colli Fiorentini are other well-regarded areas. Until recent memory, Chianti was obliged to be a blend of several indigenous grapes, red and white, with Sangiovese at the core, and aged in old, large oak casks. Modern, more robust styles are likely to be fully Sangiovese, or blended with up to 15 percent Cabernet, Merlot, and/or Syrah. Aging in small oak barrels adds sweet vanilla flavors. Riserva wines are more concentrated, higher in alcohol, and spend at least twenty-seven months in barrels.

at the table

Basic Chianti's simple, fruity, high-acid flavors are just the thing to wash down pizza or spaghetti and meatballs. Classicos have the richness for chicken cacciatore, pot roast (*bollito misto*), or sage-stuffed pork chops. Riservas need heartier foods yet, like *bistecca alla fiorentina* or roast venison.

the bottom line
Good, basic Chianti runs just $8 to $12; $10 to $18 buys a Classico version. Wines from Chianti subregions like Rùfina are a little less. Riservas start at around $16 and go to $65 and higher for rare single-vineyard wines.

what to buy CHIANTI

1994	1995	1996	1997	1998
★★★	★★★★	★★★	★★★★	★★★

1999	2000	2001	2002	2003
★★★	★★★	★★	★★	★★

recommended wines

2000 Marchesi de' Frescobaldi Nipozzano Riserva,
Rùfina ★★★★ $$$
dry, full-bodied, heavy tannin, high acidity   **drink in 1–12 years**
A hallmark in Chianti, Nipozzano impresses with dark fruit wrapped by herbs,
minerals, and smooth leather.

1999 Borgo Salcetino Lucarello Riserva, Classico ★★★ $$$
dry, full-bodied, medium tannin, high acidity   **drink now–10 years**
An elegant Chianti, with wild berry fruit deepened by fine espresso flavors.

2001 Casanuova di Nittardi, Classico ★★★ $$$
dry, full-bodied, heavy tannin, high acidity   **drink in 2–10 years**
This youthful wine gushes fresh wild cherry and almond flavors, then takes on
leather and spice like older wines.

2000 Ruffino Riserva Ducale Oro Riserva, Classico ★★★ $$$
dry, full-bodied, medium tannin, high acidity   **drink now–15 years**
Ducale Oro evokes sun-baked berries and precious minerals, regally con-
structed to impress now or last for years in the cellar.

1999 Fattoria Valtellina, Classico ★★★ $$
dry, full-bodied, heavy tannin, high acidity   **drink in 1–10 years**
Tarry minerals enrobed in dark, tannic fruit make this far more than "ordinary"
Chianti Classico.

1999 Melini La Selvanella Riserva, Classico ★★★ $$
dry, full-bodied, heavy tannin, high acidity   **drink now–15 years**
Fresh herb, dry spice, and orange peel notes mix with bushels of berry flavors.

1999 Monsanto Riserva, Classico ★★★ $$
dry, medium-bodied, heavy tannin, high acidity   **drink now–12 years**
Chianti the old-fashioned way, with a base of tart red fruit that oozes herbal,
floral, and roasted meat flavors.

2000 Rocca delle Macìe Riserva di Fizzano, Classico ★★★ $$
dry, full-bodied, heavy tannin, high acidity drink now–12 years
This has the savory flavors of a slow-cooked ragù backed with ripe berry and mineral notes—and would be delicious with the same.

2001 Palazzo Bandino, Colli Senesi ★★★ $
dry, full-bodied, heavy tannin, high acidity drink in 1–10 years
This is a holiday table in a bottle, full of sweet spice, red berry compote, and roasted meat flavors.

2001 Brancaia, Classico ★★ $$$
dry, full-bodied, heavy tannin, high acidity drink now–8 years
An engaging Chianti, full of brambly berry fruit, foresty earth, and stones.

2002 Castellare, Classico ★★ $$
dry, medium-bodied, heavy tannin, high acidity drink now–4 years
Straight-ahead Chianti, with red berry, herb, and spice flavors.

2001 Dievole Vendemmia, Classico ★★ $$
dry, medium-bodied, medium tannin, high acidity drink now–8 years
Chianti, slick as the polished marble in Florence's Uffizi.

2001 Fattoria Rodáno, Classico ★★ $$
dry, medium-bodied, heavy tannin, high acidity drink now–6 years
Strawberry and floral notes supported by coal-black tannin make for a firm and elegant wine.

2001 Fattoria Selvapiana, Rùfina ★★ $$
dry, full-bodied, heavy tannin, high acidity drink now–6 years
A veritable forest of flavors, from fresh pine to wild berry, mushrooms, and smoldering campfire.

2001 Tenimenti Angelini San Leonino, Classico ★★ $$
dry, full-bodied, medium tannin, high acidity drink now–5 years
Pull the cork to release a gush of mineral flavor sweetened by dark berries.

2001 Lanciola, Colli Fiorentini ★★ $
dry, medium-bodied, medium tannin, high acidity drink now–6 years
From the land of Michelangelo comes a wine sculpted from stone, red berries, and herbs.

WINES WE WISH WE HAD MORE ROOM FOR
2000 Castello di Bossi Berardo Riserva, Classico ★★★ $$$ dry, full-bodied, heavy tannin, high acidity, drink now–12 years; **2001 Mazzei Fonterutoli, Classico** ★★★ $$$ dry, full-bodied, heavy tannin, high acidity, drink in 1–10 years; **2001 Fattoria Galiga Codirosso** ★★ $ dry,

medium-bodied, medium tannin, high acidity, drink now–3 years; **2002 Toscolo** ★★ $ dry, medium-bodied, medium tannin, high acidity, drink now–2 years; **2002 San Fabiano Borghini Baldovinetti** ★ $ dry, medium-bodied, medium tannin, high acidity, drink now–3 years; **2002 Volpaia Borgianni** ★ $ dry, medium-bodied, medium tannin, high acidity, drink now–3 years

MONTALCINO

Brunello di Montalcino joins Barolo and Barbaresco (see p. 156) as one of Italy's greatest wines. A type of Sangiovese that grows around the village of Montalcino, Brunello is famously powerful, dry, and tannic, yet has impressive elegance. Its typical flavors are dry cherry, cedar, and leather. Brunello wines must be aged for four years, two of those in barrel, before they are sold. Riserva versions require an extra year of each. Once released, the wine ages beautifully, two decades or more for good vintages. Rosso di Montalcino is Brunello's kid brother, typically made of grapes from younger vines that produce less-concentrated flavors. Rossos can be released one year after the vintage and they are ready to drink far sooner than Brunello.

at the table

Brunello is ideal with roasted game birds, hearty rib roasts, and garlic-studded, pepper-rubbed roast leg of lamb. Vegetarians will enjoy it with grilled Portobello mushrooms or a wild mushroom ragù spooned over polenta. Softer Rosso matches well with tender, mild-flavored meats like filet mignon.

the bottom line Brunello is expensive. Bottles of any note start at $45 and climb over $100 for top Riservas. Often overlooked, Rosso di Montalcino can offer good value for $18 to $25.

recommended wines

1997 Castello Banfi Poggio all'Oro Riserva, Brunello di Montalcino ★★★★ $$$$
dry, full-bodied, heavy tannin, high acidity drink in 2–15 years
Richard Serra could have sculpted this wine, big in concept, bigger in detail, with dense blocks of blackberry, lanolin, and spice.

1999 Tenuta Caparzo, Brunello di Montalcino ★★★★ $$$$
dry, full-bodied, heavy tannin, high acidity drink in 3–15 years
A showstopper, this Brunello's deep berry flavors and wild, earthy notes will dominate any conversation.

1998 Pian dell'Orino, Brunello di Montalcino ★★★★ $$$
dry, full-bodied, heavy tannin, high acidity drink in 3–15 years
Seductively aromatic, this plays all of Brunello's deep fruit, dry, savory spice, mineral, and leather notes to soulful perfection.

1998 Poggio Antico, Brunello di Montalcino ★★★ $$$$
dry, full-bodied, heavy tannin, high acidity drink in 1–12 years
An almost delicate Brunello, with lacy layers of fruit, mineral, and spice.

1999 Tenute Silvio Nardi, Brunello di Montalcino ★★★ $$$$
dry, full-bodied, heavy tannin, high acidity drink in 3–20 years
Bawdy Brunello, full of lusty fruit and spice on a slick bed of minerals.

2001 Conti Costanti, Rosso di Montalcino ★★★ $$$
dry, full-bodied, heavy tannin, high acidity drink now–6 years
Sweet-tart fruit and salty minerality make this especially engaging.

2001 Fuligni Ginestreto, Rosso di Montalcino ★★★ $$$
dry, full-bodied, medium tannin, high acidity drink now–6 years
Single-vineyard Rosso, singularly delicious.

2001 Vitanza, Rosso di Montalcino ★★★ $$$
dry, full-bodied, heavy tannin, high acidity drink in 2–10 years
Rosso barreling toward Brunello, prodigious and intensely flavored.

2001 Il Poggione, Rosso di Montalcino ★★ $$$
dry, full-bodied, medium tannin, high acidity drink now–6 years
Here's a Rosso almost rich enough for dessert, with creamy, vanilla-laced, cherry-chocolate flavors.

2001 La Poderina, Rosso di Montalcino ★★ $$$
dry, full-bodied, medium tannin, high acidity drink now–6 years
An easy-drinking Rosso to sip while waiting for a Brunello to age.

2002 Argiano, Rosso di Montalcino ★★ $$
dry, full-bodied, medium tannin, high acidity drink now–3 years
A simple pleasure from Montalcino, with lots of juicy red berry flavors and a subtle earthiness.

2001 Casanova di Neri, Rosso di Montalcino ★★ $$
dry, full-bodied, heavy tannin, high acidity drink in 1–6 years
Robust, roasted flavors require no less than rib roasts, rare, but well charred.

OTHER TUSCAN REDS

Vino Nobile di Montepulciano Montepulciano wines were once so highly prized that they earned the name "Nobile." Now in the shadows of Chianti and Montalcino, Montepulciano falls between the two in style. Made from Prugnolo Gentile, a local variant of Sangiovese, Vino Nobile must be aged two years, one in oak, before it's released from the winery. More tannic, concentrated Riservas demand three years. Rosso di Montepulciano wines require none, and are simple, juicy reds meant for drinking soon after purchase.

Carmignano Unique to Tuscany, Carmignano is the only DOC to require Cabernet Sauvignon in its wines. Sangiovese still dominates, but Cabernet gives the wines a little more brawn and heft than Chianti's reds.

Morellino di Scansano The "little cherry of Scansano" is as charming as it sounds, a 100 percent Sangiovese wine that takes on particularly juicy cherry flavors.

Super Tuscan Sassicaia set off a revolution in Tuscany when it was first made in 1968. Made from "foreign" grapes like Cabernet, the iconoclastic wine was ranked at the lowly vino da tavola level by conservative bureaucrats, even though it was full of flavor, body, and tannin. More wines like it followed from other vintners, and these vino da tavolas were dubbed "Super Tuscans." By 1992, it was clear that these wines could be among Italy's best, and the classification IGT (*Indicazione Geografica Tipica*) was added. Wines from Bolgheri, Sassicaia's home region, are now classified with their own DOC.

at the table

Enjoy Morellino, Carmignano, and Montepulciano wines as you would Chiantis of similar levels. Full-bodied, tannic Super Tuscan wines go perfectly with dry-aged porterhouse steaks and braised lamb shanks.

the bottom line
Simple Morellino, Carmignano, and Montepulciano wines can be picked up for under $12; more substantial wines cost $15 to $25, with prices grazing $40 for special bottles. Super Tuscans are generally super expensive—top wines fetch over $100, but there are a handful for $10, many around $20, and even more for $30 to $50.

what to buy SANGIOVESE-BASED WINES

1998	1999	2000	2001	2002	2003
★★★	★★★	★★★	★★★	★★	★★

what to buy SUPER TUSCANS

1998	1999	2000	2001	2002	2003
★★★★	★★★	★★★	★★★	★★	★★

recommended
sangiovese-based wines

**2001 Marchesi Mazzei Belguardo Poggio Bronzone,
Morellino di Scansano**   ★★★★ $$$
dry, full-bodied, heavy tannin, high acidity   **drink in 2–12 years**
Beautiful wine, echoing not only typical cherry flavors, but every measure of
berry, plus orange, minerals, and exciting spice.

2000 Boscarelli, Vino Nobile di Montepulciano   ★★★ $$$
dry, full-bodied, medium tannin, high acidity   **drink now–8 years**
Nobile with a soft touch, with sweetly spiced strawberry flavors piqued by a
slight peppery edge.

2001 Costanza Malfatti, Morellino di Scansano   ★★★ $$$
dry, full-bodied, heavy tannin, high acidity   **drink now–8 years**
Morellino stays true to its name in this cherry-laden treasure.

2000 Poliziano Asinone, Vino Nobile di Montepulciano   ★★★ $$$
dry, full-bodied, heavy tannin, high acidity   **drink in 2–12 years**
Think big: big berry, big tannin, big tobacco. It's so big, in fact, that it would be
better off in the cellar for a couple of years before drinking.

2001 Pratesi, Carmignano   ★★★ $$$
dry, full-bodied, heavy tannin, high acidity   **drink in 2–10 years**
A big-boned beauty with lots of Cabernet character, this will please partisans
of Napa reds.

**1999 Fattoria di Gracciano Svetoni Calvano,
Vino Nobile di Montepulciano**   ★★★ $$
dry, full-bodied, heavy tannin, high acidity   **drink in 2–12 years**
Generous, ripe fruit and mineral flavors impress, but there's even more to
come with age.

2002 Capezzana, Barco Reale di Carmignano ★★★ $
dry, medium-bodied, medium tannin, high acidity **drink now–8 years**
A vibrant, flower-scented, smoky red.

2002 Moris, Morellino di Scansano ★★ $$
dry, medium-bodied, heavy tannin, high acidity **drink now–4 years**
Smoky, soulful, and elegant with zingy cherry flavors, this beats most Chianti for the price.

2001 Poliziano, Vino Nobile di Montepulciano ★★ $$
dry, full-bodied, medium tannin, high acidity **drink now–8 years**
Lip-smackingly good, with luscious, sweet blackberry and light spice flavors.

1999 Ruffino Lodola Nuova, Vino Nobile di Montepulciano ★★ $$
dry, medium-bodied, medium tannin, high acidity **drink now–6 years**
Contemplative wine, this Vino Nobile offers gentle cherry flavors made fragrant with leather and spice.

2002 Caparzo Sangiovese, Toscana ★★ $
dry, medium-bodied, medium tannin, high acidity **drink now–3 years**
Zippy Sangiovese, just right for grilled herb-marinated chicken.

WINE FAKERY

The counterfeit wine industry is big business. High resolution scanners and laser printers make it a cinch to slap the label of a famed $200 wine onto a bottle of swill. Corks embossed with a winery's name are scant protection since they can't be seen until the bottle is opened. But rather than lamenting their fate, winemakers are coming up with solutions rivaling those of the federal mint. Champagne house Louis Roederer, maker of the pop diva's favorite, Cristal, has embossed special codes on its bottles, that, with special equipment, tell consumers every path the wine has taken in the distribution process. Tenuta San Guido, maker of the famed Super Tuscan Sassicaia, is considering installing a microchip into each label that will provide tracking information. While the security might go some way to discourage fraud, it doesn't address the limits of lay people's ability to decode the embedded information. The best protection may be the adage, If a price sounds too good to be true, it probably is.

2001 Nottola, Rosso di Montepulciano ★★ $
dry, full-bodied, medium tannin, high acidity drink now–3 years
Juicy wine: fresh and high acid, this is perfect drinking with sausage pasta.

WINES WE WISH WE HAD MORE ROOM FOR
2001 Poggio Argentiera Capatosta, Morellino di Scansano ★★★
$$$ dry, full-bodied, medium tannin, high acidity, drink now–10 years; **2002 Bruni Marteto, Morellino di Scansano** ★★★ $$ dry, full-bodied, heavy tannin, high acidity, drink now–10 years; **2000 Val delle Rose Riserva, Morellino di Scansano** ★★★ $$ dry, full-bodied, heavy tannin, high acidity, drink in 3–10 years; **2000 Cecchi, Vino Nobile di Montepulciano** ★★ $$$ dry, medium-bodied, medium tannin, high acidity, drink now–5 years

recommended super tuscan wines

2000 Marchesi Antinori Tenuta Guado al Tasso, Bolgheri ★★★★ $$$$
dry, full-bodied, heavy tannin, high acidity drink in 2–15 years
This is so huge it's hard to get your tongue around all the luscious black fruit, oak, and spice, yet it's elegant, too.

2000 Tenuta San Guido Sassicaia, Bolgheri ★★★★ $$$$
dry, full-bodied, heavy tannin, high acidity drink in 3–20 years
Once a revolutionary, now royalty, Sassicaia rules with grace, power, and the generosity that comes with having it all.

2000 Terrabianca Il Tesoro, Toscana ★★★★ $$$
dry, full-bodied, heavy tannin, high acidity drink in 2–15 years
Merlot from Tuscany, thick as a blackberry malt, spicy as Marco Polo's baggage, with a vein of coal that could keep miners working for years.

2000 Castello Banfi Summus, Sant'Antimo ★★★ $$$$
dry, full-bodied, heavy tannin, high acidity drink in 3–15 years
Cabernet Sauvignon, Sangiovese, and Syrah seamlessly join in one monumental red, built like a mountain of fruit and minerals.

2001 Gagliole, Colli della Toscana Centrale ★★★ $$$$
dry, full-bodied, heavy tannin, high acidity drink in 3–15 years
From the Tuscan hills comes this brooding Sangiovese blended with Cabernet Sauvignon. Dense with black fruit, herbs, minerals, and leather, it needs time in the cellar, followed by thick steaks.

2001 Marchesi Mazzei Tenuta Belguardo, Maremma ★ ★ ★ $$$$
dry, full-bodied, heavy tannin, high acidity drink in 2–15 years
Hedonism in a bottle, this oozes super-ripe black fruit accented by musk.

2000 Castello del Terriccio Tassinaia, Toscana ★ ★ ★ $$$
dry, full-bodied, heavy tannin, high acidity drink in 2–15 years
Flavors straight from an Eastern bazaar fill this red wine, fragrant with sweet
spice, bitter herbs, fresh mulberries, dried cherries, and Turkish coffee.

2001 Fuligni S.J., Toscana ★ ★ ★ $$$
dry, full-bodied, medium tannin, high acidity drink now–12 years
Just as you're ready to settle into the plush, plummy fruit, this hits you with
zingy orange notes and nutty flavors.

2000 Dievole Rinasciamento, Toscana ★ ★ ★ $$
dry, full-bodied, medium tannin, high acidity drink now–8 years
The winemaker's eyes staring from the bottle dare one not to like this. Fresh
fruit and spice make that impossible.

2001 Fattoria Poggio a Poppiano Calamita, Toscana ★ ★ $$
dry, full-bodied, medium tannin, high acidity drink now–5 years
Like going on a forest stroll, gathering nuts and berries along the way.
Engaging wine.

2000 Villa Pillo Vivaldaia Cabernet Franc, Toscana ★ ★ $$
dry, medium-bodied, medium tannin, high acidity drink now–4 years
Tuscany keeps Cabernet Franc's pepper and adds its own unique herbal notes
and zingy acidity.

2001 Altesino Rosso di Altesino, Toscana ★ ★ $
dry, full-bodied, heavy tannin, high acidity drink in 2–8 years
Altesino's Brunello tendencies are apparent here: this is all power, with dark
fruit, tar, and tobacco.

2001 Monte Antico, Toscana ★ ★ $
dry, medium-bodied, medium tannin, high acidity drink now–3 years
Proof that a Super Tuscan doesn't have to be super expensive, this does the
trick with vibrant, flowery berry flavors.

WINES WE WISH WE HAD MORE ROOM FOR
2001 Tenuta Sette Ponti Oreno, Toscana ★ ★ ★ $$$$ dry, full-bodied,
heavy tannin, high acidity, drink in 2–15 years; **2001 Marchesi de'**
Frescobaldi/Robert Mondavi La Vite Lucente, Toscana ★ ★ $$$
dry, full-bodied, heavy tannin, high acidity, drink in 1–8 years; **2002 Barone**
Ricasoli Formulae, Toscana ★ ★ $ dry, full-bodied, medium tannin, high
acidity, drink now–3 years

other central italy

Tuscany isn't central Italy's only wine region. North, south, and east are five wine regions with their own winemaking traditions. Read on to see what else the area offers.

Abruzzi Abruzzi provides some of Italy's best wine bargains. Trebbiano d'Abruzzo (a different grape from Tuscan Trebbiano) balances ebullient fruit flavors with savory mineral notes. Its wines can be superb. In reds, Montepulciano d'Abruzzo provides an abundance of dark berry and spice flavors with solid tannin. Oddly, the Montepulciano grape has nothing to do with the Tuscan village of the same name (which makes its wine from Sangiovese).

Emilia-Romagna There are more wines to go with Emilia's prosciutto, Parmigiano-Reggiano, and Bolognese-sauced pastas than just frothy purple Lambrusco. Try the region's interesting whites made from Chardonnay and the unusual, nutty Albana, and the tasty, hearty reds it puts out from Sangiovese, Barbera, and Cabernet Sauvignon.

Lazio Rome's legendary *dolce vita* is fueled in part by the charmingly *frizzante* white Frascati. Based on Trebbiano and Malvasia, the wine doesn't offer much more than light citrus flavors and zippy acidity, and that's okay.

Le Marche Marche's unique white wine, Verdicchio, earns attention for its lemon and smoked almond flavors. In reds, some of the region's Sangiovese match many Chianti in brightly acidic, juicy cherry flavors. However, don't miss the full-bodied Montepulciano-Sangiovese blends from volcanic Rosso Piceno and Rosso Cònero: both are smoky and distinctive.

Umbria Though landlocked, Umbria makes one of Italy's best wines for fish: Orvieto. Made from Grechetto grapes, most examples are simple and cheap, but with care the wine can be quite interesting. The smoky, deep cherry flavors of Montefalco reds, made from the Sagrantino grape, are enjoying a renaissance of popularity today. Earthy, tannic Torgiano reds are also worthy of attention when you can find them. Look, too, for Sangiovese made by Tuscan winemakers drawn to Umbria for its relatively inexpensive land prices.

at the table

Lazio's Frascati was made for lemony octopus salads and baskets of fried calamari. Nutty, mineral-rich Albana is excellent with the region's sweet-salty prosciutto and thick chunks of nutty Parmesan cheese. Enjoy Orvieto with poached sole. Simple red Montepulciano is great with grilled meats; Riservas deserve slow-cooked lamb. Serve Sangiovese-based wines as you would Chianti and richer Montefalco wines with dry-aged prime steaks or game.

the bottom line Good quality whites sell for $9 to $22 and reds from $8 to $15. Better Rosso Cònero and Montepulciano wines can hit the $30 mark. Montefalco typically runs $30 to $70.

recommended white wines

2002 Vallona Pignoletto, Colli Bolognesi, Emilia-Romagna ★★★ $$
dry, medium-bodied, no oak, high acidity   **drink now–2 years**
Supposedly, the locals keep most of Emilia's wines for themselves, but happily, this citrus- and almond-scented gem made it out.

2002 Cataldi Madonna, Trebbiano d'Abruzzo, Abruzzi ★★★ $
dry, medium-bodied, no oak, high acidity   **drink now–2 years**
Herbs and stones, apples and spice. Lovely.

2002 Colonnara Cuprese,
Verdicchio dei Castelli di Jesi Classico Superiore, Marche ★★★ $
dry, medium-bodied, no oak, high acidity   **drink now–4 years**
With dry flavors of golden fruits and nuts sweetened by honey, it's easy to imagine the ancients serving wines like this.

2002 Poggio Pollino Monte di Cambro, Albana di Romagna,
Emilia-Romagna ★★★ $
dry, medium-bodied, no oak, high acidity   **drink now–6 years**
More zippy than most Albana (trust me), this is loaded with almond flavors joined by citrus blossom scents.

2002 Salviano, Orvieto Classico Superiore, Umbria ★★ $
dry, medium-bodied, no oak, high acidity   **drink now–2 years**
Better than basic Orvieto, this example earns smiles for ripe apple and fresh-cut herb flavors.

**2002 Tenuta di Pietra Porzia Regillo, Frascati Superiore,
Lazio** ★ ★ $
dry, medium-bodied, no oak, high acidity drink now–2 years
Frascati's freshness, plus succulent pineapple and lemon, make this an outstanding example.

2002 Ruffino, Orvieto Classico, Umbria ★ $
dry, light-bodied, no oak, high acidity drink now
Light lemon flavors make for thirst-quenching poolside sipping, alone or with
a splash of soda.

WINES WE WISH WE HAD MORE ROOM FOR
2002 Lungarotti Torre di Giano, Torgiano, Umbria ★ ★ $$ dry,
medium-bodied, no oak, high acidity, drink now–2 years; **2002 Colonnara
Lyricus, Verdicchio dei Castelli di Jesi Classico, Marche** ★ ★ $ dry,
medium-bodied, no oak, high acidity, drink now–2 years

recommended red wines

**1999 Cantina dell'Alunno, Sagrantino di Montefalco,
Umbria** ★ ★ ★ ★ $$$
dry, full-bodied, heavy tannin, high acidity drink now–12 years
Wild red berry, intense herb, and spice flavors could bring any deity to ecstasy.

1997 Lungarotti San Giorgio, Umbria ★ ★ ★ $$$$
dry, full-bodied, medium tannin, high acidity drink now–12 years
Slaying stereotypes about the modest quality of Umbrian wine, San Giorgio
has the elegance of the best Italian wines.

**1999 Il Feuduccio di S. Maria d'Orni Ursonia,
Montepulciano d'Abruzzo, Abruzzi** ★ ★ ★ $$$
dry, full-bodied, medium tannin, high acidity drink now–10 years
Positively indulgent, this oozes ripe fruit, roses, and spice. Excellent.

2001 Dezi Dezio, Marche ★ ★ ★ $
dry, full-bodied, medium tannin, high acidity drink now–8 years
No need to splurge on flowers if you bring your date a bottle of this highly per-
fumed, delicious Montepulciano.

**2001 Tenuta Cocci Grifoni Le Torri, Rosso Piceno Superiore,
Marche** ★ ★ ★ $
dry, full-bodied, medium tannin, high acidity drink now–6 years
This shows Rosso Piceno at its best, rich with red berries and savory spice.

2001 Salviano Turlo, Lago di Corbara, Umbria ★★ $$
dry, full-bodied, medium tannin, medium acidity   drink now–4 years
These suave, velvety-smooth berry and silken smoke flavors will put you in the mood for more.

2001 Colli Ripani Transone, Rosso Piceno, Marche ★★ $
dry, full-bodied, medium tannin, high acidity   drink now–6 years
Rosso Piceno comes up roses in this floral, berry-flavored red. Its refreshing acidity begs for food.

2001 Còlpetrone, Montefalco Rosso, Umbria ★★ $
dry, full-bodied, heavy tannin, high acidity   drink now–6 years
Get a smooth, delicious taste of Sagrantino's rich fruit and spice for less in this afforable, lovely Montefalco.

2001 Lamborghini Trescone, Umbria ★★ $
dry, full-bodied, medium tannin, high acidity   drink now–8 years
Look under the hood to find an engine raring to go with smoke, roasted meat, and wild berry flavors.

2002 Falesco Syrah, Lazio ★ $$
dry, full-bodied, medium tannin, high acidity   drink now–3 years
Simple Syrah, but still packed with juicy, smoky flavors, this is light enough for smoked turkey sandwiches.

southern italy

Sunshine is southern Italy's blessing and curse. It provides the means to easily ripen grapes but can also burn off the acidity that keeps the grapes balanced. Until the recent past, the sun also baked the fresh-fruit charm out of grapes fermented in the region's traditional outdoor tanks. With technological advances such as temperature-controlled fermentation, wine quality in southern Italy is soaring.

Apulia Apulia is Italy's most prolific winemaking region, though most of its production never sees these shores. What does arrive here is usually good, sometimes excellent. The heavy, aromatic wines of Salice Salentino and Copertino, made from the Negroamaro grape, are fine examples. Look also for wines from Manduria, which are made from Primitivo, a grape genetically related to California's Zinfandel.

Basilicata Grown around the Monte Vulture volcano, Basilicata's Aglianico wines are among Italy's most enchanting. Once its tannins soften, spiced mulberry and rose notes emerge.

Calabria Italy's toe makes loads of wine, but little of it is of any significant quality. The Gaglioppo-based brawny reds from Cirò, however, are worth a search.

Campania An exception to southern Italy's heavy bias toward red wines, Campania has been lauded since ancient days for its whites. Most praised was its noble Falernum. Today Campania earns praise for its hazelnut- and honey-scented Fiano di Avellino, the almond- and flower-blossom-scented Greco di Tufo, and Falanghina, the white grape upon which Falernum was based. In reds, seek out the bold, sweet-spiced Aglianico-based wines of Taurasi.

Sicily & Sardinia Ill-regarded until recently, Sicily is being transformed into a vinous Eden, as ambitious vintners take advantage of the region's diverse microclimates and indigenous grapes. Noteworthy are the spicy reds from Nero d'Avola and Frappatto and the brisk, citrusy whites from Catarratto and Grillo grapes. Surprisingly elegant wines are also being made from the international stars Merlot, Cabernet Sauvignon, and Chardonnay. Sardinia is best known for its tart yet tropical-tasting whites from Vermentino and seductively smooth but spicy red wines from Cannonau (Grenache) and Carignano (Carignan).

at the table

Flavorful Greco di Tufo is a good choice for chicken couscous or meaty fish like monkfish. More delicate Fiano di Avellino is a good choice for grilled red mullet or sand dabs in a lemon-butter sauce. Sardinian Vermentino is full of crisp lemon-lime flavors, great with platters of raw shellfish or grilled anchovies.

In reds, try Sardinian reds or Aglianico-based wines with osso buco or pork loin stuffed with prunes. Pour Primitivo as you would Zinfandel. Simple Sicilian Nero d'Avola is juicy and casual enough for meatball subs.

the bottom line
Campania's whites are a good buy at $12 to $16. Sicilian whites are usually cheaper—though exceptional ones jump to over $30. Vermentino makes a great summer wine at $10; a few rare examples reach $23.

For $10, you'll find many tasty southern Italian reds, but spend a few extra dollars for older vintages and you'll be rewarded with greater complexity. Better-than-basic Primitivo runs $15 or more. A few exceptional southern Italians cost around $40; a handful go for double that.

recommended white wines

2002 Cottanera Barbazzale, Sicily ★★★ $$
dry, medium-bodied, no oak, high acidity drink now–3 years
Seductive wine, with smooth almond and pear flavors accented by blossoms.

2002 Feudi di San Gregorio Falanghina, Sannio, Campania ★★★ $$
dry, medium-bodied, no oak, high acidity drink now–4 years
Nutty citrus and apple flow from the glass, smoky and beguiling.

2002 Montesole, Fiano di Avellino, Campania ★★★ $$
dry, medium-bodied, no oak, high acidity drink now–8 years
This Fiano is terrific in every way, from its mixed citrus fruit flavors to its notes of flowers, straw, and smoke.

2003 Argiolas Costamolino, Vermentino di Sardegna ★★ $
dry, light-bodied, no oak, high acidity drink now–1 year
Island wine, light and citrusy, with a taste of marzipan.

2002 Botromagna Gravina, Apulia ★★ $
dry, medium-bodied, no oak, high acidity drink now–2 years
Simply delightful—savory spice combines with floral apple flavors.

2003 Donnafugata Anthìlia, Sicily ★★ $
dry, medium-bodied, no oak, high acidity drink now–2 years
Sicilian sunshine in a bottle, this is full of bright fruit and light floral flavors.

2001 Rapitalà Casalj, Sicily ★ $
dry, medium-bodied, light oak, high acidity drink now–3 years
Nutty baked fruit flavors dance on the tongue in this marriage of Chardonnay with the indigenous Catarratto.

2003 Sella & Mosca La Cala, Vermentino di Sardegna ★ $
dry, light-bodied, no oak, high acidity drink now
The limey mineral flavors of this Sardegnan Vermentino provide as much refreshment as a Mediterranean breeze.

recommended red wines

1999 Cantina di Venosa Carato Venusio, Aglianico del Vulture, Basilicata ★★★★ $$$
dry, full-bodied, heavy tannin, high acidity   drink now–12 years
Super-Aglianico cubed, this is bursting with black fruit, intense smoky tannin, and wildflowers.

1999 Argiolas Turriga, Isola dei Nuraghi, Sardinia ★★★ $$$$
dry, full-bodied, heavy tannin, high acidity   drink now–12 years
Sardinia's in the big leagues with wines like this, robust, soulful, and full of ripe fruit and spice.

2000 Amativo, Salento, Apulia ★★★ $$$
dry, full-bodied, medium tannin, high acidity   drink now–10 years
A luscious wine with flavors of blackberry, animal, and spice.

2001 Donnafugata Tancredi Contessa Entellina, Sicily ★★★ $$$
dry, full-bodied, heavy tannin, high acidity   drink in 2–10 years
Cabernet puts a bright cassis sheen on Nero d'Avola's old-fashioned earthiness in this clever, well-built blend.

1997 Montesole, Taurasi, Campania ★★★ $$$
dry, full-bodied, heavy tannin, high acidity   drink now–10 years
A meaty red, this is colored by spices—sweet, savory, and piquant—plus dry roses and mulberries.

1999 Re Manfredi, Aglianico del Vulture, Basilicata ★★★ $$$
dry, full-bodied, heavy tannin, high acidity   drink now–12 years
Soft, plummy fruit hides a cast-iron backbone that can ward off any challenge, from chicken to wild boar steaks.

1998 Struzziero Taurasi Riserva, Campania ★★★ $$$
dry, full-bodied, heavy tannin, high acidity   drink now–10 years
Taurasi reaches its apex in this Riserva wine, full of berry, spice, and smoky tea flavors. Excellent.

2002 Cottanera Barbazzale, Sicily ★★★ $$
dry, full-bodied, heavy tannin, high acidity   drink in 2–12 years
Seductive from first whiff to last sip, this starts with scents and flavors of currants and moves on to flowers, tobacco, and spice.

2002 Metiusco, Salento, Apulia ★★★ $$
dry, medium-bodied, medium tannin, high acidity   drink now–6 years
Simply delicious, this offers an abundance of vivid cassis flavors.

2002 Santa Maria La Palma Le Bombarde Cannonau, Sardinia ★★★ $$

dry, medium-bodied, medium tannin, high acidity   drink now–10 years

Gracious flavors are well aimed to provide pleasure with red berry, leather, and subtle spice notes.

1998 Ca'ntele Riserva, Salice Salentino, Apulia ★★★ $

dry, full-bodied, medium tannin, high acidity   drink now–6 years

Salice goes sophisticated, with a silky robe of spicy red fruit.

2002 Spadina Una Rosa Signature Nero d'Avola, Sicily ★★★ $

dry, full-bodied, heavy tannin, high acidity   drink in 2–12 years

Dense fruit bolstered with tarry minerality and scented with roses makes for one very good Nero d'Avola.

2002 Torre Quarto Bottaccia Nero di Troia, Apulia ★★★ $

dry, full-bodied, medium tannin, high acidity   drink now–6 years

With saucy black fruit and sassy spice carried along on a voluptuous texture, what else could you want?

2000 Santadi Rocca Rubia Riserva, Carignano del Sulcis, Sardinia ★★ $$$

dry, full-bodied, medium tannin, high acidity   drink now–8 years

This charms with rustic wild berry and herbal flavors.

ANTI-MAFIA WINE

Mafia bosses might soon have to find something other than wine to drink with their pasta. The "Consortium of Hope" has been turning over confiscated Mafia lands to cooperatives eager to create honest jobs for unemployed youth and adults in Sicily. Fearful that the wrong message would be sent if lands once productive under the Mafia became barren under state control, the Consortium of Hope project is building restaurants, vineyards, farms, and summer camps. And, to emphasize the point that it's possible for non-Mafia-controlled enterprises to provide jobs, wine labels from the Monte Jato cooperative proudly state, "From Sicilian land confiscated from the Mafia." Since one cannot live by wine alone, wheat and vegetables cultivated on seized properties are being turned into pasta and sauces. Proceeds from sales of the products support the growth of anti-Mafia programs.

2002 Planeta La Segreta, Sicily ★★ $$
dry, full-bodied, medium tannin, high acidity   drink now–4 years
Terrific, everyday wine, great for an occasional glass, or with midweek stew.

1999 Cantina Sociale Cooperativa Copertino Riserva, Apulia ★★ $
dry, medium-bodied, medium tannin, high acidity   drink now–6 years
Spicy floral notes add compelling accents to tart berry flavors in this unusual acidic red.

2003 Feudo Monaci Primitivo, Apulia ★★ $
dry, full-bodied, heavy tannin, high acidity   drink now–5 years
Simple but tasty and black as night, this tannic Primitivo is built for well-charred meat.

2001 Maretima Primitivo, Apulia ★★ $
dry, full-bodied, medium tannin, high acidity   drink now–4 years
What does the barren tree on the label indicate? If taste holds the answer, all the fruit went into this juicy wine.

2002 Masseria del Pilone Primitivo, Salento, Apulia ★★ $
dry, full-bodied, medium tannin, high acidity   drink in 2–8 years
Intense flavors are packed somewhere in this wine. Give them time to find their way out.

2001 Tasca d'Almerita Regaleali, Sicily ★★ $
dry, medium-bodied, medium tannin, high acidity   drink now–5 years
Lovely red fruit with hints of eucalyptus, this is the sort of wine to have on an autumn night.

2001 La Corte Zinfandel, Apulia ★ $$
dry, full-bodied, heavy tannin, high acidity   drink now–3 years
This tastes nothing like California Zin, but tart red berries and spice make for good, simple drinking.

2002 Promessa Negroamaro, Apulia ★ $
dry, full-bodied, medium tannin, high acidity   drink now–3 years
Promises come in small packages. This one's wrapped in black, with dark fruit and mineral flavors.

2001 San Francesco Cirò Rosso Classico, Calabria ★ $
dry, full-bodied, medium tannin, high acidity   drink now–3 years
An earthy, *animale* wine for steak, grilled rare.

spain

Spain devotes more land to vines than any country on Earth, yet, remarkably, it has only been in the past twenty years or so that it started broadly promoting its wines on the world stage. Since then, the country has revealed some of the world's best wine values, from light, refreshing whites to seductive reds—and many charming rosés.

on the label

Spanish wines are generally labeled by region, following a designation system called the *Denominación de Origen* (DO), which lays out the rules regarding permitted grape varieties and techniques in each area. Additionally, many bear a statement that indicates how long a wine has been aged at the estate or *bodega* before release. *Joven* (young) or *sin Crianza* wines see little or no time in oak barrels. *Crianza, Reserva,* and *Gran Reserva* each require respectively longer periods of aging in oak barrels and bottles before release. A few regions also note the grape varieties on the wine label: for instance, Albariño in Rías Baixas.

rioja

white wines

Young white Riojas are refreshing, bright with flavors of citrus and crisp apples. Gran Reservas, which have been aged before they are sold, are completely different, with rich, complex, nutty flavors. Pick them up when you see them before they become part of wine lore.

at the table

Garlicky sautéed shrimp with a squeeze of lemon is perfect with young, well-chilled, zesty white Rioja. Older versions are delicious chilled only slightly, then served with Serrano ham and Manchego cheese, or even braised pork loin.

the bottom line Great quality, low prices: white Rioja is a bargain. Fresh, clean, modern versions to drink immediately are nearly always below $11; rare, prized whites, aged ten years or more, run $17 to $55 depending on age and scarcity.

recommended wines

1994 R. López de Heredia Viña Tondonia Viña Gravonia ★★★★ $$$
dry, medium-bodied, medium oak, high acidity   drink now–10 years
A decade old, these oxidized flavors aren't for everyone, but the baked quince, dried citron, herb, and mineral flavors make it one iconic, special wine.

2002 Cune Monopole ★★★ $
dry, medium-bodied, light oak, high acidity   drink now–8 years
Flowers and minerals play against quince and citrus in this lovely wine.

2003 Muga ★★★ $
dry, medium-bodied, medium oak, high acidity   drink now–8 years
Sultry and smoky on the surface, bright and peachy underneath, white Rioja
rarely offers such pleasure as this.

2002 Bodegas Montecillo ★★ $
dry, light-bodied, no oak, high acidity   drink now
Crisp as a Granny Smith apple, and, with its minerality, even more refreshing.

2002 Marqués de Cáceres Antea ★ $
dry, medium-bodied, light oak, high acidity   drink now–2 years
Simple citrus flavors and hints of oak are made for chilling out.

rosé wines

With fresh berry and herb flavors, Rioja's young *rosados* can be
delightful. Rare, aged versions take on an intoxicating smoky
quality, making them some of Spain's most compelling wines.

at the table
Young rosés from Rioja are great summer sippers, on their own
or with salads and light food. Older rosados can stand up to
salty ham or garlic shrimp.

the bottom line Young, fresh Rioja rosados run
about $8 to $12; older vintages can reach $20.

recommended wines

1993 R. López de Heredia Viña Tondonia ★★★★ $$$
dry, medium-bodied, high acidity   drink now–6 years
Berry, burnt orange, and abundant minerals make this a memorable rosé.

2003 Muga ★★ $
dry, medium-bodied, high acidity   drink now–2 years
Forget about sweet, simple rosé: this is all savory spice and dry berry.

2003 El Coto ★ $
dry, medium-bodied, high acidity   drink now
Easy Rioja rosé, light and citrusy with a strawberry edge.

red wines

Rioja is Spain's Bordeaux and Burgundy combined; powerful, regal, yet also delicate. Other regions like Priorat or Ribera del Duero may be more in vogue, but Rioja's reds have proved their worth for centuries. Tempranillo is Rioja's dominant grape, customarily blended with Garnacha, Cabernet Sauvignon, or local varieties. By tradition, most vintners age their wines in American oak barrels, which impart trademark coconut and vanilla flavors to Rioja's base of cherry and spice. Crianza reds must be aged two years, one in barrel, before release. Reservas require three years total, one in oak; Gran Reservas, five years total, two in oak. Crianzas often taste oakier than Reservas since they aren't given as long a time for their oak flavors to soften.

at the table

Rioja reds are elegant yet substantial, especially delicious with any cut of lamb, roasted or grilled. The wine's vanilla and spice profile makes it especially good with meats braised with dry fruit. Try it, too, with Cabrales, Spain's famed blue cheese.

the bottom line Young Rioja Crianzas can be found for about $9 to $20; Reservas for $12 to $65, and Gran Reservas for $20 to $100 and above.

what to buy RIOJA REDS

1994	1995	1996	1997	1998
★★★★	★★★★	★★★	★★	★★★

1999	2000	2001	2002	2003
★★	★★	★★	★★	★★

recommended wines

1995 Cune Imperial Gran Reserva　　　　　　★★★★ $$$
dry, full-bodied, heavy tannin, high acidity　　　drink now–20 years
Majestic in scale and grace, this combination of spice, smoke, leather, pomegranate, and berries is what Rioja's all about.

spain rioja reds

1996 R. López de Heredia Viña Tondonia Reserva ★★★★ $$$
dry, full-bodied, medium tannin, high acidity   **drink now–20 years**
A window into the past, this is traditionally styled Rioja redolent with smoky tart fruit, herbs, leather, spice, and mouthwatering astringency.

1998 Dominio de Conte Reserva ★★★ $$$
dry, full-bodied, medium tannin, high acidity   **drink now–10 years**
This Reserva offers velvety fruit fragrant with floral and spice notes.

1998 Finca Valpiedra Reserva ★★★ $$$
dry, full-bodied, medium tannin, high acidity   **drink now–10 years**
The stone on the label is iconic of what's inside: deep minerality saturating suave, beautiful fruit.

2000 Señorío de Cuzcurrita ★★★ $$$
dry, full-bodied, heavy tannin, high acidity   **drink now–8 years**
Full of sappy fruit flavors, this is new-wave Rioja, but it still has the leather and spice of the old stuff.

1996 Bodegas Campillo Reserva ★★★ $$
dry, full-bodied, medium tannin, high acidity   **drink now–9 years**
A few extra years in the bottle have served this nicely, softening the fruit and accenting the cuminlike spice.

1995 Bodegas Montecillo Gran Reserva ★★★ $$
dry, medium-bodied, medium tannin, high acidity   **drink now–8 years**
Ten years old, this is remarkably fresh for a Gran Reserva, with flavors of crushed pepper and blackberries.

1998 Castillo Labastida Reserva ★★★ $$
dry, medium-bodied, medium tannin, high acidity   **drink now–8 years**
Lovely, elegant wine, with red berry and spice flavors tuned just right.

2000 Sierra Cantabria Cuvée Especial ★★★ $$
dry, full-bodied, heavy tannin, high acidity   **drink now–10 years**
Like a farmers' market in midsummer: you'll find bushels of fruit in the flavors of this Rioja, from peaches to cherries and berries.

1999 Baron de Ley Reserva ★★ $$
dry, full-bodied, medium tannin, high acidity   **drink now–8 years**
Baronial in body, generous in spirit, this offers an abundance of red fruit flavors with wisps of smoke.

1998 Faustino V Reserva ★★ $$
dry, full-bodied, medium tannin, high acidity   **drink now–6 years**
Solid Rioja, traditional, tasty, and easy to find.

2000 Darien Crianza ★★ $
dry, medium-bodied, medium tannin, high acidity   drink now–6 years
Tart cherry, leather, and herbal notes put grace before power.

2002 Osoti ★★ $
dry, full-bodied, medium tannin, high acidity   drink now–3 years
Organic farming brings a harvest of vibrant fruit and spice.

2000 Ramón Bilbao Tempranillo ★★ $
dry, full-bodied, medium tannin, high acidity   drink now–6 years
Deliciously smooth dark berry flavors with a bit of oaky spice would be delicious with smoked pork loin.

2003 Noemus Tinto ★ $
dry, medium-bodied, medium tannin, high acidity   drink now–2 years
A rambunctious little treat, full of verve and lively, fresh berry flavors.

WINES WE WISH WE HAD MORE ROOM FOR
2000 Pagos del Camino Garnacha ★★★★ $$$ dry, full-bodied, heavy tannin, high acidity, drink now–12 years; **2000 Remírez de Ganuza Reserva ★★★ $$$$** dry, full-bodied, heavy tannin, high acidity, drink now–10 years; **2001 Solabal Crianza ★★ $$** dry, full-bodied, heavy tannin, high acidity, drink now–8 years; **2000 Conde de Valdemar Crianza ★★ $** dry, full-bodied, medium tannin, high acidity, drink now–6 years; **2002 Pago Malarina Vallobera ★★ $** dry, medium-bodied, medium tannin, high acidity, drink now–4 years

ribera del duero, toro, rueda

For more than a century, Ribera del Duero had one fabled red wine—Vega Sicilia's Unico. It wasn't until the early 1980s that another vintner, Alejandro Fernández, showed that the region had more than one success story to tell. The critical success of his wine, Pesquera, started an avalanche of interest, making Ribera del Duero one of Spain's hottest wine regions today. Its wines are made mostly from Tinto Fino, a local variant of Tempranillo; some vintners blend in small amounts of Bordeaux varieties like Cabernet Sauvignon. Generally, they are similar to

Rioja, if more concentrated. More concentrated still are the lusty, bull's blood–colored reds from the Toro region, some forty miles downriver. Between the two red regions lies Rueda, which specializes in aromatic whites from the Verdejo grape, augmented sometimes by Sauvignon Blanc.

at the table

Think big when pairing the bold reds of Ribera del Duero and Toro: thick, marbled sirloins or hearty stews. Vervy Verdejo is refreshing with pesto pasta or goat cheese salad.

the bottom line

A few Ribera reds command prices up to $600, but $12 to $50 buys excellent quality. Toro reds run $10 to $40. Rueda's Verdejo provides price relief at $8 to $15.

what to buy RIBERA DEL DUERO

1998	1999	2000	2001	2002	2003
★★★	★★	★★	★★★	★	★★

recommended white wines

2003 Buil & Giné Nosis Verdejo, Rueda ★★★ $
dry, medium-bodied, no oak, high acidity drink now–2 years
Fresh as a dew-covered lawn, this will keep you cool in deepest summer.

2003 Viña Clavidor Verdejo, Rueda ★★ $
dry, medium-bodied, no oak, high acidity drink now–2 years
Fun summertime wine, full of zingy lime and peach flavors.

2002 Blanco Nieva Verdejo, Rueda ★ $
dry, light-bodied, no oak, high acidity drink now
Take in these snappy green apple flavors while sitting by the pool.

recommended red wines

2000 Condado de Haza Reserva, Ribera del Duero ★★★★ $$$
dry, full-bodied, heavy tannin, high acidity drink in 2–20 years
Glorious, gargantuan wine worthy of acclaim for its black berry, black walnut, and roasted meat flavors underlined with oak and floral undertones.

1999 Finca Sobreño Reserva Selección Especial, Toro ★★★ $$$
dry, full-bodied, heavy tannin, high acidity drink now–12 years
Big-boned but still elegant, lush berry, sweet oak, and earthy flavors are just right for winter meals of roasted meats and chestnuts.

1998 Zumaya Reserva Tempranillo, Ribera del Duero ★★★ $$
dry, full-bodied, heavy tannin, high acidity drink now–10 years
Polished mineral flavors weave tightly through silky red fruit and well-weathered leather flavors for a classy Ribera.

2001 Valdubón Crianza, Ribera del Duero ★★ $$
dry, full-bodied, medium tannin, high acidity drink now–6 years
Woodsy flavors introduce this wine, but dark fruit flavors steal the show.

2001 Vega Real Crianza, Ribera del Duero ★★ $$
dry, full-bodied, heavy tannin, high acidity drink in 2–10 years
This red packs a punch of dark cherry and coconut flavors; put it away for a few years to mellow out.

2002 Bodegas Covitoro Cermeño, Toro ★ $
dry, medium-bodied, medium tannin, medium acidity drink now
With a slight chill and some tapas on a warm day, this light, fruity Toro red will be mighty enjoyable.

navarra, catalonia, & between

Just east of Rioja, Navarra makes wines similar to those of its neighbor, but uses more Garnacha and French varieties in blends. Dry Navarra rosés (*rosados*) are particularly famous. Penedès is best known for sparkling Cava, but it has its share of fine wines from local and international varieties. The steep, mineral-rich, mountain vineyards of Priorat produce some of Spain's most sultry, full-bodied reds from Garnacha, and a very few, very special, nutty, full-bodied whites. North of Priorat, Costers del Segre is responsible for seductive wines from Spanish and French varieties. Between Navarra and Catalonia is Somontano, which is gaining recognition for its tasty, berry-flavored blends.

at the table

Penedès Muscat can hold up to wine-killing asparagus; other white blends are good for chicken. Richer Priorat whites are delicious with crab and lobster. For tapas, try dry Navarra rosados. Reds from these regions demand hearty foods like braised lamb shanks, oxtails, or roast beef.

the bottom line Most good Navarra or Penedès whites and rosés run $12 or less; reds start at $9 and cost up to $20 or more. Rare Priorat whites run about $20; its reds average $20 to $80, and run up to $250. Costers del Segre reds run $12 to $20; Somontano's wines run $9 to $29.

recommended
white & rosé wines

2003 Conreria d'Scala Dei Les Brugueres, Priorat 🍷 ★★★★ $$
dry, medium-bodied, no oak, high acidity   drink now–10 years
Hundred-year-old vines carved into Priorat's steep slopes show spectacular results in rich flavors of peach, pear, and lime interwoven with minerality.

2001 Torres Milmanda, Penedès 🍷 ★★★ $$$
dry, full-bodied, heavy oak, high acidity   drink now–10 years
No-holds-barred oak flavors are equally matched by intense flavors of citrus confit, almonds, and minerals.

2003 Marqués de Alella Parxet Pansa Blanca, Alella 🍷 ★★ $
dry, light-bodied, no oak, high acidity   drink now
A delightful dance of summer fruit from lands north of Barcelona.

2003 Masia Perelada Rosado, Catalunya 🍷 ★★ $
dry, medium-bodied, high acidity   drink now–2 years
Looking for a rosé that's dry, spicy, and a little fruity? Set your speed dial to this little number.

2003 Sumarroca Muscat, Penedès 🍷 ★★ $
dry, light-bodied, no oak, high acidity   drink now
Lime blossom flavors, fine as Spanish lace.

2003 Vega Sindoa Rosé, Navarra 🍷 ★★ $
dry, medium-bodied, high acidity   drink now–2 years
Restrained berry flavor, mischievous spice, and a velvety texture demonstrate why Navarra rosés are held in high regard.

recommended red wines

2001 Pasanau La Morera de Montsant, Priorat ★ ★ ★ ★ $$$
dry, full-bodied, heavy tannin, high acidity drink in 1–12 years
A masterpiece of spicy red-berry fruit, smoke, and herb notes sculpted from Priorat's steep slopes. Pasanau's La Planeta is even more intense.

1998 Torres Mas La Plana Cabernet Sauvignon, Penedès ★ ★ ★ $$$
dry, full-bodied, heavy tannin, high acidity drink now–12 years
World-class Cabernet, full of berry, black mineral, and seductive musk notes.

2000 Fill del Temps Gran Selecció, Terra Alta ★ ★ ★ $$
dry, full-bodied, medium tannin, high acidity drink now–10 years
Sweet spice and dried mulberry flavors give this a Moorish feel.

2002 Guelbenzu Evo, Ribera del Queiles ★ ★ ★ $$
dry, full-bodied, medium tannin, high acidity drink now–8 years
A wonderful marriage of Spanish and French grape varieties, this oozes cassis and green peppercorn flavors with Iberian flair.

2000 Monjardin Deyo, Navarra ★ ★ ★ $$
dry, full-bodied, medium tannin, high acidity drink now–6 years
Velvety Merlot, painted in earth tones of roasted meat and bitter spice.

2002 Agrest de Guitard, Penedès ★ ★ $
dry, medium-bodied, medium tannin, high acidity drink now–6 years
A bargain-priced, Bordeaux-styled Spaniard. Lovely.

2002 René Barbier Tempranillo, Penedès ★ $
dry, medium-bodied, medium tannin, high acidity drink now–3 years
Tasty Tempranillo, with appealing cherry and spice flavors.

other regions

Lesser known, yet lacking none of the progressive energies found throughout Spain, vintners in Valencia, Utiel-Requena, Jumilla, Yecla, and Alicante in eastern Spain are moving away from bulk wine production to make better wines from Monastrell (Mourvèdre), Garnacha, and Bobal. The same goes for regions in Spain's arid midsection, Valdepeñas, Ribera del Guadiana, and La Mancha. In Galicia on Spain's Atlantic coast, Albariño stars in some of Spain's best whites.

at the table

Albariño's rich texture and bright acidity make it a brilliant match with steamed lobster or seared scallops. Reds from central and eastern Spain are good with meaty paella or hard cheeses.

the bottom line High-quality Albariños run $15 to $20. Reds from the relatively unknown central and southern wine regions range from $8 to $20.

recommended white wines

2003 Bodegas Campante Gran Reboreda, Ribeiro ★★★ $$
dry, medium-bodied, no oak, high acidity   drink now–4 years
Tropical breezes sway over Galicia, at least in this wine, full of ripe tropical fruit flavors with a fresh herbal edge.

2002 Fillaboa Albariño, Rías Baixas ★★ $$
dry, medium-bodied, no oak, high acidity   drink now–2 years
Hazelnut notes add an interesting dimension to Albariño's ripe citrus flavors.

2003 Morgadío Albariño, Rías Baixas ★★ $$
dry, medium-bodied, no oak, high acidity   drink now–2 years
With grapefruit, almond, and mineral flavors, this is ready for a clambake.

2002 Haciendas Durius Viura-Sauvignon Blanc,
Tierra de Castilla y León ★ $
dry, medium-bodied, no oak, high acidity   drink now
A real zinger, with grassy lemon-lime and kiwi flavors and a creamy edge.

recommended red wines

2002 Finca Sandoval, Manchuela ★★★★ $$$
dry, full-bodied, heavy tannin, high acidity   drink now–12 years
Beautiful wine from a beautiful bottle, this velvety treasure shows off what old-vine Garnacha can do.

2001 Dominio de Tares Cepas Viejas, Bierzo ★★★ $$$
dry, full-bodied, medium tannin, high acidity   drink now–8 years
This engages all the senses: gorgeous color, seductive aromas, flavors of berry, smoke, and minerals, velvet texture—and a Braille label.

BY ANY OTHER NAME

The three most important Spanish red grapes and the single most important white remain virtually the same wherever they're grown, though the names of all four change:

Garnacha Grenache (France and the U.S.), Cannonau (Sardinia)

Tempranillo Tinto Fino (Ribera del Duero), Tinto del Pais (Ribera del Duero), Tinto de la Rioja (Rioja), Tinto de Toro (Toro), Cencibel (La Mancha and Valdepeñas), Tinta Roriz (Portugal), Ull de Llebre (Catalan name in Penedès), or Ojo de Liebre (Spanish name in Penedès)

Monastrell Mourvèdre (France), Mataro (Australia, California), Esparte (Australia)

Macabeo Viura (Rioja), Maccabéo (France), Maccabeu (France).

2001 El Vínculo, La Mancha ★★★ $$
dry, full-bodied, heavy tannin, high acidity   drink in 1–8 years
This is so delicious with dark berry and herb flavors that it's hard to believe El Vínculo makes a Reserva, too.

2001 Viña Alarba Pago San Miguel, Calatayud ★★★ $$
dry, full-bodied, heavy tannin, high acidity   drink now–10 years
Deep berry flavors cement the wall of mineral flavors this puts up.

2002 Casa Castillo Monastrell, Jumilla ★★★ $
dry, full-bodied, heavy tannin, high acidity   drink now–8 years
Spanish Monastrell is rarely so intense as this blackberry-laden wonder.

2001 Son Bordils Negre, Illes Balears ★★ $$
dry, full-bodied, heavy tannin, high acidity   drink now–6 years
A wine from the islands off the coast of Valencia, this indulges with smoky fruit and wild herb flavors.

2002 Codice, Tierra de Castilla ★★ $
dry, full-bodied, medium tannin, high acidity   drink now–4 years
Lots of juicy berry flavor for less than ten bucks.

2000 Gandia Ceremonia Reserva de Autor, Utiel-Requena ★★ $
dry, full-bodied, heavy tannin, high acidity   drink in 1–8 years
Bobal adds feral charm to this dark, juicy Cabernet-Tempranillo blend.

portugal

Portugal isn't large, but it's a colossus when it comes to the variety of wines it produces. Historically, most attention has been paid to sweet Port and Madeira, but Portugal's wine scene has changed dramatically since the early 1990s. With better facilities and new techniques, Portugal has been able to make the most of its rich array of indigenous grape varieties, resulting in unique and fascinating wines.

on the label

With a multitude of grape varieties growing in a limited amount of space, blends are the norm. Most Portuguese wines found in the U.S. are labeled by region, called the *Dominação de Origem Controlada* (DOC). Each DOC specifies the grape varieties and farming methods allowed within that particular area. Wines labeled *Reserva* must be at least half a percent higher in alcohol (indicating more richly flavored grapes) than the minimum set by DOC rules. *Garrafeira* identifies wines that have been aged for at least two years in wood casks and another year in bottles. Wines labeled by variety must be made from at least 85 percent of the named grape.

white wines

grapes & styles

Vinho Verde, or "green wine," is Portugal's best-known white. Made in the demarcated area of the same name, its "greenness" applies to its youth as well as its refreshing flavor—light, low-alcohol, high-acid, with a slight sparkle. Most Vinho Verde is

Featured Wine-Growing Regions

meant to be consumed soon after release, so bottles don't even bother to include a vintage dating. Vinhos Verdes made from superior grapes, especially Alvarinho (Spain's Albariño) grapes, are fuller in body, lusher in flavor, and can hold up for a year or two. Whites from other regions of the country like Alentejo, Dão, Douro, Bairrada, and Bucelas range widely in content and flavor and can be quite good.

at the table

For a country with practically as much coastline as land, it's a good thing that Vinhos Verdes are ideal for simple seafood like steamed clams or mussels or mild white fish like porgy. Low in alcohol, they're a good choice to wash down light lunches of any sort. Richer single-variety Vinho Verde is delicious with crab cakes. Whites from other regions can often provide a substitute for Chardonnay; try them with richer dishes, like the uniquely Portuguese combination of pork with clams.

the bottom line Most Vinhos Verdes are cheap: about $5 to $8. Alvarinho versions are pricier but worth the $11 to $19. Whites from other regions go for $6 to $15.

recommended wines

2003 Evel, Douro ★ ★ ★ $
dry, medium-bodied, no oak, high acidity drink now–3 years
From a land of powerful reds comes this graceful white, which, with minerals, apples, and citrus, is no pushover itself.

2003 Aveleda Trajadura, Vinho Verde ★ ★ $
dry, medium-bodied, no oak, high acidity drink now–2 years
Very *verde,* this offers a parade of green flavors, from apple to herbs and green almonds, with loads of minerals underneath.

2003 Casa de Vila Verde, Vinho Verde ★ ★ $
dry, medium-bodied, no oak, high acidity drink now–1 year
A bit flashier than most Vinho Verde, with fresh peach, melon, and lemon.

2003 Monte Velho, Alentejano ★ ★ $
dry, medium-bodied, no oak, high acidity drink now–3 years
Steam some mussels in a garlicky broth and open a bottle of this mineral- and lime-laden wine.

2003 Quinta da Romeira Arinto, Bucelas ★ ★ $
dry, medium-bodied, no oak, high acidity drink now–2 years
A veritable fruit salad of flavors, from pineapples to peaches and pears, brightened with orange.

2003 Quintas de Melgaço QM Alvarinho, Vinho Verde ★ ★ $
dry, medium-bodied, no oak, high acidity drink now–2 years
Spice and minerals course through this Alvarinho's crisp apple-citrus flavors.

2003 Muralhas de Monção, Vinho Verde ★ $
dry, medium-bodied, no oak, medium acidity drink now
Fresh grapes and almonds make for a light, refreshing quaff.

red wines

grapes & styles

Not so long ago, the best that could be said of most Portuguese reds exported to the U.S. was that they were charmingly rustic and cheap. You'll still find examples like that, but increasing numbers of noble, sophisticated wines deserve the admiration of wine connoisseurs everywhere. Inevitably, jet-setting Merlot and Cabernet Sauvignon have their promoters, but Portugal's most compelling wines are made from indigenous varieties such as Baga, Touriga Franca, Touriga Nacional, and Tinta Roriz. These wines tend to be full-bodied, dry, and tannic, with some of the same dark fruit and sweet spice flavors found in Port wines. Many age exceptionally well. Portuguese reds are almost always high in acidity.

at the table

Aromatic spicy reds like those from Dão, Bairrada, Douro, and Ribatejo need full-flavored foods such as garlicky, peppery roast leg of lamb or goulash. Full-bodied Garrafeira wines are wonderful with prime rib or suckling pig. Simple reds are the perfect wine for grilled *linguiça* sausages or burgers.

the bottom line There are bargains galore in Portuguese reds. High quality can be found for $8 to $12. More substantial wines, some outstanding, cost between $15 and $22. A handful of exceptions run $50 to $100.

recommended wines

2000 Quinta da Manuela, Douro ★★★★ $$$$
dry, full-bodied, heavy tannin, high acidity drink in 2–20 years
Lovers of great Port beware: with deep fruit, minerals, tobacco, and spice, this might sway you away from the sweet stuff.

2001 Luis Pato Vinha Pan, Beiras ★★★★ $$$
dry, full-bodied, heavy tannin, high acidity drink in 2–12 years
Master of Baga, Luis Pato expertly conducts a symphony of dark fruit and minerals. Serve in place of a great Cab.

portugal**reds**

1999 Casa Ferreirinha Vinha Grande, Douro ★★★★ $$
dry, full-bodied, heavy tannin, high acidity   **drink in 2–15 years**
A superb smoky, spicy red with the depth and restraint of great Bordeaux.

**2001 Domaines Barons de Rothschild (Lafite) Quinta do Carmo
Reserva, Alentejano** ★★★ $$$
dry, full-bodied, heavy tannin, high acidity   **drink in 3–12 years**
With Rothschild style, this is rich with ripe fruit, toasty oak, and coffee notes.

1998 Cartuxa, Evora ★★★ $$
dry, medium-bodied, medium tannin, high acidity   **drink now–8 years**
Wonderfully fragrant, this is like walking into a garden overgrown with flowers,
herbs, and brambly bushes laden with berries.

**1995 José Maria da Fonseca Periquita Clássico Special Reserve,
Terras do Sado** ★★★ $$
dry, medium-bodied, heavy tannin, high acidity   **drink now–10 years**
One of Portugal's most famous wineries shows its best side after ten years'
age with a suite of mineral, dry fruit, and animal notes.

2000 Porca de Murça Reserva, Douro ★★★ $$
dry, full-bodied, medium tannin, high acidity   **drink now–10 years**
A tangle of wild berry and herb flavors marbled with animal notes.

2002 Quinta das Tecedeiras Reserva, Douro ★★★ $$
dry, full-bodied, heavy tannin, high acidity   **drink in 2–12 years**
Delicious now, this violet-scented, berry-full wine will only get better.

2001 Evel, Douro ★★★ $
dry, full-bodied, medium tannin, high acidity   **drink now–12 years**
Smooth as silk velvet, this Douro red carries suave berry and lanolin flavors.

2000 Quinta de Cabriz Superior, Dão ★★★ $
dry, medium-bodied, medium tannin, high acidity   **drink now–6 years**
Spicy, tart cherry flavors lifted by high acidity mouthwateringly demand food.

2000 Quinta dos Aciprestes, Douro ★★★ $
dry, full-bodied, medium tannin, high acidity   **drink now–8 years**
Hedonistic wine, this is rich with ripe, dark fruit scented by rose petals.

2001 Cortes de Cima Incógnito, Alentejano ★★ $$$
dry, full-bodied, medium tannin, high acidity   **drink now–6 years**
Fully Syrah, these intense blackberry flavors steal the show at dinner.

2002 J. Portugal Ramos Marquês de Borba, Alentejo ★★ $
dry, full-bodied, medium tannin, high acidity   **drink now–6 years**
Zingy acidity lifting smoky berry notes make this a flexible house red.

2000 Quinta de S. João Batista Castelão, Ribatejo ★ ★ $
dry, full-bodied, medium tannin, high acidity drink now–4 years
Robust and gentle at once, this wine's berry flavors have a lacy, floral edge.

2000 Altano, Douro ★ $
dry, full-bodied, medium tannin, high acidity drink now–4 years
An enjoyable, affordable quaffer with rich, mouthwatering berry flavor.

WINES WE WISH WE HAD MORE ROOM FOR
2001 Casa de Santar Reserva, Dão ★ ★ ★ $$ dry, medium-bodied, medium tannin, high acidity, drink now–8 years; **1999 Herdade de Santa Marta, Alentejano** ★ ★ $ dry, medium-bodied, medium tannin, high acidity, drink now–6 years; **2001 Quinta de Bons-Ventos, Estremadura** ★ ★ $ dry, full-bodied, medium tannin, high acidity, drink now–5 years; **2001 Quinta de Parrotes, Alenquer** ★ ★ $ dry, full-bodied, medium tannin, high acidity, drink now–5 years

---

LOW-CARB WINE, HIGH HYPE

Perhaps it was inevitable. With low-carbohydrate diets continuing to be thought of as the yellow brick road to weight loss, America's first deliberately "low-carb" wines have entered the market. Since May 2004, carb-conscious folks can openly imbibe without guilt, courtesy of the folks at Brown-Forman, owners of Fetzer Vineyards and Jack Daniel's distillers, and makers of One.6 Chardonnay and One.9 Merlot. The names refer to the grams of carbohydrates in one 5-ounce glass of wine. What did they have to do to achieve such low numbers? Not much, since all dry wines can be considered low-carb: after all, they are made by converting the sugars (i.e., the carbs) in grape juice to alcohol. According to the USDA, the average 5-ounce glass of red has 2.5 grams of carbs, the average white, 1.17 grams. Both these figures are well under the 7 grams of carbohydrates that the U.S. Treasury's Alcohol and Tobacco Tax and Trade Bureau defines as "low-carb" for wine. The verdict? Carbophobes might want to go easy on sweet wines (which contain more sugar, and therefore carbs), but feel free to enjoy a glass of red—any red—with that cheese steak (hold the roll, of course).

germany

German Riesling sales have skyrocketed in the past year, and it's no wonder: few wines in the world regularly offer such vivid fruit and electric acidity. But that's not all Germany has to offer: read on to discover a wide array of other fascinating whites, from bone-dry to syrup-sweet.

grapes & styles

Of all German grape varieties, it's Riesling *über alles* in terms of quality and quantity. Off-dry wines are the norm, though growing numbers are fermented dry. But even when there's a little sugar in the wines, high acid levels balance out the sweetness. Müller-Thurgau is Germany's second grape in terms of quantity, but more interesting wines are made from Gewürztraminer, Grauburgunder (Pinot Gris), Kerner, Bacchus, Scheurebe, and Silvaner. German reds can be good in warmer years. Keep an eye out for Spätburgunder (Pinot Noir) and Dornfelder.

on the label

German vintners are finally giving up the Gothic script, but even the holdouts are worth the effort to decipher. Their wine labels are thoroughly informative, listing the winery, region, village, and sometimes the vineyard in which the grapes were grown, plus lot and cask numbers. Grape varieties are usually given, too.

Additionally, German wines are classified by quality. Basic, "quality" wine (as opposed to "ordinary" wine) is classified QbA or *Qualitätswein*, short for *Qualitätswein bestimmter Anbaugebiete*. Higher in distinction are QmP wines, often called *Prädikatswein*, which is short for *Qualitätswein mit Prädikat,* or "quality wine with distinction." Within this caste are several levels that relate to the ripeness of grapes at harvest. In ascending order of ripeness, the categories are *Kabinett, Spätlese, Auslese, Beerenauslese* (BA), and *Trockenbeerenauslese* (TBA).

Ripeness doesn't always indicate sweetness. Depending on the balance of acidity and sugar, it's possible that a Kabinett wine can taste sweeter than an Auslese. Some winemakers helpfully put *trocken* ("dry") or *halbtrocken* ("half-dry") on their labels (check the back labels, too) to indicate that a wine is dry regardless of its Prädikat; for example, "Spätlese trocken" means the wine is a dry Spätlese wine.

Starting with the 2000 vintage, a parallel classification system was introduced to simplify matters, though it's questionable how much simpler it actually made things. Wines designated *Classic* and *Selection* have Prädikat levels of ripeness, "Selection" being superior. In theory, both wines are dry, but stylistic differences among producers and regions make these designations less than absolute.

In general, you can expect most Auslese wines to be medium-sweet, and all BA and TBA wines to be sweet, with a haunting luxuriousness from the botrytis, or "noble rot," that infects the grapes before harvest. *Eiswein,* a separate category, is a sweet wine made from grapes left to freeze on the vine before harvest. (For more information about these sweet wines, see Fortified & Dessert Wines, p. 285).

Liebfraumilch is an inferior product that is to fine wine what plastic-wrapped American cheese singles are to English farmhouse Cheddar. Avoid it.

lay of the land

Regional differences in German wines are often overlooked, but there are significant differences in terrain, climate, and winemaking traditions among Germany's wine regions. Here's a breakdown of regional styles to expect.

Mosel-Saar-Ruwer That anyone can harvest grapes from the dangerously steep vineyards that rise from the shores of the Mosel River and its tributaries the Saar and Ruwer is a wonder. But the delicate, yet powerfully flavored, citrus- and mineral-laden Rieslings are worth the effort. Those from Mosel tend to be fuller-bodied than those from the cooler Saar or Ruwer.

Pfalz Pfalz is practically tropical compared to cooler regions in Germany, allowing grapes that can't grow elsewhere to thrive here. Riesling is still central, but the region's dynamic vintners do wonderful things with Scheurebe, Gewürztraminer, Weissburgunder, and Grauburgunder (Pinots Blanc and Gris, respectively), too.

Rheingau Riesling is so central to the Rheingau that the grape's name often doesn't appear on labels of the region's wines. Rheingau wines are often fuller-bodied and drier than those from Mosel.

Rheinhessen Most wine spewing from Rheinhessen factories is the insipid stuff that destroyed the image of German wines. However, subregions within Rheinhessen, especially the steep Rheinterrassen, make some excellent wines.

Other Regions Similar in climate to Pfalz, both Nahe and Baden offer many of the same sorts of wines. Especially good are the aromatic, broad-textured Pinot Blanc and Pinot Gris of

Baden, and the spicy, mineral-laden Rieslings from Nahe. More steely than spicy are the Rieslings from Mittelrhein. Franken is beloved in Germany for its bone-dry wines from Silvaner, Kerner, Bacchus, and Müller-Thurgau grapes, as well as the squat round bottle, called a *Bocksbeutel,* in which Franken wines are traditionally found.

white wines

RIESLING

It's no wonder German Riesling captures the hearts of so many wine lovers. Electric acidity powers the grape's citrus, peach, and tropical fruit flavors, and its ability to absorb the mineral qualities of the soil it grew in makes each wine special to the place it was grown. Rieslings are bright and brilliant in their youth, yet they can also age for years, even decades. Over time, they develop deeper, more complex mineral flavors, as well as oddly compelling "petrol" or kerosene-like aromas.

at the table

German Rieslings are exceptionally versatile. The slight sweetness combined with the high acidity of off-dry versions can make a good foil for sweet-spicy dishes like kung pao chicken or Thai green curries. Riesling's bright citrus flavor perks up any manner of seafood, while fuller-bodied, drier examples are fine matches for pork chops or even pan-roasted medallions of venison. Sweet versions, which are unctuous in texture yet sharp in acidity, are ideal with foie gras or rich patés.

the bottom line
Renewed interest in Riesling has caused a rise in prices, but fine bottles of simple Rieslings from excellent producers can still be found for as little as $8. The $12 to $20 range brings a sharp ascent in quality. Sublime wines may reach $90 or more.

what to buy RIESLING

1999	2000	2001	2002	2003
★★★★	★★	★★★★	★★★	★★★

recommended wines

2002 A. Christmann Idig Königsbach, Pfalz ★★★★ $$$
dry, full-bodied, no oak, high acidity drink now–15 years
Some like it hot; others like it dry—very dry. This offers both, as it smolders with smoke and a warm confit of Indian-summer fruits, yet finishes stone-dry, laden with minerality. Spectacular.

2003 Dr. Loosen Ürziger Würzgarten Spätlese,
Mosel-Saar-Ruwer ★★★★ $$$
off-dry, medium-bodied, no oak, high acidity drink now–10 years
Deliciously unctuous Ürziger, this oozes golden flavors, like mangos, yellow plums, and Queen Anne cherries.

2002 Weingut Karlsmühle Kaseler Nies'chen Kabinett,
Mosel-Saar-Ruwer ★★★★ $$
off-dry, medium-bodied, no oak, high acidity drink now–15 years
It's hard to imagine a better Kabinett wine: though regally bearing the weight of layers of tropical fruit, mineral, truffle, smoke, and citrus, this remains remarkably light and graceful.

2001 Schmitt's Kinder Marsberg Spätlese Trocken,
Franken ★★★ $$$
dry, medium-bodied, no oak, high acidity drink now–10 years
Franken wines have a reputation for steely seduction; this lives up to it, with a diamond-crusted bed of irresistible tropical and floral flavors.

2003 Weingut Bassermann-Jordan Forster Jesuitengarten
Spätlese, Pfalz ★★★ $$$
off-dry, medium-bodied, no oak, high acidity drink now–12 years
Some think that quinces, not apples, were the fruits of temptation. One sip of this wine's spicy quince flavors, and it's easy to believe that it's true, especially when they are so lively and fresh.

2002 Guntrum Oppenheimer Sackträger Classic Spätlese Trocken,
Rheinhessen ★★★ $$
dry, medium-bodied, no oak, high acidity drink now–12 years
This is *trocken* (dry), and how! Yet with such a bounty of flowers, mango, and berry flavors, this smoky wine is no desert.

2002 Joh. Haart Piesporter Goldtröpfchen Spätlese,
Mosel-Saar-Ruwer ★★★ $$
off-dry, medium-bodied, no oak, high acidity drink now–10 years
This is less than three years old and showing its petrol side, deliciously sweetened by ripe pear and citrus notes.

2003 Kruger-Rumpf Münsterer Dautenpflänzer Spätlese, Nahe ★★★ $$

off-dry, medium-bodied, no oak, high acidity   **drink now–12 years**

One sip and your tongue will rumba throughout dinner with this orchestra of wild fruit flavors. Delicious.

2003 Künstler Reichestal Kabinett, Rheingau ★★★ $$

off-dry, medium-bodied, no oak, high acidity   **drink now–8 years**

Delicious, exciting drinking, this offers a panoply of ripe pear and dry apricot flavors, beautifully balanced.

2003 Leitz Dragonstone, Rheingau ★★★ $$

medium-sweet, medium-bodied, no oak, high acidity   **drink now–8 years**

Though a bit sweeter than is currently in vogue, this orange- and berry-scented wine has the acidity to slay any hint of cloying.

2003 Reichsgraf von Kesselstatt Scharzhofberger Spätlese, Mosel-Saar-Ruwer ★★★ $$

off-dry, medium-bodied, no oak, high acidity   **drink now–12 years**

A luscious parade of fruit flavors, balanced by surprisingly electric acidity.

2003 Reichsrat von Buhl Armand Kabinett, Pfalz ★★★ $$

off-dry, medium-bodied, no oak, high acidity   **drink now–8 years**

Vibrant acidity and smoky minerals rounded out by citrus make one mouthwatering, versatile Riesling.

2002 Selbach-Oster Zeltinger Sonnenuhr Kabinett, Mosel-Saar-Ruwer ★★★ $$

dry, medium-bodied, no oak, high acidity   **drink now–12 years**

Johannes Selbach's fine touch crafts an elegant wine of light citrus, pineapple, and smoky minerals.

2002 von Othegraven Maria v.O., Mosel-Saar-Ruwer ★★★ $$

off-dry, medium-bodied, no oak, high acidity   **drink now–8 years**

The simplest of Othegraven's intricately flavored wines is far from minimalist, with layers of dry fruit, smoke, and minerals.

2002 von Volxem, Saar ★★★ $$

dry, medium-bodied, no oak, high acidity   **drink now–12 years**

This swings from one tropical fruit to the next, grounded by stony minerality.

2002 Weingut Albert Merkelbach Kinheimer Rosenberg Spätlese, Mosel-Saar-Ruwer ★★★ $$

off-dry, medium-bodied, no oak, high acidity   **drink now–15 years**

Citrus and tropical fruits are superbly woven with aromatic herbs, delicious to drink now but promising more to come in the next decade.

2002 Weingut Dr. Deinhard Ruppertsberger Reiterpfad Kabinett, Pfalz ★ ★ ★ $$

off-dry, medium-bodied, no oak, high acidity   **drink now–10 years**

Die Hard, Deinhard, whatever; this will keep you at the edge of your seat in anticipation of the next thrilling flavor.

2002 Gunderloch Nackenheimer Rothenberg Spätlese, Rheinhessen ★ ★ $$$

off-dry, medium-bodied, no oak, high acidity   **drink now–8 years**

Give this a few minutes and an herbal ambrosia of fruit will emerge.

2002 Dr. Wagner Ockfener Bockstein Kabinett, Mosel-Saar-Ruwer ★ ★ $$

off-dry, medium-bodied, no oak, high acidity   **drink now–8 years**

Dry lime and mineral flavors carry a pleasant ribbon of pine flavor.

2002 Egon Müller Scharzhof, Mosel-Saar-Ruwer ★ ★ $$

off-dry, medium-bodied, no oak, high acidity   **drink now–6 years**

Rieslingmeister Egon Müller strikes a fine balance of tropical and citrus notes.

2002 Weingut Karl Erbes Ürziger Würzgarten Auslese, Mosel-Saar-Ruwer ★ ★ $$

off-dry, medium-bodied, no oak, high acidity   **drink now–5 years**

On the drier side of Auslese, this has sweet spice and dry lime flavors that seem carved from a chunk of honeycomb.

2002 Weingut Spreitzer Oestricher Doosberg, Rheingau ★ ★ $$

off-dry, medium-bodied, no oak, high acidity   **drink now–6 years**

Solid Riesling, with ripe apple and sweet lime flavor accented by nuts.

2002 Carl Graff Erdener Treppchen Spätlese, Mosel-Saar-Ruwer ★ ★ $

off-dry, medium-bodied, no oak, high acidity   **drink now–8 years**

Vervy citrus and mineral flavors energize the palate for more.

2003 Künstler Estate, Rheingau ★ ★ $

off-dry, medium-bodied, no oak, high acidity   **drink now–6 years**

An archetype of Rheingau Riesling: plush fruit restrained by minerals and acidity.

2002 Lingenfelder Bird Label, Pfalz ★ ★ $

off-dry, medium-bodied, no oak, high acidity   **drink now–3 years**

Citrus and almond flavors are pleasurable at any time, from brunch to a dinner of chicken Caesar.

2003 Mönchhof Robert Eymael Estate, Mosel-Saar-Ruwer ★ ★ $

off-dry, medium-bodied, no oak, medium acidity   **drink now–3 years**

The warmth of the year shows in the juiciness of this wine's fruit flavors.

2003 Reichsrat von Buhl Maria Schneider Jazz Medium-Dry, Pfalz ★★ $
dry, medium-bodied, no oak, high acidity   **drink now–8 years**
A veritable bebop of minerals, dry spice, and citrus flavors.

2002 Weingut Rudolf Eilenz Ayler Kupp Kabinett, Mosel-Saar-Ruwer ★★ $
off-dry, medium-bodied, no oak, medium acidity   **drink now–6 years**
Soft as velvet, this ripe wine pampers your tongue with mixed tropical fruit flavors laden with minerals.

2002 Weingut Stephan Ehlen Erdener Treppchen Kabinett, Mosel-Saar-Ruwer ★★ $
off-dry, medium-bodied, no oak, high acidity   **drink now–8 years**
A fount of mineral oil flavors jet from glass to palate, with nut and citrus to back them up.

2002 Zilliken Butterfly Medium-Dry, Mosel-Saar-Ruwer ★★ $
off-dry, medium-bodied, no oak, high acidity   **drink now–6 years**
If not for the steely minerals, the charming apple and citrus flavors might just flutter away.

2003 Selbach Dry (Fish Label), Mosel-Saar-Ruwer ★ $
off-dry, light-bodied, no oak, high acidity   **drink now–2 years**
The multicolored fish on the label says it all: pour this zippy, citrusy wine at your next fish dinner.

2002 Weingut G. Dickenscheid Kabinett, Rheinhessen ★ $
off-dry, medium-bodied, no oak, high acidity   **drink now–6 years**
This offers a lot more than just fruit for the money—there are interesting mushroom notes, too.

OTHER WHITE WINES

Riesling might be king, but a number of grapes in Germany could qualify as princes and princesses. Like their Alsatian counterparts Pinot Gris and Pinot Blanc, Grauburgunder and Weissburgunder make lush and aromatic wines. Scheurebe shows intriguing, funky charms with flavors ranging from cassis to grapefruit to animal. Kerner, Huxelrebe, and Bacchus are distinctive hybrids that do well in Franken. Delicious wines are made from fragrant Gewürztraminer and Muskateller (Muscat), but far more common and far less aromatic are Silvaner and Müller-Thurgau, which, with notable exceptions, are made into tart, insipid wines.

at the table

The high-acid, off-dry, aromatic Riesling model holds for most German whites. Enjoy Grauburgunder with roast chicken or turkey. The herb, flower, spice, and stone qualities of Scheurebe, Muskateller, and Gewürztraminer make them terrific with sweet and spicy foods, like many Asian or Caribbean dishes.

the bottom line Non-Riesling German wines tend to be overlooked. You'll find most for under $20, although a few from revered producers hit the $40 mark.

what to buy OTHER WHITE WINES

1999	2000	2001	2002	2003
★★★★	★★	★★★★	★★	★★

recommended wines

2002 Munzberg Weissburgunder Spätlese Trocken, Pfalz ★★★ $$
dry, medium-bodied, no oak, high acidity   drink now–8 years
Weissburgunder, nicely sculpted from a block of waxy minerals and lime.

2003 Valckenberg Gewürztraminer, Pfalz   ★★★ $
off-dry, medium-bodied, no oak, high acidity   drink now–3 years
Subtle scents of honeysuckle will bring sweet sighs of pleasure with every sip. It's affordable, too.

**2003 Pfeffingen Ungsteiner Herrenberg Scheurebe Spätlese,
Pfalz**   ★★ $$
off-dry, medium-bodied, no oak, medium acidity   drink now–4 years
Funky, feral Scheurebe cleans up its act, but limeade and herb flavors are far from conventional.

2003 Guntrum Scheurebe Kabinett, Rheinhessen   ★★ $
off-dry, medium-bodied, no oak, medium acidity   drink now–4 years
Like a beacon, this red-colored bottle draws you in to offer unique flavors of peach, green peppercorn, herbs, and almonds.

2003 J.L. Wolf Pinot Gris, Pfalz   ★★ $
dry, medium-bodied, light oak, high acidity   drink now–6 years
Plush Pinot Gris takes a sharp turn toward savory austerity, as minerals and dry citrus flavors take over.

TOP 10 OVERLOOKED & UNDERAPPRECIATED WINES

1. Dry Rosés Dry rosés are light and refreshing enough for aperitifs as well as flavorful enough to match with hearty vegetable and light meat dishes.

2. Loire Valley Cabernet Franc Wines from Chinon, Bourgeuil, and Saumur all offer Cabernet Franc's peppery red berry flavors with acidity, power, and finesse.

3. Dolcetto from Piedmont From simply, cheerful, cherry-laden wines to dark brooding, tobacco-scented reds, Dolcetto assumes many poses, most affordable.

4. Greek wines Beyond Retsina, Greece offers an array of soulful reds plus racy, mineral-laden whites.

5. Finger Lakes whites The region's cool hillside vineyards produce the best Gewürztraminer and Riesling in the U.S.

6. Sparkling wine There's one for every occasion, from a Cava with salads to sparkling red Shiraz with steak.

7. Portuguese reds Powerful yet fine, plus the excitement that comes from unique grape varieties.

8. Cru Beaujolais These can echo good Burgundy at a fraction of the cost.

9. Madeira Sweet flavors with rocketing acidity lets Madeira glide easily from dinner to dessert.

10. Sherry From bone-dry to molasses-sweet , there's a Sherry for everything.

2002 Konigschaffhausen Flaneur Müller-Thurgau, Baden   ★ ★ $
dry, light-bodied, no oak, high acidity   **drink now–3 years**
Flowery scents add delicacy to a bed of peach and dry spice flavors.

2002 Thungersheim Müller-Thurgau Halbtrocken, Franken   ★ $
off-dry, medium-bodied, no oak, medium acidity   **drink now–2 years**
Light pear and almond flavors would be tasty alone, but a squeeze of lemon adds extra charm.

2002 Weingut Köster-Wolf Müller-Thurgau Halbtrocken,
Rheinhessen   ★ $
off-dry, light-bodied, no oak, medium acidity   **drink now**
Müller's simplicity takes a nutty turn in this picnic wine in a 1-liter bottle.

austria

With racy acidity, explosive flavors, and a profound sense of the land from which they came, Austrian whites wines are among the most thrilling anywhere.

grapes & styles

Riesling's shadow is long, stretching from Germany to Austria, but once it crosses the Alps it morphs into a drier yet richer form. Grüner Veltliner, Austria's most widely grown grape, also offers dry flavors ranging from citrus to herb, mineral, smoke, and even lentil. Rounder and fuller than Riesling, great Grüner Veltliners can also offer spell binding depth. Other white wines are made from the prolific Welschriesling and the rarer Furmint, which is also the basis of Hungary's famed Tokaji wines. Winemakers from Styria love Sauvignon Blanc for its fine balance of citrus and herb flavors. Chardonnay (sometimes called Morillon) is also found.

White wines dominate, but Austrian reds are increasingly garnering attention. Availability is still limited, but with quality running as high as the pricetag, it's worth seeking out juicy Zweigelt, delicate Blauer Portugieser, peppery Blaufränkisch (Lemberger), or Blauburgunder (Pinot Noir).

on the label

Austrian wine labels routinely list grape variety and region. In addition, Austria uses a classification system and indication of ripeness similar to Germany's (see Germany, page 204), though Austrian ripeness standards are higher and the wines are likely to be drier than Germany's.

The Wachau region uses its own classification scheme: *Steinfeder* indicates the lightest wines, meant for early drinking; *Federspiel* signifies weightier wines, and *Smaragd* wines—named after a local lizard that basks in the sun—are richer still, dry, and capable of long aging.

NIEDERÖSTERREICH

Kamptal
Kremstal
Wachau
Traisental
Carnuntum
Neusiedlersee
Thermenregion
Neusiedlersee-Hügelland

Weinviertel
Donauland

VIENNA

Danube River

SALZBURG

BURGENLAND

STYRIA

▢ Featured
Wine-Growing
Regions

lay of the land

Niederösterreich Niederösterreich, or "Lower Austria," produces the most wine in the country. The area, which spreads along the Danube from the northwest corner of Austria west to Slovakia, is conventionally broken down into eight regions: Carnuntum, Donauland, Thermenregion, Traisental, Weinviertel, Kamptal, Kremstal, and Wachau. The latter three claim some of the country's most intense Rieslings and Veltliners.

Burgenland Austria's warmest region provides Tokaji-like sweet wines from the Neusiedlersee and the Neusiedlersee-Hügelland subregions. Mittelburgenland and Südburgenland specialize in red wines.

Styria Bordering Slovenia and not so far from northern Italy, Styria (Steiermark) specializes in Welschriesling, Muskateller, Sauvignon Blanc, and Chardonnay.

Vienna Surrounded by important wine regions, Vienna isn't just an island of cosmopolitan culture, it's a wine region itself. Most of Vienna's fresh Veltliner never makes it farther than the local wine taverns, but a couple of excellent bottlings manage to find their way overseas.

white wines

GRÜNER VELTLINER

Most Grüner Veltliners are simple, everyday wines with snappy fruit flavors. Exceptional examples can be as striking as wine gets, with flavors recalling grapefruit, nuts, herbs, flowers, smoke, pepper, and even lentils. The best can age for decades.

at the table

Simple Grüner Veltliners can fill in for any simple white. More complex versions can highlight the freshness of sushi. Lusher Smaragd-level wines can handle Wienerschnitzel. The variety's pleasantly vegetal flavors make it uniquely able to stand up to foods that kill most wines, like asparagus and artichokes.

the bottom line Liter bottles of a few simple but quality Grüner Veltliners offer outstanding value for $11; more complex wines run from $15 to $50 or higher.

what to buy WHITE WINES

1999	2000	2001	2002	2003
★★★★	★★★★	★★★	★★★	★★

recommended wines

2002 Rudi Pichler Terrassen Smaragd, Wachau   ★★★★ $$$
dry, medium-bodied, no oak, high acidity   drink now–15 years
Grüner's potential for smoky lentil, herb, and ripe citrus flavors is expertly realized in this masterpiece.

2003 Weingut Bründlmayer Alte Reben, Kamptal   ★★★ $$$
dry, medium-bodied, no oak, high acidity   drink now–8 years
These old vines (*alte Reben*) give plenty of fresh-squeezed grapefruit flavors supported by abundant minerals.

2003 Weingut Knoll Federspiel, Wachau   ★★★ $$$
dry, medium-bodied, no oak, high acidity   drink now–4 years
Behind the Baroque label resides a Palm Beach rococo of breezy lime and mineral flavors.

2002 Johann Donabaum Spitzer Point Smaragd, Wachau ★★★ $$
dry, medium-bodied, no oak, high acidity   drink now–12 years
Intense minerals, smoky spice, and apple flavors can take on toro like a pro.

2002 Nikolaihof Hefeabzug, Wachau   ★★★ $$
dry, medium-bodied, no oak, high acidity   drink now–12 years
Biodynamic Grüner Veltliner, filled with salty cashew and citrus flavors.

2003 Gritsch Mauritiushof Singerriedel Smaragd, Wachau ★★ $$$
dry, full-bodied, no oak, high acidity   drink now–12 years
A ripe vintage brings in a bounty of mixed fruit, made more complex by linger-
ing smoke and spice.

2003 Loimer Lois, Kamptal   ★★ $
dry, medium-bodied, no oak, high acidity   drink now–2 years
Groovy Grüner, done in shades of green, from apple to grass to lime. Fun stuff.

2003 Undhof Salomon Hochterrassen, Kremstal   ★★ $
dry, light-bodied, no oak, high acidity   drink now–3 years
Wonderfully fresh, with a bright, zippy spirit.

RIESLING

Those not ready to dip into Grüner Veltliner's sometimes funky
disposition have plenty of excellent Rieslings to enjoy. Austrian
Rieslings are typically drier than those from Germany and fuller-
bodied than their Alsatian counterparts.

at the table

Riesling displays the same supreme adaptability in Austria as it
does elsewhere, marrying beautifully with anything from fish to
roast duck to baked ham.

the bottom line There are a few good Austrian
Rieslings for less than $15, but expect to pay $15 to $30 for better
wines, and up to $90 for single-vineyard and reserve bottlings.

recommended wines

2002 Franz Hirtzberger Hochrain Smaragd, Wachau ★★★★ $$$$
dry, full-bodied, no oak, high acidity   drink now–12 years
Lovers of full-throttle Riesling should race to get this wine: with waves of tropi-
cal fruit fueled by smoking minerals, it's superb.

2002 Prager Steinriegl Federspiel, Wachau
★ ★ ★ ★ $$$
dry, full-bodied, no oak, high acidity   drink now–15 years

Layer upon layer of mixed fruit, stone, truffles, and smoke prove, once again, that Prager is one of the world's Riesling masters.

2002 Alzinger Loibenberg Smaragd, Wachau
★ ★ ★ $$$$
dry, medium-bodied, no oak, high acidity   drink now–12 years

This strikes an impressive balance of super-ripe fruit contrasted against intense minerals and earthy mushroom notes.

2003 Hirsch Gaisberg Zöbing April, Kamptal
★ ★ ★ $$$
dry, medium-bodied, no oak, high acidity   drink now–10 years

Apples, pears, and toasted almonds with citrus undertones make fine drinking all year long.

2002 Lagler Federspiel Von den Terrassen, Wachau
★ ★ ★ $$$
dry, medium-bodied, no oak, high acidity   drink now–10 years

Lithe and lean, this spins graceful pirouettes of mineral and grapefruit flavors.

2003 Loimer Seeberg, Kamptal
★ ★ ★ $$$
dry, medium-bodied, no oak, high acidity   drink now–12 years

Fresh-squeezed lime and mint jazz up this refreshing pour.

2003 Gritsch Mauritiushof 1000-eimerberg Smaragd, Wachau
★ ★ ★ $$
dry, medium-bodied, no oak, high acidity   drink now–8 years

Like an unexpected bouquet of spring flowers, this lovely Riesling is bound to bring a smile to your face, especially with its notes of Meyer lemon.

2003 Domäne Wachau Terrassen Federspiel, Wachau
★ ★ ★ $
dry, medium-bodied, no oak, high acidity   drink now–10 years

Luscious peach, herb, and mineral flavors offer great pleasure for a modest sum.

2003 Schloss Gobelsburg Urgestein, Kamptal
★ ★ $$
dry, medium-bodied, no oak, high acidity   drink now–5 years

Straightforward, well-honed Riesling, forged from minerals and fruit.

OTHER WHITE WINES

Austria's vineyards reflect its multinational heritage, with Weissburgunder (Pinot Blanc), Sauvignon Blanc (sometimes called Muskat-Sylvaner), and Chardonnay (Morillon) settled here for more than a century. Welschriesling, Grauburgunder (Pinot Gris), and Muskateller (Muscat) make fragrant wines. Furmint makes fascinating wines in the eastern part of the country

at the table

Serve Austrian Sauvignon Blanc as you would a Sancerre, with delicate fish and vegetable dishes. Weissburgunder and Welschriesling are good with baked, herbed chicken breasts or lunch salads. Grauburgunder and Chardonnay have the weight for grilled salmon steaks or roast pork. Muskateller's floral notes can hold up to asparagus or artichokes.

the bottom line Welschriesling, Weissburgunder, Muskateller, and Furmint sell for between $9 and $35. Sauvignon Blanc and Chardonnay cost $13 to $50.

recommended wines

2001 Wieninger Alte Reben Nussberg, Wien ★★★★ $$
dry, full-bodied, no oak, high acidity   drink now–8 years
This field blend of different grape varieties offers a gorgeous collage of fruits, herbs, and nut flavors.

2003 Leth Roter Veltliner, Wagram ★★★ $$$
dry, medium-bodied, no oak, high acidity   drink now–6 years
Rare Roter Veltliner shows its worth with ripe fruit plus floral and stony notes.

2002 Weingut Erwin Sabathi Merveilleux Sauvignon Blanc, Südsteiermark ★★★ $$$
dry, medium-bodied, light oak, high acidity   drink now–4 years
Wine well named, this offers simply marvelous flavors of lemon confit, green peppercorn, and passion fruit.

2002 Lackner-Tinnacher Ried Gamitz Muskateller, Südsteiermark ★★★ $$
dry, medium-bodied, no oak, high acidity   drink now–6 years
It's easy to get swept away with this whirlwind of citrus blossom, lemon, and mineral flavors.

2002 Tscheppe Pössnitzberg Pinot Gris, Südsteiermark ★★★ $$
dry, full-bodied, light oak, high acidity   drink now–10 years
Ripe baked pear and spice are underlined by tart citrus and steely minerals.

2002 Jaungegg Muri Chardonnay, Südsteiermark ★★ $$
dry, full-bodied, light oak, high acidity   drink now–8 years
This silken Chardonnay sparkles with minerals alongside its pear flavors.

switzerland

Swiss wines are among the most impeccably crafted in the world. Unfortunately, Switzerland's thirst for its own wines has made them difficult to find in the U.S. Still, a few internationally minded, generous-hearted vintners are trying to ease America's deprivation. Try them when you can.

grapes & styles

Chasselas, Switzerland's most common grape, can be light and floral, austerely mineral, mouthwateringly citrusy, or succulently pear-filled depending on where it's grown. Valais vintners call it Fendant. Other Swiss whites are made from Müller-Thurgau (known locally as Riesling-Sylvaner), Sylvaner (Johannisberg), Pinot Gris, Marsanne (Ermitage), and Petite Arvine. Pinot Noir and Gamay are the most common red grapes, often combined for a blend called "Dôle." Merlot reigns in the Italian-speaking region of Ticino; Syrah grows in the francophone Valais. Oeil de Perdrix ("partridge eye") is a rosé wine.

on the label

Swiss wines are normally labeled by grape variety and region. Assume whites without a varietal label are made from Chasselas. Unlabeled reds are likely to be blends.

at the table

Different wherever it grows, Chasselas must be paired according to region. Profoundly mineral, Chasselas from Valais (Fendant) is perfect with raw oysters, chalky goat cheese, and fish terrines. Heavier wines from the Vaud (and sometimes Valais) pair well with Vacherin cheese, skate in a beurre blanc, or smoked fish. Vivacious Neuchâtel whites are great with shrimp cocktails. Pinot Gris and Petite Arvine can be enjoyed like heavier Chasselas—fondue is perfect. Drink Ticino Merlot as you would a Pomerol and Pinot Noir as you would a Burgundy. Dôle is a good choice with lamb chops or duck.

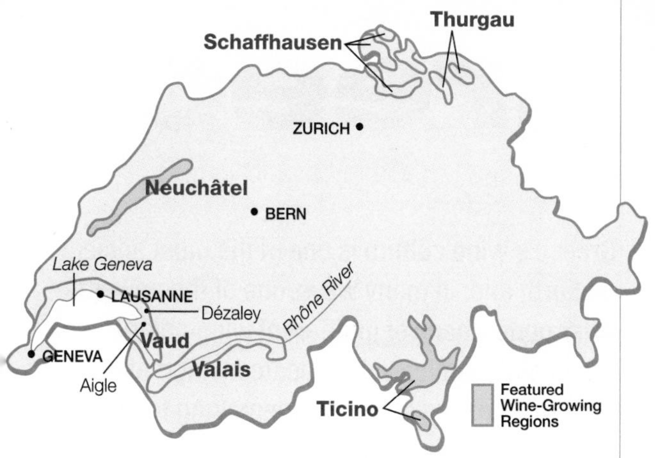

the bottom line Limited availability, high production costs, and high quality make Swiss wines dear, at $15 to $85, with most between $20 and $30.

recommended wines

1999 Tenimento dell'Ör Sottobosco Rosso del Ticino ★★★★ $$$
dry, medium-bodied, medium tannin, high acidity **drink now–12 years**
This Merlot-based blend is an elegant treasure of smoky, restrained red fruit

1999 Castello di Morcote Merlot, Ticino ★★★ $$$
dry, medium-bodied, medium tannin, high acidity **drink now–10 years**
More northern Rhône in profile than Bordeaux-like, this Merlot is laden with minerals, tobacco, and smoke.

2001 Bianco Rovere Bianco di Uve Merlot, Ticino ★★★ $$
dry, medium-bodied, medium oak, high acidity **drink now–6 years**
A very unusual white wine made from Merlot grapes, this shows incredible finesse, with fine minerals and diaphanous-textured fruit.

2002 Château d'Auvernier, Neuchâtel ★★★ $$
dry, medium-bodied, no oak, high acidity **drink now–6 years**
A tight balance of crisp green apple and mineral notes, perfectly in tune.

2002 Robert Gilliard Fendant Les Murettes Pétillant ★★★ $$
dry, light-bodied, no oak, high acidity **drink now–2 years**
Light on the tongue, this lemony Fendant would make a great oyster wine.

greece

Greece's wine culture is one of the most ancient on Earth and, in many ways, one of the newest. After generations of indifferent winemaking, a new breed of dynamic, well-educated winemakers has arrived, applying modern winemaking techniques to grape varieties that would have been recognized by the ancients. The result: past, present, and future, all in one bottle.

grapes & syles

As one noted Greek winemaker said, "If it finds its way into the ground in Greece, it will grow." Greece claims thousands of indigenous grape varieties. Savatiano is the most common white grape. It often provides the basis for Greece's distinctive Retsina, a pine-flavored white wine, and can also make fruity, unresinated wines. Assyrtiko makes powerful, mineral-laden, bone-dry whites on the island of Santorini. Pink-skinned grape Moscofilero makes for wonderfully floral whites and exotically spiced rosés. Roditis wines play sun off earth with charmingly floral yet deeply mineral flavors.

Xinomavro provides the basis for a large number of Macedonian reds. It does exceptionally well in the cool-climate region of Náoussa. In its youth the grape lives up to its name—"acid black." With age it takes on the dark berry, leather, truffle, and smoke qualities of fine Barolo. In the Peloponnese heartland, Agiorgitiko is the alpha-to-omega red grape. In the flatlands it makes copious quantities of cheap, plummy, easy-to-drink wines; from the hillsides of Neméa, it offers plenty of fruit, but more structure. International varieties Merlot, Cabernet Sauvignon, and Chardonnay have established presences in Greece, too, and can be especially good when blended with indigenous grapes.

white wines

at the table

Fresh, simple Greek whites are terrific with mezes such as stuffed grape leaves and salads. Drink Retsina (yes, Retsina) with strongly-flavored dishes like smoky eggplant salad or salty taramasalata. Assyrtiko was made for grilled red mullet or *spanakopita*. Spicy, floral Moscofilero is delightful with Moroccan *bisteeya* or a saffron-and-chile-laced seafood stew.

the bottom line
Greek white wines are bargains at less than $10. A few scratch $15, and even fewer catch sight of the $20 mark.

recommended wines

2003 Domaine Gerovassiliou Malagousia, Epanomi ★★★ $$
dry, medium-bodied, no oak, high acidity drink now–2 years
One sip packs an amazing array of hypnotic flavors, from lime to peach, pineapple, jasmine, and thyme.

2003 Domaine Spiropoulos, Mantinia ★★★ $
dry, medium-bodied, no oak, high acidity drink now–4 years
Moscofilero can be a little slip of a wine, but this example adds citrus and pear oomph to its light floral side.

2003 Gentilini Robola, Cephalonia ★★★ $
dry, light-bodied, no oak, high acidity drink now–2 years
Mineral notes evoke the chalk quarry that sits across the road from this winery; pear and tangerine flavors sweeten them nicely.

2001 Pape Johannou Vineyards Ai Lia Vineyard Assyrtiko, Corinth ★★★ $
dry, medium-bodied, no oak, high acidity drink now–3 years
Vibrant lime, herb, and mineral notes are carried on a luscious, creamy texture in this mainland Assyrtiko.

2003 Sigalas, Santorini ★★★ $
dry, medium-bodied, no oak, high acidity drink now–4 years
If not for the layers of smoky minerals from volcanic soils, one might swear this very good Assyrtiko was actually Riesling. (It isn't.)

2003 Domaine Tselepos Moscofilero, Mantinia ★★ $
dry, medium-bodied, no oak, high acidity drink now–3 years
Light floral flavors deepened by sweet lime and green apple flavors recall early spring—a great sip in the dog days of summer.

2003 Gai'a Nótios, Peloponnese ★★ $
dry, medium-bodied, no oak, high acidity drink now–3 years
Roditis' peach and lemon notes share the limelight with Moscofilero's flowers.

2003 Mercouri Foloï, Pisatis ★★ $
dry, light-bodied, no oak, high acidity drink now–2 years
Among Mercouri's treasures are its summer estate concerts; this light white with its pear and honey-lemon flavors makes a great accompaniment.

2003 Oenoforos Asprolithi, Patras ★★ $
dry, light-bodied, no oak, high acidity drink now–2 years
Chalky soils strut their stuff through flavors of pear, lime, and light honey.

red wines

at the table

Throw some lamb sausages or herbed chicken on the grill, open a bottle of juicy, fruity Neméa or Cretan red and you're as good as lounging in the Greek isles. Pair reserve-level reds with leg of lamb, stuffed tomatoes, or pork chops. Náoussa reds bear impressive resemblance to Nebbiolo from northern Italy. Roast venison, wild mushroom risotto, or aged cheeses are ideal.

the bottom line Lots of Greece's reds are bargains at less than $9. Add a few dollars and the wines become significantly more complex. A few exceptional wines cost $20 or so.

recommended wines

1999 Kir-Yianni Ramnista, Náoussa   ★ ★ ★ ★ $$
dry, full-bodied, medium tannin, high acidity   drink now–8 years
Think of this single-vineyard Xinomavro as very good, modern Barolo—*à la grecque* of course.

2001 Domaine Mercouri, Vin de Pays des Letrinon   ★ ★ ★ $$
dry, full-bodied, heavy tannin, high acidity   drink now–8 years
A real tongue twister, this fascinating, delicious wine combines sweet cherry, sour sumac, salty mineral, and bitter charred meat flavors.

2000 Papantonis Meden Agan, Neméa   ★ ★ ★ $$
dry, full-bodied, heavy tannin, high acidity   drink now–12 years
Suave cherry and spice share space with herb and animal notes. Excellent.

2000 Pape Johannou Vineyards, Neméa   ★ ★ ★ $$
dry, medium-bodied, heavy tannin, high acidity   drink now–8 years
Dry berry flavors are held together by herbaceous notes and earthy spice.

1998 Tsantalis Metoxi Agioritikos, Mount Athos   ★ ★ ★ $$
dry, full-bodied, medium tannin, high acidity   drink now–8 years
Limnio and Cabernet form a mosaic of red berry, mineral, and spice.

2002 Ioannis Hatzis Xynomavro, Amyntaion   ★ ★ $$
dry, medium-bodied, medium tannin, high acidity   drink now
This has old-fashioned, sophisticated, smoky red berry charm.

eastern europe

Viticulture has figured prominently in several East European countries for centuries. Economic liberalization has brought investors and a revival of family wineries eager to raise the profile of the region's wines. Thus far the results range from hopeful to impressive, always with good value.

grapes & styles

Slovakia Fame has yet to come, but Slovakia deserves notice for superbly crafted Rieslings, reminiscent of those of Austria.

Hungary No other Hungarian wine eclipses the superb nectars from illustrious Tokaj, but others are trying. For the moment there is a tug of war between local and international varieties. Hungary's famously powerful red Egri Bikavér ("Bull's Blood") is now apt to be a blend of indigenous grapes and Cabernet Sauvignon and/or Merlot, and no worse for it.

Romania Some legends have it that Dionysius was born in Romania. True or not, Romania has a vibrant wine culture. Most wines, white and red, are slightly sweet.

Moldova Moldova's modern wine industry dates to the early 19th century, when French settlers planted Cabernet and Merlot. Riesling does well here, too.

Bulgaria Bulgaria's export-oriented wine industry relies on good-quality international varietals to push its good name.

Slovenia Contiguous to Italy's Friuli and Veneto and Austria's Styria wine regions, Slovenia's vinous credentials have long been in relatively good order. Look for fine wines resembling those of her neighbors but at lower prices.

Croatia Wine is grown in several parts of Croatia, but the country's Dalmatian coast, with its Adriatic influences, shows the most promise. Indigenous grapes, both white and red, are still the rule here. Red grape Plavac Mali, a relative of California's Zinfandel (genetically identical to Croatian Crljenak) is the most well known.

white wines

at the table

Pair wines made from international grape varieties such as Pinot Grigio, Chardonnay, or Riesling as you would their equivalents from other countries. Hungary's Furmint and Croatia's Posip (possibly the same grape) have intriguing nut and herb flavors that make them an attractive choice for chicken stews like gumbo (not too many chiles) or chicken paprikash. Try them, too, with a wedge of kasseri or kashkaval cheese.

the bottom line You can find decent white wines for under $5. Some Rieslings and Furmints cost $12 to $18. A few excellent Slovenians hit $30.

recommended wines

2002 Château Belá Riesling, Sturovo Region, Slovakia ★ ★ ★ ★ $$
dry, medium-bodied, no oak, high acidity   drink now–12 years
Egon Müller is a Riesling magician in Germany; in Slovakia, he conjures up the vibrant flavors of classic Riesling of the highest level.

2002 Batic Sivi Pinot, Vipavska Dolina, Slovenia   ★ ★ ★ $$
dry, medium-bodied, light oak, high acidity   drink now–8 years
An elegant Pinot Grigio, full of minerals and captivating fruit.

2001 Movia Ribolla, Brda, Slovenia   ★ ★ ★ $$
dry, full-bodied, no oak, high acidity   drink now–8 years
Summer fruit, honeycomb, and abundant minerals make a Ribolla that trumps nearly every example made across the Italian border.

2001 Monarchia Nyakas Pince Budai Pinot Gris, Buda, Hungary   ★ ★ ★ $
dry, medium-bodied, no oak, high acidity   drink now–6 years
Multilayered as strudel, this has the richness of Hungarian pastry, from baked apples to butter and nuts.

1998 Vinakoper Malvazija, Capo d'Istria, Slovenia   ★ ★ $$
dry, medium-bodied, no oak, high acidity   drink now–5 years
Here's a Malvasia with the nutty richness of a sweet wine, done dry.

2002 Katunar Zlahtina, Island of Krk, Croatia   ★ ★ $
dry, medium-bodied, no oak, high acidity   drink now–3 years
Get a taste of the Adriatic in this mineral-laden white, rich in dry, herbal fruit.

2001 Marko Polo Posip Cara, Korcula, Croatia   ★ ★ $
dry, full-bodied, no oak, high acidity   drink now–6 years
If Marco Polo had tasted this treasure chest of exotic fruit, spice, and minerals, he may never have left home.

red wines

at the table

Enjoy Merlot and Cabernet as you would their versions from other countries. Think roast beef, stews, or steak. Plavac Mali can be enjoyed like Zinfandel; it's particularly good with barbecued meats, ribs, pork shoulder, or lamb. Perhaps inevitably, hearty Egri Bikavér ("Bull's Blood") is good with braised oxtails.

the bottom line When you can find Eastern European reds, they'll likely cost between $6 and $10. Buy two, since off bottles are common. Plavac Mali costs $12 to $25; some ambitious Hungarian and Slovenian reds scratch $30.

recommended wines

2000 Takler Regnum Szekszárdi Cuvée, Szekszard, Hungary ★★★ $$$$
dry, full-bodied, heavy tannin, high acidity   drink in 2–12 years
This Cabernet-Merlot blend aims high, with berry, mineral, and tobacco flavors that mingle deliciously.

1999 Santomas Big Red Reserve, Koper, Slovenia ★★★ $$
dry, full-bodied, medium tannin, high acidity   drink now–8 years
This red gets its size from layer upon layer of smoke, herb, and mineral notes bound together by wild berry flavors.

2000 Monarchia Borászat Egri Cuvée, Egri, Hungary ★★★ $
dry, full-bodied, medium tannin, high acidity   drink now–8 years
This keeps the weight and the wild herb flavors of Egri's famous Bull's Blood wines, yet replaces some of the typical roughness with elegance.

1998 Movia Pinot Nero, Brda, Slovenia ★★ $$$
dry, medium-bodied, medium tannin, high acidity   drink now–8 years
Does Brda have a spiritual connection with Burgundy? The finesse of this Pinot Noir says possibly.

2000 Dingac Ivo Skaramuca Vineyard, Peljesac Peninsula, Croatia ★★ $$
dry, full-bodied, medium tannin, high acidity   drink now–5 years
Big berry flavors get a unique twist with earthy spice and lamb notes.

2002 Tilia Cabernet Sauvignon, Vipavska Dolina, Slovenia ★★ $
dry, full-bodied, medium tannin, high acidity   drink now–6 years
More Loire Valley Cabernet Franc than Cabernet Sauvignon, this has delicious, peppery red fruit flavors.

2001 Vetus Mons Reserve Cabernet Sauvignon, Rose Valley, Bulgaria ★★ $
dry, medium-bodied, medium tannin, high acidity   drink now–4 years
Much like a good, modest Bordeaux, this has straightforward red currant and black peppercorn flavors.

middle east & north africa

Wine had its beginnings in the diverse lands of the Caucasus and Fertile Crescent. Used for sacred and profane purposes, praised by poets and condemned by moralists, wine enjoys a unique place in the region's lore and culture. In North Africa, the wine industry took off during the French colonial period. In the 1950s and early 1960s, Tunisia, Morocco, and Algeria accounted for two-thirds of the international wine trade. After periods of decline, wine industries throughout these lands are improving, and many bargains can be found.

grapes & styles

Algeria, Morocco, Tunisia This trio of North African nations traces its wine industry to the French, who ruled them from 1830 to the early 1960s. A sharp decline in winemaking after independence has been reversed and the mostly Rhône varieties now yield some good wines.

Lebanon Lebanese wines have been appreciated since the days of the Phoenicians. The civil war of the 1970s to 1990s ravaged the vineyards, but they are now restored and expanded, and the wines from local and international grape varieties are once again worthy of the world's attention.

Israel/Palestine Winemaking has continued nearly uninterrupted in this part of the world from its ancient beginnings to the turbulent present. For decades, most Israeli wine was thick and

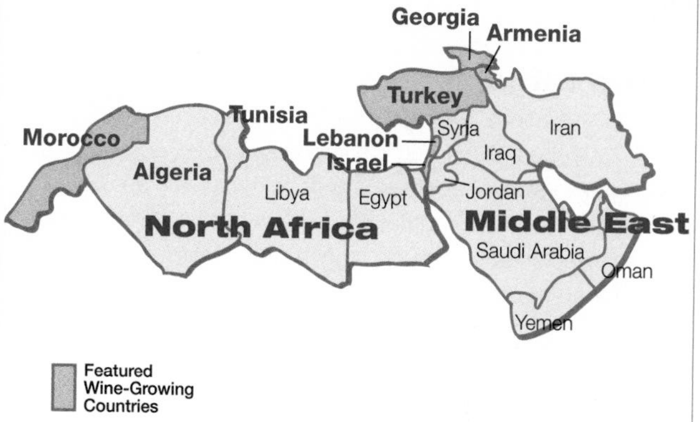
Georgia
Armenia
Turkey
Tunisia
Morocco
Lebanon
Syria
Iran
Iraq
Israel
Algeria
Libya
Egypt
Jordan
North Africa
Middle East
Saudi Arabia
Oman
Yemen
Featured
Wine-Growing
Countries

simple, coming from the humid coastal plain. Better wines are now produced in cooler Galilee, the Syrian Golan Heights, and the Judean hills west of Jerusalem, many made from international varieties such as Chardonnay, Sauvignon Blanc, and Merlot. Most Palestinian wine is made by monastic communities on the West Bank.

Turkey Turkey's secular government has encouraged winemaking in this overwhelmingly Muslim country since the foundations of the republic in the 1920s. But despite vast vineyards, relatively little wine is made—Turks prefer the fiery anise spirit *raki*. The wines that are exported can be quite good. Look especially for wines made from indigenous varieties, like Narince for white wines and reds from Okuzgozu.

Georgia Possibly the most verdant country of the former Soviet Union, the record of Georgian viticulture is longer than that of any nation on earth. Of the hundreds of indigenous varieties, spicy Saperavi dominates the reds; nutty, mineral-laden Rkatsiteli is the most common white. Semi-sweet red and white wines are the norm—and they can be delicious, especially with smoked or spicy meats—but export-minded vintners are making more dry wines, too.

Armenia Armenians have grown grapes since Noah beached his ark on their Mt. Ararat millennia ago. Most wine is poor in quality and distilled into their famed brandy, but some of their semi-sweet and dry wines are worth picking up the next time you find yourself in an Armenian grocery.

white wines

at the table

Made in conditions reminiscent of California, Lebanese and Israeli Sauvignon Blanc and Chardonnay can be enjoyed like Californian versions. Lebanese blends from native grapes have the complexity and power that can hold up to a variety of meats such as sweetbreads or lamb's tongue salad. Try them also with Lebanese specialties like fish in *tarator* (a sauce of tahini, lemon juice, garlic, and parsley), or spice-rubbed roast chicken stuffed with almond-and-raisin-studded rice. These wines can age beautifully, too, taking on richer, nuttier flavors over time. Turkish whites are tasty with fish kebabs. Georgian Rkatsiteli is delicious with roast pork or chicken tabak.

the bottom line Reliable Lebanese and Israeli whites cost between $10 and $18; the best reach $50. The few North African whites worth drinking cost about $8. For about the same price Georgian and Turkish whites are a good deal.

recommended wines

1998 Château Musar, Bekaa Valley, Lebanon ★★★★ $$$
dry, full-bodied, medium oak, high acidity drink now–12 years
Looking for a glorious wine adventure? This will take you on a journey through flavors of exotic spice, honeycomb, glistening minerals, toasted almonds, and baked quince.

2001 Tbilvino Tsinandali, Kakheti, Georgia ★★★ $
dry, medium-bodied, no oak, high acidity drink now–3 years
If one wine best shows Georgia's potential as a great wine country, this is it, laden with minerals and citrus confit flavors.

2003 Château Kefraya La Dame Blanche, Bekaa Valley, Lebanon ★★ $
dry, light-bodied, no oak, high acidity drink now–2 years
Light and limey, this is as refreshing as a Mediterranean breeze.

2003 Château Ksara Blanc de Blancs, Bekaa Valley, Lebanon ★★ $
dry, light-bodied, light oak, high acidity drink now–2 years
Like biting into a peach while lazing by the cedars of Lebanon.

NV Cremisan Blanc de Blancs, Bethlehem, Palestine ★★ $
dry, light-bodied, no oak, high acidity drink now–2 years
No room at the inn? These light lemon-almond flavors might provide comfort.

2002 Golan Heights Winery Chardonnay, Galilee, Israel ★ $
dry, medium-bodied, no oak, high acidity drink now–3 years
These simple lemon and pear flavors go nicely with baked snapper.

2003 Kavaklidere Emir de Nevsehir, Çankaya, Turkey ★ $
dry, light-bodied, no oak, high acidity drink now
Charming wine, this apple- and lime-flavored white will be perfect with fish kebabs or chilled shrimp.

2002 Les Trois Domaines Blanc, Guerrouane, Morocco ★ $
dry, medium-bodied, no oak, high acidity drink now–2 years
These lemon and salted almond flavors seem designed for Moroccan cuisine—though they'll be just as refreshing with lemon-stuffed roast chicken.

2003 Recanati Sauvignon Blanc, Shomron, Israel ★ $
dry, medium-bodied, no oak, high acidity drink now–2 years
Shomron morphs into shamrock in this Sauvignon Blanc, green with flavors of clover, green pepper, and lemon.

red wines

at the table

Enjoy Lebanon's Cabernet or Merlot wines as you would simple Bordeaux reds; lamb chops are ideal. Israeli reds are modeled on those of California. Pair them similarly—steaks or roast prime rib. Indigenous Lebanese blends need something more substantial like braised lamb shanks. North African reds are good with simple bistro foods: grilled sausages, *steak frites,* or couscous royale. Kebabs, especially those made with ground lamb and chile, are delicious with Turkish reds. The roast-eggplant-based *imam bayildi* is also ideal.

the bottom line
Lebanese reds start at $12 and reach $50; Israeli reds are priced similarly, but top out at $40. For between $7 and $10, North African reds are worth trying in place of a simple French or Italian red. Good Turkish reds can be had for $10 to $15; most in the mid-$20s are not worth it. Georgian reds cost $10 to $25.

recommended wines

1997 Château Musar, Bekaa Valley, Lebanon ★★★★ $$$
dry, full-bodied, medium tannin, high acidity **drink now–15 years**
One of the world's most unique, iconic wines shows a range of flavors as intricate as any oriental carpet.

2000 Château Kefraya, Bekaa Valley, Lebanon ★★★ $$
dry, full-bodied, heavy tannin, high acidity **drink now–10 years**
This captures the essence of the Levant in a bottle, as it exudes scents and flavors of mountain herbs, mulberry, lamb, cedar, and mastic.

2000 Château Ksara, Bekaa Valley, Lebanon ★★★ $$
dry, full-bodied, heavy tannin, high acidity **drink now–8 years**
A mesmerizing combination of mulberry and myrrh, infused with notes of pine and frankincense.

2000 Château Ksara Cuvée Spéciale Cabernet Sauvignon,
Bekaa Valley, Lebanon ★★ $$
dry, full-bodied, medium tannin, high acidity **drink now–6 years**
Cabernet, scented by wild herbs, makes one terrific wine for rosemary-laced lamb roasts.

1999 Château Musar Hochar Père et Fils, Bekaa Valley,
Lebanon ★★ $$
dry, medium-bodied, medium tannin, high acidity **drink now–3 years**
Musar's second-tier wine may not offer the sublime depth of its flagship wine, but these layers of mulberry, animal, and spice flavors sure make fascinating drinking at a fraction of the price.

2002 Tbilvino Odjaleshi, Lechkhumi, Georgia ★★ $$
off-dry, medium-bodied, medium tannin, high acidity **drink now–5 years**
Adjust your palate before tasting this. It's moderately sweet, but not cloying. With ripe pomegranate, berry, and spice flavors and plenty of acidity, it would find a great mate with Chinese barbecue.

2002 Château Kefraya Les Bretèches, Bekaa Valley, Lebanon ★★ $
dry, medium-bodied, medium tannin, high acidity **drink now–4 years**
Here's the perfect wine for ground lamb kebabs—smoky, lightly spiced, and perfumed by wild herbs.

2003 Golan Heights Winery Sion Creek Red, Galilee, Israel ★★ $
dry, medium-bodied, medium tannin, high acidity **drink now–3 years**
A blend of Sangiovese, Syrah, Gamay Noir, Pinot Noir, and Napa Gamay, it's no surprise this simple pleasure has international flair.

WINE FOR THE AFTERLIFE

All the talk about red wine's possible healthful benefits has taken an ancient twist: it seems that ancient Egyptian pharaohs thought it was good for the afterlife, too. It's long been known that ancient Egyptians made grape wine and enjoyed drinking it: a wine jar inscribed with vintage and vintner information was found in King Tutankhamun's tomb when it was unearthed in 1922. What wasn't known was whether the good king was tippling white or red wine as he made his way through the stages of the afterlife. Though grape variety remains unknown, in winter 2004, a team of Spanish researchers chemically analyzed the residue on the inside of the jars and concluded that the wine was red. Perhaps the boy-king wanted to take advantage of red wine's heart-healthy properties to make sure that his heart was in good shape as it was weighed by the jackal-headed god Anubis before final acceptance into the realm of immortality.

2000 Kavaklidere Okuzgozu-Bogazkere Selection Kirmizi, Turkey ★★ $
dry, medium-bodied, medium tannin, high acidity   **drink now–4 years**
Dry rose petal, cherry, and spice scents and flavors make for savory Turkish delight in a bottle.

2001 Recanati Reserve Merlot, Galilee, Israel ★★ $
dry, full-bodied, medium tannin, high acidity   **drink now–6 years**
Red berry flavors entwined with smoky oak and brightened with jazzy acidity show Merlot's wild side.

2000 Getup Vineyards Areni, Vayots Dzor, Armenia ★ $
dry, light-bodied, medium tannin, high acidity   **drink now–3 years**
For a country known more for sweet reds, this is Sahara dry, with tart berry and spice.

2000 Les Trois Domaines Rouge, Guerrouane, Morocco ★ $
dry, full-bodied, medium tannin, high acidity   **drink now–3 years**
With juicy red berry and mixed spice flavors, this would be terrific with *merguez* couscous.

australia

Over the next couple of decades, Australia may become the world's greatest wine-producing country. From $7 Chardonnay to its exalted, triple-digit Shiraz blends and luscious, sweet stickies, Australia has it all, at consistently higher quality than anywhere else.

on the label

Australian wines are typically labeled by grape variety even when they are blends. Most also list a "geographical indication" (GI) if 85 percent of the wine was grown in the named region.

white wines

CHARDONNAY

Many Australian Chardonnays are loaded with sun-rich, tropical fruit flavors and oak, but there's a trend toward more restraint, with leaner, more balanced wines helped along by plantings in cooler regions like the Clare Valley or Western Australia.

at the table

Lean, citrusy Chardonnay can be enjoyed with leaner fish such as grouper or red snapper, grilled, baked, or in ceviche. Heavier, oaky wines need richer food, like battered soft-shell crabs, Thai fried pompano, or holiday birds.

the bottom line Australian Chardonnay starts around $7 for reasonable quality but spending more will make a difference. Between $20 and $30, quality is typically excellent; world-class examples might hit $70 or more.

Featured Wine-Growing Regions

NORTHERN TERRITORY

Coral Sea

WESTERN AUSTRALIA

QUEENSLAND

SOUTH AUSTRALIA Riverland

BRISBANE

Barossa and Eden Valleys

Mudgee

Hunter Valley

Clare Valley

NEW SOUTH WALES

PERTH

SYDNEY

ADELAIDE

CANBERRA

Frankland

McLaren Vale

VICTORIA

Margaret River

Indian Ocean

Padthaway Coonawarra

Yarra Valley

MELBOURNE

Tasman Sea

Mornington Peninsula

Tasmania

recommended wines

2001 Yering Station Reserve, Yarra Valley ★ ★ ★ ★ $$$
dry, full-bodied, medium oak, high acidity drink now–12 years
With sumptuous flavors of brioche, lemon curd, and salted butter, this Australian Chardonnay could stand in for top-flight Meursault.

2002 Giant Steps, Yarra Valley ★ ★ ★ $$$
dry, full-bodied, medium oak, high acidity drink now–8 years
Giant, indeed, this walks with a gargantuan stride of ripe fruit, caramel, smoke, and stone.

2002 Cape Mentelle, Margaret River ★ ★ ★ $$
dry, medium-bodied, light oak, high acidity drink now–6 years
Margaret River's cool climate shows here in crisp apple and mineral flavors. Very good Chardonnay.

2001 Frankland Estate Isolation Ridge Vineyard, Frankland River ★ ★ ★ $$
dry, medium-bodied, light oak, high acidity drink now–8 years
For those weary of flabby Aussie Chard, have a sip of this stony zinger—ripe, restrained, and beautiful.

2003 Tyrrell's Wines Reserve, Hunter Valley ★★★ $$
dry, medium-bodied, medium oak, high acidity   **drink in 1–8 years**

Still a baby, this wine shows only hints of what's to come with its light pineapple, mango, and mineral flavors.

2003 Wolf Blass Gold Label, Adelaide Hills ★★ $$
dry, medium-bodied, medium oak, high acidity   **drink now–6 years**

A toasty, creamy Chardonnay, this has rich, yeasty, leesy flavors to add depth to its subtle, restrained fruit.

2001 Bimbadgen Grand Ridge, Hunter Valley ★★ $
dry, medium-bodied, light oak, high acidity   **drink now–3 years**

Zingy citrus flavors energize this buttery, rich Chardonnay. It's a definite crowd pleaser, able to swing from drinks before dinner right into a barbecue.

2002 Callanans Road, Mornington Peninsula ★★ $
dry, medium-bodied, medium oak, medium acidity   **drink now–3 years**

A panoply of fruit in a box of oak, studded with stones. Tasty.

2002 Greg Norman Estates, Victoria ★★ $
dry, medium-bodied, medium oak, medium acidity   **drink now–2 years**

Good-value Chardonnay from a professional golfer, perfect for lunch at the clubhouse after nine holes.

2003 De Bortoli Willowglen, South Eastern Australia ★ $
dry, medium-bodied, light oak, high acidity   **drink now–2 years**

A fair deal for eight bucks, with juicy pineapple and citrus flavors.

2003 Kirralaa, South Eastern Australia ★ $
dry, medium-bodied, light oak, medium acidity   **drink now–2 years**

From Mondavi's Australian project with Rosemount Estates, Kirralaa offers a nice, affordable Chardonnay with sunny fruit and stone flavors.

WINES WE WISH WE HAD MORE ROOM FOR

2001 Grosset Piccadilly, Adelaide Hills ★★★ $$$ dry, medium-bodied, medium oak, high acidity, drink now–10 years; **2001 Leeuwin Estate Prelude Vineyards, Margaret River** ★★★ $$$ dry, full-bodied, medium oak, high acidity, drink now–8 years; **2002 Chateau Reynella, McLaren Vale** ★★★ $ dry, full-bodied, light oak, high acidity, drink now–8 years; **2002 Rosemount Estate Show Reserve, Hunter Valley** ★★★ $ dry, medium-bodied, medium oak, high acidity, drink now–8 years; **2002 Tuck's Ridge, Mornington Peninsula** ★★ $$ dry, medium-bodied, light oak, high acidity, drink now–3 years; **2003 Blackwing, South Australia** ★★ $ dry, medium-bodied, no oak, medium acidity, drink now–2 years; **2003 Banrock Station, South Eastern Australia** ★ $ dry, medium-bodied, light oak, medium acidity, drink now–1 year

OTHER WHITE WINES

Look past Aussie Chardonnay and you're liable to find some of the most interesting white wines on earth. Don't mock screw-capped Australian Riesling, especially from cooler regions like Clare Valley and Frankland: they are excellent, with spicy citrus and tropical flavors. Sauvignon Blanc is full of zingy citrus and herb flavors, tamer than New Zealand's. With pear, orange, and nutty notes, Semillon frequently outshines other country's varietal versions, developing seductive marmalade qualities with age. Some of Oz's best whites are from Rhône varieties, especially the flowery Viognier and the honey-nut goodness of Marsanne, sometimes blended with Roussanne.

at the table

Pair Australian Riesling with bright, vibrantly flavored foods, like Thai seasoned shrimp, or seared tuna with a mango relish. Semillon is at home with richer dishes like grilled lobster. Marsanne can be enjoyed similarly. Pair grassy Sauvignon Blanc with herb-marinated chicken breasts or goat cheese salads. Floral Viognier is delicious with dishes with a lot of fresh herbs or greens, such as a parsley-heavy tabbouleh salad, or chicken breast stuffed with spinach and mozzarella.

the bottom line There are plenty of very good single-variety and blended white wines for $10 to $15. Semillon runs from $10 to $30. Riesling starts around $11, up to $35 for some of the best on the planet. Superb Rhône-style wines fetch a similar price.

recommended wines

2002 Frankland Estate Isolation Ridge Vineyard Riesling, Frankland River ★★★★ $$
dry, medium-bodied, no oak, high acidity   **drink now–20 years**
A study in minerality, lightened by floral and summer fruits. Buy a case to put in the cellar: it will only get better with time.

2002 Leeuwin Estate Art Series Riesling, Margaret River ★★★ $$
dry, medium-bodied, no oak, high acidity   **drink now–8 years**
Profoundly mineral and lemon-limey, this is impressive Riesling.

2002 Wirra Wirra Vineyards Hand Picked Riesling, South Australia ★ ★ ★ $$

dry, medium-bodied, no oak, high acidity   drink now–8 years

This is fuller in body than most Aussie Riesling, as if to make room for all the luscious fruit.

2003 Primo Estate La Biondina, Adelaide ★ ★ ★ $

dry, medium-bodied, no oak, high acidity   drink now–3 years

French Colombard—erstwhile grape of bland bulk wines—never had it so good, with flavors as crisp as celery and refreshing as grapefruit.

2002 Browns of Padthaway Verdelho, Padthaway ★ ★ $$

dry, medium-bodied, no oak, high acidity   drink now–3 years

A terrific choice when you're looking for something different, this Verdelho offers the herbs of Sauvignon and the richness of Chardonnay.

2003 Kirrihill Estates Riesling, Clare Valley ★ ★ $$

dry, medium-bodied, no oak, high acidity   drink now–6 years

Forget frou-frou tropical cocktails when you can have all the pineapple-and-lime goodness of this elegant wine.

2003 Pike & Joyce Sauvignon Blanc, Adelaide Hills ★ ★ $$

dry, light-bodied, no oak, high acidity   drink now–2 years

A palate awakener, with zingy lemon and light herb flavors.

2002 Bimbadgen Grand Ridge Verdelho, Hunter Valley ★ ★ $

dry, medium-bodied, no oak, high acidity   drink now–2 years

Spicy orange and lime flavors and a waxy, aloelike texture make this a great summer sipper.

2002 Fox Creek Semillon-Sauvignon Blanc, South Australia ★ ★ $

dry, medium-bodied, no oak, high acidity   drink now–2 years

This is as citrusy, green, and refreshing as sipping lemonade on a fresh-mown lawn—and more sophisticated.

2002 Penfolds Koonunga Hill Semillon-Chardonnay, South Eastern Australia ★ ★ $

dry, medium-bodied, no oak, high acidity   drink now–6 years

Fresh pear and light lemon flavors make for a nice springtime lunch wine.

2003 Zilzie Viognier, Victoria ★ ★ $

dry, medium-bodied, light oak, high acidity   drink now–3 years

Peach blossoms turn into pineapples in this rich, unctuous Viognier.

WINES WE WISH WE HAD MORE ROOM FOR

2003 Leasingham Bin 7 Riesling, Clare Valley ★ ★ ★ $ dry, medium-bodied, no oak, high acidity, drink now–8 years; **2002 Peter Lehmann Riesling, Eden Valley** ★ ★ $$ dry, light-bodied, no oak, high acidity, drink now–8 years; **2003 Pierro Semillon-Sauvignon Blanc, Margaret River** ★ ★ $$ dry, medium-bodied, no oak, high acidity, drink now–3 years; **2003 Wolf Blass Gold Label Riesling, Eden Valley/Clare Valley** ★ ★ $ dry, medium-bodied, no oak, high acidity, drink now–8 years

red wines

SHIRAZ

No grape says "Australia" like Shiraz. Robust, but exuberant in its freshness; spicy, but loaded with juicy berry flavors; sweet, but also scented with savory eucalyptus, Shiraz can seem entirely different from Syrah, its French equivalent. Some of the differences are due to winemaking practices, others to Australia's sweet sunshine. There is a range of styles from which to choose, from lean, spicy versions aged in French oak to others laden with the coconut-vanilla notes of American oak. Warmer regions like the Barossa Valley and the McLaren Vale yield dark and dense wines, while cooler regions such as the Clare Valley and Margaret River in Western Australia make more restrained Shiraz.

at the table

Inexpensive Shiraz are great for cookouts, especially for meats basted with sweet and spicy barbecue sauce. Heavier, high-quality versions require braised meats, or a nutty, creamy cheese like farmhouse Cheddar. More restrained Shiraz are delicious with rack of lamb or wild mushroom pastas.

the bottom line
You'll find no shortage of simple Shiraz for under $10, but you'll do far better at $15 and above. Prices rise radically from there, all the way up past $200.

what to buy SHIRAZ

1999	2000	2001	2002	2003
★★★	★★	★★★	★★★	★★★

recommended wines

2001 D'Arenberg The Dead Arm, McLaren Vale ★★★★ $$$$
dry, full-bodied, heavy tannin, high acidity drink in 2–20 years
Ominously named, epically flavored, this is as intense as Shiraz can get, yet it's still graceful.

2002 Fox Creek Short Row, McLaren Vale ★★★ $$$
dry, full-bodied, medium tannin, high acidity drink now–10 years
This oozes Australia, with ripe black fruit, wild herbal scrub, eucalyptus, and peppery enthusiasm.

1999 Leasingham Classic Clare, Clare Valley ★★★ $$$
dry, full-bodied, heavy tannin, high acidity drink now–12 years
Classic indeed, this has the lush fruit and spice of Aussie Shiraz, tempered by Clare's cooler climes. Perfect with roast lamb.

1999 Penfolds St. Henri, South Australia ★★★ $$$
dry, full-bodied, heavy tannin, high acidity drink in 3–15 years
If Shiraz needs a patron saint, Henri would qualify, with dense yet elegant fruit, animal, and spice flavors.

2000 Rosemount Estate Balmoral Syrah, McLaren Vale ★★★ $$$
dry, full-bodied, heavy tannin, high acidity drink in 2–12 years
Nearing its fifth year, this Balmoral is still a kid. Maturity will bring its dark fruit, peppery oak, and prickly mineral flavors into harmony.

1999 Turramurra Estate, Mornington Peninsula ★★★ $$$
dry, full-bodied, heavy tannin, high acidity drink now–8 years
More Syrah than Shiraz, this echoes the greats of the northern Rhône, with dark berry, smoke, and black pepper flavors.

2001 Harbord, Barossa Valley ★★★ $$
dry, full-bodied, heavy tannin, high acidity drink now–10 years
Dark cherry fruit, sweet spice, and an appealing earthiness make this Shiraz simply delicious.

2000 Hewitson Barossa, Barossa Valley ★★★ $$
dry, medium-bodied, medium tannin, high acidity drink now–10 years
Finesse goes farther than brawn in this elegant wine, laden with berry, lavender, and mineral flavors.

2001 Peter Lehmann The Barossa, Barossa Valley ★★ $$
dry, full-bodied, heavy tannin, high acidity drink now–6 years
Lip-smackingly thick and juicy; deliciously spicy.

2001 Bimbadgen Grand Ridge, Hunter Valley ★★ $
dry, medium-bodied, medium tannin, high acidity   drink now–3 years
Pomegranate, spice, and gamey fruit are as seductively appealing in flavor as the wine is in price.

2002 Tyrrell's Old Winery, Hunter Valley/McLaren Vale ★ $
dry, medium-bodied, medium tannin, high acidity   drink now–2 years
Flexible Shiraz, simple and affordable enough for a party, but impressive at the dinner table, too.

WINES WE WISH WE HAD MORE ROOM FOR

2001 Frankland Estate Isolation Ridge Vineyard, Frankland River ★★★ $$ dry, full-bodied, heavy tannin, high acidity, drink now–10 years; **2001 Mak, Clare Valley** ★★★ $$ dry, full-bodied, heavy tannin, high acidity, drink now–8 years; **2002 Elderton, Barossa Valley** ★★ $$$ dry, full-bodied, heavy tannin, high acidity, drink in 1–8 years; **2001 Sheep's Back Old Vine, Barossa Valley** ★★ $$ dry, full-bodied, medium tannin, high acidity, drink now–6 years; **2002 Wirra Wirra Vineyards Scrubby Rise, South Australia** ★★ $ dry, medium-bodied, medium tannin, high acidity, drink now–3 years; **2002 Black Swan, South Eastern Australia** ★ $ dry, full-bodied, medium tannin, high acidity, drink now–2 years

---

SCREW IT

You might not want to retire your fancy corkscrew yet, but opportunities to use it are quickly becoming fewer. Tired of rising percentages of "corked" wines—wines infected with TCA (trichloroanisole), which gives them a wet-cardboard scent—vintners are exchanging corks for screw-caps. The majority of these wines are coming from Australia, but vintners from New Zealand, California, and even tradition-bound France are jumping on board. Evidence shows that screw-topped white wines taste fresher than their cork-sealed equals and age beautifully. But the issue of cork taint is still murky, since TCA can sometimes infect the walls of a winery itself, creating the unlikely but real possibility of a cork-tainted, non-cork-sealed wine. While that sort of TCA infection might be improbable, screw-caps still have image problems among a public more used to seeing this type of enclosure on cheap wine. In response, a California company has come up with an image-enhancing hybrid: the screw-cap cork.

CABERNET SAUVIGNON

Though Shiraz is the Australian grape par excellence, Cabernet Sauvignon is by no means an also-ran. Full of ripe cassis, blackberry, chocolate, mint, and eucalyptus, the best can spar with Napa's finest. Versions from cool-climate Western Australia show a Bordeaux-like elegance. Coonawarra examples are earthy and dense, while those from Barossa tend to be minty.

at the table

Simple, inexpensive Cabs can be enjoyed in much the same way as their Shiraz equivalents. For the rest, the choice is simple: steaks, thick, juicy, with lots of char. Have weightier versions with stews or braised short ribs: their tannin will cut right through the fat. More elegant wines are perfect with filet mignon.

the bottom line Simple Cabernet Sauvignon can be

purchased for less than $10. Far better wines sell for $10 to $20; exceptional, world-class wines pass $100.

what to buy CABERNET SAUVIGNON

1999	2000	2001	2002	2003
★★★	★★	★★★	★★★	★★★

recommended wines

2001 D'Arenberg The Coppermine Road,
McLaren Vale   ★★★★ $$$$
dry, full-bodied, heavy tannin, high acidity   **drink in 3–20 years**
Have patience for this one: when the dark berry, cassis, mint, chocolate, and mineral flavors melt together, they'll only be more delicious.

1999 Leasingham Classic Clare, Clare Valley   ★★★★ $$$
dry, full-bodied, heavy tannin, high acidity   **drink now–15 years**
A stunner, this herb-scented, dark-fruited Cabernet Sauvignon has power, wildness, and grace all at once.

2000 Dominique Portet, Yarra Valley   ★★★ $$$
dry, full-bodied, heavy tannin, high acidity   **drink now–12 years**
A smoky, wild blackberry- and bramble-scented Cabernet Sauvignon from a Bordeaux-born winemaker.

2000 Elderton, Barossa Valley ★★★ $$$
dry, full-bodied, heavy tannin, high acidity drink in 1–12 years
Not for the faint of heart: smoky tar and tannin flavors need time to soften, but plenty of berry, nut, and mineral flavors are waiting to take over.

2001 Kirrihill Estates, Clare Valley ★★★ $$
dry, full-bodied, medium tannin, high acidity drink now–10 years
Cassis, cassis, and more cassis. Beautiful.

2001 Penley Estate Phoenix, Coonawarra ★★★ $$
dry, full-bodied, medium tannin, high acidity drink now–10 years
This Phoenix soars with lovely cherry and fine mineral flavors. Penley's Reserve is excellent, too.

2002 Rosemount Estate Hill of Gold, Mudgee ★★★ $$
dry, full-bodied, heavy tannin, high acidity drink now–8 years
A chewy Cabernet Sauvignon, dense with fruit and tobacco flavors.

2002 Kirralaa, South Eastern Australia ★★ $
dry, full-bodied, medium tannin, high acidity drink now–3 years
Peppery, berry goodness from a joint venture between California's Mondavi and Australia's Rosemount wineries.

2002 Lindemans Reserve, South Australia ★★ $
dry, full-bodied, medium tannin, high acidity drink now–3 years
Deliciously juicy, this offers lots of fresh cherry- berry flavors for little money.

2002 McWilliam's Hanwood Estate, South Eastern Australia ★★ $
dry, full-bodied, medium tannin, high acidity drink now–3 years
A surprisingly elegant Aussie Cab at the price.

2002 Wolf Blass Yellow Label, South Australia ★ $
dry, full-bodied, medium tannin, high acidity drink now–2 years
Pull the cork, throw a burger on the barbie, and enjoy the simple berry flavors.

OTHER RED WINES

If the Australian climate has smiled on Shiraz, it has been just as encouraging to other Rhône varieties such as Grenache and Mourvèdre, encouraging rich berry, herb, mineral, and smoke flavors. Merlots are well made. Pinot Noir, difficult to grow in most places, is an increasing presence in the market with some fine, ripe—but not overly ripe—flavors. Blends of Shiraz and other grapes, Cabernet Sauvignon in particular, are responsible for a few exquisite wines.

at the table

A California-like climate brings forth wines that can be paired as you would their California equivalents.

the bottom line Simple Merlot remains under $10, though $10 to $20 buys better. Pinot Noir is expensive in Australia as it is elsewhere: a smattering run under $15, but most run $20 to $35, and past $40 for some excellent wines. Rhône blends can be affordable at under $15. Shiraz-Cabernet blends can be had cheap, at $7 or so, but pay $12 to $40 for some of the best, and over $200 for a few exalted bottles.

recommended wines

2001 By Farr Pinot Noir, Geelong ★★★ $$$
dry, medium-bodied, medium tannin, high acidity drink now–6 years
Gossamer elegance, drawn in light strawberry and fine herb flavors.

2001 Fox Creek Reserve Merlot, McLaren Vale ★★★ $$$
dry, full-bodied, medium tannin, high acidity drink now–8 years
Australia is not known for Merlot, but a few more like this berry-packed mineral treasure could change that.

2000 Grosset Gaia, Clare Valley ★★★ $$$
dry, full-bodied, heavy tannin, high acidity drink in 1–15 years
Grosset is a master of terroir-driven wines, and it shows in this red-fruited Bordeaux blend, heady with the earthy, minty aromas of Australia's countryside.

**2000 Joseph Moda Cabernet Sauvignon-Merlot,
McLaren Vale/Coonawarra** ★★★ $$$
dry, full-bodied, heavy tannin, high acidity drink now–15 years
A unique Aussie red, this gets its wonderful sweet spice and floral notes, as well as its berry-rich base, from a portion of partially dried grapes.

2001 Tim Adams The Fergus Grenache, Clare Valley ★★★ $$
dry, medium-bodied, heavy tannin, high acidity drink now–8 years
The Mediterranean comes to the Clare in this wine, rich in wild herb, lavender honey, and tart red berry flavors.

2002 Wirra Wirra Vineyards Church Block, McLaren Vale ★★★ $$
dry, full-bodied, medium tannin, high acidity drink now–3 years
Church is rarely so hedonistic, with lush dark berry and wild herb flavors.

BOTTLE HUNTING

It's frustrating: you read about a wine, call around town to find it, and come up empty-handed. Though I try to write about wines that will be available around the country, I'm not always successful. Sometimes it's a matter of production; if only a small amount of a wine is made, then it can't be everywhere. Often, however, small-production wines would be more widely available if some state laws didn't make it so difficult or expensive to bring them to market. Connecticut, for instance, requires a winery or importer to pay $100 to register each vintage of each wine it wants to sell in the state—and it can only sell one vintage at a time. Unless the registree expects to sell large quantities of a wine, it may make little economic sense to pay that fee. Many states also operate under franchise laws, in which distributors are given extensive rights to their supplier's wines. Designed to avoid corruption by powerful liquor companies, these laws pose their own problems in that a supplier can be required to remain with its wholesaler for years, even if the wholesaler isn't marketing or selling its wine. Texas law requires suppliers to register their label (and pay) before they can even send samples to wholesalers in the state who may or may not agree to sell the wine. So the next time you are frustrated by finding only big national brands in your wine shop, take some of the blame off the shopkeeper or the wine writer and call your state representatives.

2002 D'Arenberg The Stump Jump Grenache-Shiraz, McLaren Vale ★★★ $
dry, full-bodied, heavy tannin, high acidity   drink now–3 years
Like a Châteauneuf-du-Pape—but only around $11.

2001 Mad Fish Cabernet Sauvignon-Merlot-Cabernet Franc, Western Australia ★★ $
dry, medium-bodied, medium tannin, high acidity   drink now–3 years
A fun, affordable red with earthy, lip-smacking berry flavors.

2001 Callanans Road Pinot Noir, Mornington Peninsula ★ $
dry, medium-bodied, medium tannin, high acidity   drink now–2 years
Simple Pinot with light berry and smoke flavors.

new
zealand

A generation ago, New Zealand had only its excellent lamb to impress gastronomes. Today, pioneering Kiwi winemakers seduce with thrilling Sauvignon Blanc and sophisticated Pinot Noir. As vineyards replace sheep pastures, New Zealand's eager vintners are gaining some attention for other wines, too. And the lamb's still great.

on the label

No difficulty here: by custom, New Zealand wines are labeled by grape variety, vintage, and place of origin.

white wines

SAUVIGNON BLANC

Today, New Zealand Sauvignon Blanc is often the model against which all others are judged. New Zealand vintners tend to eschew oak, allowing the fruit's distinctively pungent herb, grapefruit, and gooseberry flavors to sing *a cappella*. The most-lauded examples come from Marlborough and Wairarapa.

at the table

Pungent New Zealand Sauvignon Blanc can match asparagus, artichokes, and vinaigrette-dressed salads, all notorious adversaries of wines, not to mention any manner of fish or chicken

the bottom line Most New Zealand Sauvignon Blancs run $10 to $20; a few rise higher.

KUMEU •
AUCKLAND • **Waiheke Island**

Gisborne

Hawkes Bay

Tasman Sea

Nelson WELLINGTON **Wairarapa**
Marlborough • BLENHEIM **Martinborough**

Canterbury • WAIPARA
• CHRISTCHURCH

Pacific Ocean

Central Otago
QUEENSTOWN

Featured
Wine-Growing
Regions

recommended wines

2003 Cloudy Bay, Marlborough ★★★ $$$
dry, medium-bodied, no oak, high acidity **drink now–3 years**
The wine that put New Zealand on the map still charts a firm course.

2003 Villa Maria Reserve, Clifford Bay ★★★ $$$
dry, medium-bodied, no oak, high acidity **drink now–6 years**
Villa Maria can't be beat for consistency and value. Their top Sauvignon
seduces with guava and grapefruit flavors.

2003 Craggy Range Winery Te Muna Road Vineyard,
Martinborough ★★★ $$
dry, medium-bodied, no oak, high acidity **drink now–3 years**
Classic New Zealand Sauvignon flavors in beautiful measure.

new zealand **sauvignon blanc**

2003 Mills Reef Reserve, Hawkes Bay ★★★ $
dry, medium-bodied, no oak, high acidity drink now–5 years
Pink and green usually clash, but here guava, light berry, and lime flavors make an excellent combination.

2003 Goldwater New Dog, Marlborough ★★ $$
dry, medium-bodied, no oak, high acidity drink now–2 years
Goldwater's Sauvignon Blanc offers a rush of lime and fennel-like flavors.

2003 Matariki, Hawkes Bay ★★ $$
dry, medium-bodied, no oak, high acidity drink now–2 years
Matariki sings a gentle tune of grapefruit and spice flavors with a floral edge.

2002 Fern, Marlborough ★★ $
dry, medium-bodied, no oak, high acidity drink now–2 years
Exuberant Sauvignon Blanc, with tropical and grass flavors.

OTHER WHITE WINES

Though New Zealand Sauvignon gets all the buzz, the country actually grows more Chardonnay. Most of it isn't as distinctive, but there are some excellent versions. New Zealand examples have a leaner, more citrus- and mineral-directed profile than those from California or Australia. More noteworthy are such Alsatian varieties as Riesling, Pinot Gris, and Gewürztraminer, which thrive in the country's sunny but cool climes. These wines are always on the dry side.

at the table

Light, unoaked Chardonnay (often identified on the label as such) makes a fine complement to light but flavorful fish like red snapper or brook trout. Oaked versions have the weight for richer fish like grilled salmon. Riesling and Gewürztraminer are great with moderately spiced Asian dishes or roast chicken rubbed with Indian spices. The heavier texture of Pinot Gris weighs in well with pan-roasted duck breast; its rich citrus flavors will perk up with a side of kumquat confit.

the bottom line The lure of New Zealand Sauvignon Blanc pulls Chardonnay prices up with it, to $10 to $40. However, it also keeps prices low on the country's excellent Riesling, Gewürztraminer, and Pinot Gris: snap them up at $10 to $20 before word gets out.

recommended wines

2002 Escarpment Station Bush Vineyard Pinot Gris, Martinborough ★ ★ ★ $$$
dry, full-bodied, light oak, high acidity drink now–8 years
Like violets growing through a bed of rocks, floral scents seep through stony flavors, softened by pear fruit.

2002 Kumeu River Maté's Vineyard Chardonnay, Kumeu ★ ★ ★ $$$
dry, medium-bodied, light oak, high acidity drink now–6 years
From the northern part of New Zealand comes a Chardonnay as close to Chablis as one could imagine.

2002 Millton Opou Vineyards Chardonnay, Gisborne ★ ★ ★ $$
dry, full-bodied, medium oak, high acidity drink now–10 years
Sun-baked autumn fruit and mineral flavors, soulfully crafted.

2002 Peregrine Pinot Gris, Central Otago ★ ★ ★ $$
dry, full-bodied, light oak, medium acidity drink now–6 years
On the Rubenesque side of Pinot Gris, this oozes baked apricot and honey.

2003 Amisfield Pinot Gris, Central Otago ★ ★ $$
dry, medium-bodied, no oak, high acidity drink now–3 years
The zippy side of Pinot Gris, full of crisp pear and orange zest flavors.

2002 Carrick Riesling, Central Otago ★ ★ $$
dry, medium-bodied, no oak, high acidity drink now–5 years
Flowery citrus flavors add a delicate note to this mineral-laden Riesling.

2003 Villa Maria Private Bin Riesling, Marlborough ★ $
dry, light-bodied, no oak, high acidity drink now–2 years
Citrus and polished minerals add up to good, clean Riesling at a great price.

red wines

PINOT NOIR

"Burgundian" may be a buzzword, but it's used sincerely when it comes to New Zealand's Pinot Noir. The grape grows best in the cool-climate zones of Martinborough and Central Otago, where it develops a rich, velvety texture that carries deep red berry and herb flavors.

251

at the table

New Zealand Pinot Noir marries conveniently with roast lamb (New Zealand or otherwise) and pan-roasted pork or veal chops, but it also has the delicacy to pair with tuna or salmon.

the bottom line New Zealand Pinot Noir starts around $15 and can run up to $60.

recommended wines

2001 Pegasus Bay Prima Donna, Waipara ★★★ $$$$
dry, medium-bodied, heavy tannin, high acidity   **drink now–9 years**
Prima Donna, perhaps, but this one's worth the trouble: give it time in the glass so the dark fruit and mineral flavors sing.

2001 Fromm Winery La Strada Clayvin Vineyard, Marlborough ★★★ $$$
dry, medium-bodied, medium tannin, high acidity   **drink now–6 years**
A Fellini-like road of wildflowers and mad-capped berries paved with stone.

2002 Huia, Marlborough ★★★ $$$
dry, medium-bodied, medium tannin, high acidity   **drink now–8 years**
An exceptionally complex Pinot, with dark cherry fruit and smoky minerals.

2002 Te Kairanga, Martinborough ★★ $$$
dry, medium-bodied, medium tannin, high acidity   **drink now–6 years**
Burgundy-like Pinot Noir, with light, fine raspberry, herb, and stone flavors.

2002 Lawson's Dry Hills, Marlborough ★★ $$
dry, medium-bodied, medium tannin, high acidity   **drink now–3 years**
Herb and animal flavors in a robe of spicy fruit seem made for lamb.

2003 Roaring Meg, Central Otago ★★ $$
dry, medium-bodied, medium tannin, high acidity   **drink now–4 years**
Named after a stream, Roaring Meg babbles dark fruit and herb flavors.

2003 Kim Crawford, Marlborough ★ $$
dry, medium-bodied, medium tannin, high acidity   **drink now–3 years**
As simple and tasty as a spoonful of fresh raspberry jam.

2002 Matua Valley, Marlborough ★ $
dry, light-bodied, medium tannin, high acidity   **drink now–3 years**
Charming berry and herb flavors make a great choice with grilled lamb.

OTHER RED WINES

While Pinot Noir does well in the cooler reaches of the country, Cabernet Sauvignon, Merlot, and Syrah are happier in warmer regions like Hawkes Bay, where they can develop smooth berry and chocolate flavors. Syrah resembles some northern Rhône wines in its spice and leaner fruit flavors.

at the table

More robust cuts of lamb such as roast leg or shoulder pair well with New Zealand Cabernet or Merlot, as would a wild mushroom pasta or roast venison. Try Syrah with braised lamb.

the bottom line Cabernet or Merlot, alone or in combination, start around $15 and can reach double that. Syrah runs $30 to $40.

recommended wines

2002 Craggy Range Winery Gimblett Gravels Vineyard Merlot, Hawkes Bay ★★★ $$$
dry, full-bodied, heavy tannin, high acidity   drink in 2–10 years
Want to know what Merlot should taste like? Have a sip of this lavender-scented treasure, laden with dark fruit and minerals.

2001 Matariki Syrah, Hawkes Bay ★★★ $$$
dry, medium-bodied, heavy tannin, high acidity   drink now–8 years
This Syrah may be far from its French homeland, but there's no mistaking its smoky, salt-and-pepper flavors coated thick with red berries.

2001 Mills Reef Elspeth Mere Road Vineyard Syrah, Hawkes Bay ★★★ $$$
dry, medium-bodied, heavy tannin, high acidity   drink now–6 years
A pepper-pot of a wine, this Syrah pulls mineral and spice from every inch of soil it comes near.

1999 Herzog, Marlborough ★★★ $$
dry, full-bodied, heavy tannin, high acidity   drink in 1–10 years
St-Émilion comes to Marlborough in this powerful Bordeaux blend.

2002 Esk Valley Merlot-Cabernet Sauvignon, Hawkes Bay ★★ $$
dry, full-bodied, medium tannin, high acidity   drink now–6 years
A wine that punches with a black fruit, pepper, and carbon-crusted fist.

argentina & chile

Wine has flowed in South America since Spanish conquistadors brought grape cuttings to the continent in the 1500s. It wasn't until the 1980s, though, that U.S. consumers discovered South America's wines, especially those from Chile and Argentina. Recent deep investments have yielded some higher-cost wines, but South American producers still offer a range of wines for all budgets.

argentina

Argentina has developed the world's fifth largest wine industry. Lately, rustic wines have given way to suave wines, full of sultry fruit and hypnotic spice flavors.

on the label

Argentine vintners customarily label their wines by grape variety and region. Proprietary blends sometimes take their own name and list grape varieties on the back label.

white wines

Chardonnay dominates Argentina's white wine scene with wines that range in style from big and buttery to light and steely. Sauvignon Blanc is nearly always refreshing, but most interesting is the grape Torrontés, which is made into light, absolutely charming wines full of lime blossom flavors. The best come from the region of Salta in Argentina's north.

Chile

SALTA

Cafayate

Pacific
Ocean

Argentina

LA RIOJA

Aconcagua

VALPARAISO

Casablanca

SANTIAGO

Puente Alto

Maipo

Maipú

Rapel

Luján de Cuyo

Colchagua

Central Valley

San Rafael

Curicó

MENDOZA

Maule

BUENOS AIRES

Atlantic
Ocean

CONCEPCIÓN

Featured
Wine-Growing
Regions

at the table

Torrontés is a delightful aperitif, alone or with hors d'oeuvres. Take it to the table for shrimp tempura served with a fruity sauce. Light Argentine Chardonnay can be enjoyed with grilled halibut or salade Niçoise. Match Argentina's oaky Chardonnay as you would Californian versions—crab cakes or baked salmon are terrific options.

the bottom line Most of Argentina's whites are priced low. Torrontés can be found for $6 to $15. Good Chardonnay starts at $10, with a small number reaching $40.

recommended wines

2002 Luca Chardonnay, Mendoza ★★★ $$$
dry, full-bodied, heavy oak, high acidity drink in 1–8 years
Honey-baked pear and tropical fruit shoot skyward with deep minerality and oak flavors.

2003 Crios de Susana Balbo Torrontés, Cafayate ★★★ $
dry, medium-bodied, no oak, high acidity drink now
A beautifully restrained Torrontés from Cafayate in Salta, subtle but unmistakably floral. Beautiful.

**2003 Bodegas Salentein Finca El Portillo Sauvignon Blanc,
Mendoza** ★★ $
dry, light-bodied, no oak, high acidity drink now–1 year
Refreshingly simple, with grassy lemon flavors.

2002 Los Cardos Chardonnay, Luján de Cuyo ★★ $
dry, medium-bodied, no oak, high acidity drink now–3 years
Lovely wine, this offers breezy pineapple flavors and a zesty disposition.

2003 Michel Torino Don David Torrontés, Cafayate ★★ $
dry, light-bodied, no oak, high acidity drink now
Charming as charming can be, this Torrontés recalls a breezy walk through a citrus grove during blossom time.

2001 Terrazas de los Andes Reserva Chardonnay, Mendoza ★★ $
dry, full-bodied, medium oak, high acidity drink now–6 years
Like a lush California Chardonnay, this Mendoza version is rich in sun-filled fruit and vanilla-flavored oak.

red wines

Argentina grows lots of Cabernet Sauvignon and Merlot, but it also provides sanctuary for Malbec and Bonarda. Malbec is native to Bordeaux, but gets little respect at home. In Argentina it shows sophisticated dark fruit and chocolate flavors. Bonarda, from northern Italy, has a similar profile, though with an appealing rusticity. Syrah and Sangiovese also show promise.

at the table

Argentina's wine was made for its famed grass-fed beef. Serve Malbec with thick-sliced prime rib, Chateaubriand, or grilled portobello mushrooms. Bonarda is ideal with braised short ribs or pasta with thick tomato sauce. Lamb's gamey flavors are perfect with Argentine Cabernet Sauvignon.

the bottom line Argentina's battered economy has kept Argentine wine prices affordable. There are many good values at $10, better ones for $15, and world-class wines for up to $85.

what to buy RED WINES

1999	2000	2001	2002	2003
★★★	★★	★★	★★★★	★★★

recommended wines

2001 Tikal Jubilo, Mendoza　　　　　　　　★★★★ $$$
dry, full-bodied, heavy tannin, high acidity　　　drink in 2–12 years
As heavy in flavor as the bottle is in weight, this offers a veritable catalog of dense, dark fruit, mineral, and herb flavors.

**2002 La Posta Estela Armando Vineyard Bonarda,
Mendoza**　　　　　　　　　　　　　　　★★★★ $$
dry, full-bodied, heavy tannin, high acidity　　　drink now–10 years
Beautiful Bonarda, restrained at first sip but rich with dark fruit and animal flavors.

2001 Susana Balbo Cabernet Sauvignon, Mendoza　　★★★ $$$
dry, full-bodied, heavy tannin, high acidity　　　drink in 2–12 years
Pure Argentina, dashing but soulful with vivid fruit and mineral flavors.

257

argentina**reds**

2002 BenMarco Malbec, Mendoza ★★★ $$
dry, full-bodied, heavy tannin, high acidity   drink in 1–8 years
Powerful Malbec pumped up with a bit of Bonarda, this makes perfect drinking for gauchos and city slickers alike.

2000 Broquel Cabernet Sauvignon, Mendoza ★★★ $
dry, medium-bodied, heavy tannin, high acidity   drink now–6 years
Impressive Cabernet for the money, the floral flavors of the oak meld beautifully with tannic dark berry flavors.

2001 Salentein Reserve Pinot Noir, Mendoza ★★ $$$
dry, medium-bodied, medium tannin, high acidity   drink now–3 years
Lightly earthy berry flavors make good drinking with roast lamb.

2002 Felipe Rutini Merlot, Tupungato ★★ $$
dry, full-bodied, medium tannin, high acidity   drink now–4 years
This Merlot pleases with soft plum and berry flavors with a slight herbal edge.

2001 Zuccardi Q Tempranillo, Mendoza ★★ $$
dry, full-bodied, heavy tannin, high acidity   drink now–6 years
Rare in Argentina despite the country's Spanish heritage, Tempranillo offers lip-smacking tart berry, mineral, and dry spice flavors here.

2001 Catena Cabernet Sauvignon, Mendoza ★★ $
dry, full-bodied, medium tannin, high acidity   drink now–5 years
A classic Cab, with red berry, pepper, and mineral flavors.

2002 Michel Torino Don David Malbec, Cafayate Valley ★★ $
dry, medium-bodied, heavy tannin, high acidity   drink in 1–6 years
An Italianate Malbec, with red fruit and high acidity that would be terrific with tomato-sauced pastas.

2002 Trapiche Oak Cask Malbec, Mendoza ★★ $
dry, full-bodied, medium tannin, high acidity   drink now–4 years
Smoky dark fruit tangos seductively with black-tea-like tannin.

2002 Alamos Bonarda, Mendoza ★ $
dry, full-bodied, heavy tannin, high acidity   drink now–3 years
Big and beefy, this Bonarda is built for burgers.

WINES WE WISH WE HAD MORE ROOM FOR
2001 Cheval des Andes, Mendoza ★★★ $$$$ dry, full-bodied, heavy tannin, high acidity, drink in 3–12 years; **2002 Luca Syrah, Mendoza** ★★★ $$$ dry, full-bodied, heavy tannin, high acidity, drink in 2–15 years; **2002 Los Cardos Malbec, Luján de Cuyo** ★★ $ dry, full-bodied, medium tannin, medium acidity, drink now–3 years

chile

Cradled between a long coastline and the heights of the Andes, Chile was made for growing grapes. Chilean vintners have long taken advantage of their good fortune, making full-flavored wines at low prices. Today they also make world-class wines— yet there are still plenty of affordable choices.

white wines

Chile puts out lots of Chardonnay, in styles from light and citrusy to full-bodied and tropical. More interesting are its Sauvignon Blancs, which might actually be Sauvignon Vert, a similar though rarely seen variety. Regardless of name, its wines are tangy with green fruit flavors. Chile also offers a few fine, dry Rieslings.

at the table

Chilean Sauvignon Blanc is delicious with steamed mussels or fish soups. Lighter Chardonnay is lovely with chicken Caesar salads; oaky versions can match lobster or roast turkey.

the bottom line

You'll pay by weight for Chilean white wines. Light-bodied, simple wines cost under $10; weightier wine (in quality as much as body) run $12 to $20. A few rich Chardonnays cross the $40 threshold.

recommended wines

2003 Concha y Toro Terrunyo El Triángulo Vineyard Sauvignon Blanc, Casablanca Valley ★★★ $$
dry, medium-bodied, no oak, high acidity drink now–2 years
Consistently one of the finest lines of wine from Chile, Terrunyo earns its stripes with juicy, tangy citrus and grassy flavors.

2002 Undurraga Reserva Chardonnay, Maipo Valley ★★★ $
dry, medium-bodied, medium oak, high acidity drink now–3 years
Honeyed apples, minerals, and nuts come together impressively here.

2002 Casa Lapostolle Cuvée Alexandre Chardonnay,
Casablanca Valley ★ ★ $$
dry, medium-bodied, medium oak, high acidity   drink now–3 years
Sumptuous Chardonnay, filled with ripe tropical fruit and vanilla-laden oak flavors.

2003 Santa Rita Reserva Sauvignon Blanc, Casablanca Valley ★ ★ $
dry, medium-bodied, no oak, high acidity   drink now–2 years
Fresh mango flavors sing along with orange, all backed by bright grassy notes.

2003 Aromo Chardonnay, Maule Valley ★ $
dry, medium-bodied, no oak, medium acidity   drink now–2 years
Moderate pear and tropical flavors, moderately priced.

2003 Cousiño-Macul Doña Isidora Riesling, Maipo Valley ★ $
off-dry, light-bodied, no oak, medium acidity   drink now–3 years
A charmer with apple blossom and light mineral flavors.

red wines

Cabernet Sauvignon and Merlot have been grown in Chile since the 19th century, giving them plenty of time to call the country home. At top levels, Chilean Bordeaux blends belong among the world's best wines. Much of what is identified as Merlot seems to be the largely forgotten Bordeaux grape, Carmènere. It produces similar, if more smoky (and interesting) wines. Recent plantings of the Rhône's Syrah also show the grape's smoky side.

at the table

Fruity, inexpensive Chilean reds are an obvious choice for cookouts and parties. Have them with grilled sausages, burgers, or sweet-sauced chicken. More complex wines demand more complex dishes, like seared beef or pork tenderloin with mushroom sauce or mustard-coated rack of lamb. Serve elite reds as you would a great Napa Cabernet or Bordeaux. Venison served with a wild berry jus or classic beef Wellington would be perfect.

the bottom line Though there are plenty of Chilean reds for under $10, spend $12 to $20 for far better, if not thrilling wines. Top cuvées match the finest California can offer, and, at nearly $100, are similarly priced.

recommended wines

2000 Domaines Barons de Rothschild Le Dix de Los Vascos,
Colchagua ★★★ $$$
dry, full-bodied, medium tannin, high acidity   drink in 2–10 years
A wine designed to resemble Grand Cru Bordeaux, this Cabernet Sauvignon
gets close to the mark with elegant cassis, nut, and peppery flavors.

1999 Domus Aurea Cabernet Sauvignon Clos Quebrada de Macul
Vineyard, Maipo Valley ★★★ $$$
dry, full-bodied, heavy tannin, high acidity   drink in 2–10 years
Layer upon layer of berry fruit, bitter herb, and oily mineral flavors build into an
impressive wine that needs time and food.

2002 Leyda Reserve Cahuil Vineyard Pinot Noir,
Leyda Valley ★★★ $$
dry, medium-bodied, medium tannin, high acidity   drink now–5 years
Possibly the finest Pinot in Chile, Leyda emerges with surprising, elegant, pure
raspberry and mineral flavors.

2001 Miguel Viu Manent Special Selection San Carlos Vineyard
Malbec, Colchagua Valley ★★★ $$
dry, full-bodied, heavy tannin, high acidity   drink in 1–10 years
Malbec rarely crosses the Andes to good effect, but this one has abundant
blackberry, cedar, and spice flavors.

2002 2 Brothers Big Tattoo Red, Colchagua ★★ $
dry, full-bodied, heavy tannin, medium acidity   drink now–3 years
Worth buying for the good cause (fifty cents of each sale go to cancer
research funds), but the wine's good, too, with spicy, lush fruit.

2002 Concha y Toro Marqués de Casa Concha Merlot, Peumo ★★ $
dry, full-bodied, heavy tannin, medium acidity   drink now–8 years
Sophisticated and rustic at once, this is packed with sultry dark fruit, coffee,
camphor, and leather flavors.

2002 Undurraga Reserva Carmenère, Colchagua Valley ★★ $
dry, full-bodied, medium tannin, high acidity   drink now–6 years
Carmenère's got its funk on here, with tart berry, toasted coffee, and wild
herbal flavors.

2002 Santa Rita 120 Merlot, Lontue Valley ★ $
dry, medium-bodied, medium tannin, high acidity   drink now–3 years
Fine berry and peppery flavors hark back to the days when good, cheap
Chilean wines were easy to find.

south africa

South Africans are a people in a hurry, looking to recapture the worldwide acclaim their wines had before the bane of apartheid. Given the quality of the country's Sauvignon Blanc, not to mention the growing array of excellent Bordeaux-style reds, it's clear that their efforts are paying off. Keep your eye on this spot, for the wines will only get better.

grapes & styles

The paradigm for South African wines is France in both grape varieties and style. Cabernet Sauvignon, Merlot, Syrah (generally called Shiraz), Chenin Blanc, Chardonnay, and Sauvignon Blanc are strongly represented in wines that offer subtle flavors, rather than the heavy fruit and oak typical of many New World versions. South Africa's own grape, Pinotage, is a hybrid of Pinot Noir and Cinsault. For decades, a virus has infected many South African vines, giving their grapes deeply smoky, vegetal flavors.

on the label

South African wines are almost always labeled according to grape variety and region of origin. A few proprietary blends take their own name.

white wines

Except for parts of France's Loire Valley, South Africa favors Chenin Blanc (also called "Steen") more than any other wine region. The best versions resemble great Loire Chenin Blanc,

but most South African Chenin is leaner, less musky, and very affordable. Chardonnay tends to be medium-bodied and full of mineral flavors here, and Sauvignon Blanc offers some of the pungent herb and citrus flavors of New Zealand's but with appreciable restraint.

at the table

Melon, citrus, and mineral flavors make South African Chenin Blanc a nice sipping wine on its own or a good match to grilled shrimp, vegetables, or fish kebabs. The country's lean, minerally Chardonnay matches well with white fish dishes or steamers. Pair grassy Sauvignon Blanc with chilled oysters or herb-marinated chicken breasts.

the bottom line Decent South African Chenin Blanc typically runs $8 to $10; a few reach $20 or more, but these tend to be difficult to find. Chardonnay registers between $8 and $39, with high quality available in the mid-to-high teens. South Africa's Sauvignon Blanc puts up stiff competition to New Zealand's at just $8 to $25.

263

recommended wines

2003 De Trafford Chenin Blanc, Walker Bay ★ ★ ★ $$
dry, medium-bodied, light oak, high acidity   **drink now–8 years**
Austere and indulgent at once; intense mineral flavors are finely knitted together by hints of oak.

2002 Mulderbosch Chardonnay, Stellenbosch ★ ★ ★ $$
dry, medium-bodied, medium oak, high acidity   **drink now–8 years**
World-class Chardonnay: citrusy, mineral-laden, and filled out with a restrained measure of oak.

2003 Clos Malverne Sauvignon Blanc, Stellenbosch ★ ★ ★ $
dry, medium-bodied, no oak, high acidity   **drink now–4 years**
Modest at first, when this wine gets going, minerals take its citrus and herb flavors to a whole other dimension.

2003 De Wetshof Estate Bon Vallon Chardonnay sur Lie, Robertson ★ ★ ★ $
dry, medium-bodied, no oak, high acidity   **drink now–6 years**
Beautiful wine, heady with aromas of baked bread and fresh-squeezed lemon.

2003 Vansha, Paarl ★ ★ ★ $
dry, medium-bodied, no oak, high acidity   **drink now–3 years**
Chenin and Sauvignon Blanc combine to great effect here, joining herb and mineral notes to soft fruit and light spice.

2002 Neil Ellis Chardonnay, Stellenbosch ★ ★ $$
dry, medium-bodied, light oak, high acidity   **drink now–3 years**
Fragrant with stones and blossoms, this is like stumbling into a patch of wildflowers among the rocks.

2002 Bouchard Finlayson Blanc de Mer, Overberg ★ ★ $
dry, medium-bodied, no oak, high acidity   **drink now–3 years**
Exuberant fruit joins with sophisticated mineral notes for a fascinating wine.

2003 Bowe Joubert Sauvignon Blanc, Stellenbosch ★ ★ $
dry, medium-bodied, no oak, high acidity   **drink now–2 years**
This is textbook South African Sauvignon, nicely done with fruit, herbal notes, and minerals.

2003 Ken Forrester Chenin Blanc, Stellenbosch ★ ★ $
dry, medium-bodied, no oak, high acidity   **drink now–8 years**
Deliciously fresh, light tropical-fruit flavors will morph into even more delicious dried summer-fruit flavors with age.

2002 Nederburg Chardonnay, Western Cape ★ ★ $
dry, medium-bodied, medium oak, high acidity   drink now–8 years
Fine Chardonnay, this strikes a nice balance between ripe, apple-like fruit, oak, and mineral flavors.

2003 Uitkyk Sauvignon Blanc, Stellenbosch ★ ★ $
dry, medium-bodied, no oak, high acidity   drink now–3 years
Look elsewhere for summer Sauvignon. This has fruit and minerals, but also a seductive smokiness that gives it warmth and heft.

2003 Goats do Roam, Western Cape ★ $
dry, light-bodied, no oak, high acidity   drink now–1 year
Tongue-in-cheek fun, with juicy fruit and zingy acidity.

WINES WE WISH WE HAD MORE ROOM FOR
2002 Rustenberg Chardonnay, Stellenbosch ★ ★ ★ $$ dry, full-bodied, medium oak, high acidity, drink now–8 years; **2003 Fleur du Cap Sauvignon Blanc, Coastal Region** ★ ★ $ dry, medium-bodied, no oak, high acidity, drink now–3 years; **2003 Kanu Chenin Blanc, Stellenbosch** ★ ★ $ dry, medium-bodied, no oak, high acidity, drink now–3 years

red wines

Generous sunshine allows grapes to ripen easily in South Africa, while cool breezes from the Atlantic and Indian oceans keep acid levels high. This combination makes for red wines with ripe fruit flavors yet a fine acid balance, often with smoke and mineral flavors, too. Single-variety wines from Cabernet Sauvignon, Merlot, and Shiraz can be excellent; don't miss the Rhône-style blends, either. Simple Pinotage wines are light and juicy, like Beaujolais Nouveau; more complex versions are full-bodied, with spice and berry flavors and velvety tannin.

at the table
Outdoor barbecues provide the perfect setting for simpler South African reds. The smokier, more complex reds are especially suited to roast game. Cabernet and Merlot are fine choices for leg of lamb or pork tenderloin. South African Shiraz is more subdued than its Australian kin, but equally peppery. Try it with an adobo-style pork roast or lamb tagine. Concentrated Pinotage is especially good with venison.

the bottom line Simple South African reds start at $7; more complex wines cost around $18 to $24. Wines to brag about sell for $40 or more.

recommended wines

2001 Wildekrans Pinotage, Walker Bay ★ ★ ★ ★ $
dry, full-bodied, heavy tannin, high acidity   drink in 2–12 years
Four-star Pinotage. Juicy black berries, herbs, and a little musk make for completely seductive drinking.

2001 Rustenberg John X. Merriman, Stellenbosch ★ ★ ★ $$$
dry, full-bodied, heavy tannin, high acidity   drink in 2–12 years
This Bordeaux blend actually tastes like Bordeaux, with an earthy African twist.

2000 Camberley Cabernet Sauvignon-Merlot, Stellenbosch ★ ★ ★ $$
dry, full-bodied, heavy tannin, high acidity   drink in 2–12 years
Just delicious, with luscious red and black fruit flavors and violet aromas.

1999 Clos Malverne Auret Cabernet Sauvignon-Pinotage, Stellenbosch ★ ★ ★ $$
dry, full-bodied, heavy tannin, high acidity   drink now–8 years
With smoky bramble berry flavors, this is perfect for spit-roasted meat.

2001 Meinert Devon Crest, Devon Valley ★ ★ ★ $$
dry, full-bodied, heavy tannin, high acidity   drink in 1–10 years
A high-octane red (15% alcohol), dense with delicious berry and spice.

1999 Le Bonheur Prima, Stellenbosch ★ ★ ★ $
dry, full-bodied, heavy tannin, high acidity   drink now–10 years
Ripe fruit wrapped by ribbons of pine and herb flavors.

2002 Hamilton Russell Vineyards Pinot Noir, Walker Bay ★ ★ $$$
dry, medium-bodied, medium tannin, high acidity   drink now–6 years
Smoky red berry flavors brightened by acidity make good drinking with grilled salmon steaks.

2002 Ridgeback Shiraz, Paarl ★ ★ $$$
dry, full-bodied, heavy tannin, high acidity   drink in 1–6 years
Shiraz that tastes like Syrah, with earthy, peppery, suitably smoky flavors.

2002 Fairview Pegleg Carignan, Coastal Region ★ ★ $$
dry, medium-bodied, medium tannin, high acidity   drink now–3 years
Cherry flavors energized by high acidity make this a vibrant Carignan.

WE'RE NOT A GANG, WE'RE A CLUB

I hope by now you'd agree it's exciting to read about the multitude of wines in the world. But wouldn't it be even better to taste them? It's impossible to taste them all, of course, but you can hit a lot of wines at once at an organized wine tasting. Where legal, wine shops frequently hold tastings to give customers a chance to experience different wines. Sometimes winemakers promoting their wares will turn up to answer questions, too. There are also tasting clubs that wine lovers can join: The American Wine Society (www.americanwinesociety.com) has affiliates across the U.S. for enthusiasts and professionals, while the Wine Brats (www.winebrats.org) draw youthful crowds to their wine-appreciation events. There are so many wine-tasting opportunities, actually, that there are two wine-event calendars, www.localwineevents.com and www.wineevents-calendar.com, that tell you what's happening the world over every night of the week. Check them out, and get tasting.

2001 Plaisir de Merle Cabernet Sauvignon, Paarl ★★ $$
dry, medium-bodied, heavy tannin, high acidity **drink in 2–8 years**
Tart dark berries get a lift from minerals and acid.

2003 Indaba Shiraz, South Africa ★ $
dry, full-bodied, medium tannin, high acidity **drink now–2 years**
Simple, spicy berry flavors will wash down burgers nicely.

WINES WE WISH WE HAD MORE ROOM FOR
2001 Beaumont Ariane, Walker Bay ★★★ $$ dry, full-bodied, heavy tannin, high acidity, drink in 1–10 years; **2001 De Trafford Cabernet Sauvignon, Stellenbosch** ★★★ $$ dry, medium-bodied, heavy tannin, high acidity, drink in 1–10 years; **2000 Flagstone Dragon Tree Cabernet Sauvignon-Pinotage, Western Cape** ★★★ $$ dry, full-bodied, heavy tannin, high acidity, drink now–8 years; **2001 Hercules Paragon Shiraz, Western Cape** ★★ $$$ dry, full-bodied, medium tannin, high acidity, drink now–6 years; **2001 Kanonkop Pinotage, Simonsberg/Stellenbosch** ★★ $$$ dry, full-bodied, heavy tannin, high acidity, drink now–8 years

champagne
& other
sparkling
wines

Nothing says "party" like bubbly. Whether it's a simple sparkler from California, a crisp Cava, or a valorous vintage Champagne, sparkling wines bring festivity to any event. With wines available for all price ranges, there's no reason for life not to be a perpetual party.

at the table

Sparkling wines are usually enjoyed as an aperitif, but they can be good at dinner, too. Lighter sparkling wines are wonderful at brunch or with cold cuts (try Prosecco and prosciutto, for instance). Medium-bodied sparklers are lovely with steamed crab or chicken. Richer wines are wonderful with smoked salmon or sable and have the weight to stand up to roast pork loin or porcini pasta. Dedicated steak lovers can enjoy bubbly with dinner, too: try Australia's unique sparkling red Shiraz.

champagne

Skirting the northernmost point at which fine wines can be made in France, Champagne makes the best of a difficult situation. The region's climate is warm enough to grow fine wine grapes, but too cool to regularly ripen them enough to make good table wine. What the grapes lack in sugar, they make up for in acidity, which makes them perfect for sparkling wines. In Europe, only sparkling wines made in France's Champagne region using a technique known as *méthode champenoise* are entitled to be called "Champagne."

grape & styles

Champagne vintners work almost exclusively with three permitted grape varieties: Chardonnay, Pinot Noir, and Pinot Meunier. Most Champagnes are blends of the three, but wines labeled *Blanc de Blancs* ("white of whites") are 100 percent Chardonnay; *Blanc de Noirs* ("white of blacks") wines are made from red grapes Pinot Noir and/or Pinot Meunier. Rosé wines are made either by adding a touch of red wine, or by macerating pigment-rich black grape skins with pressed white juice.

on the label

All Champagnes will say Champagne on the label. Most Champagnes don't bear a vintage date: instead, vintners blend wines from several years to create a consistent house style. These non-vintage cuvées can be quite luxurious. Vintage Champagnes are made in years when grapes ripen especially well—typically about four years in a decade. Some Champagnes also bear the name of the vineyard from which they came: vineyards considered excellent are classified Premier Cru, and the best are designated Grand Cru.

Most Champagne is *Brut,* or dry, but there are variations of sweetness. From driest to sweetest, the categories of Champagne are: *Brut Nature* (or *Brut Zéro, Pas Dosé,* or *Sans-Dosage), Extra Brut, Brut, Extra Dry/Extra Sec, Sec/Dry,* and *Demi-Sec*. These categories are relative.

the bottom line Expect to pay $25 to $40 for good, basic non-vintage wines, $40 to $85 for vintage wines, and well over $100 for the most exalted bottles and cuvées de prestige.

what to buy VINTAGE CHAMPAGNE

1990	1991	1992	1993	1994	1995
★★★★	NV	NV	★★	NV	★★★

1996	1997	1998	1999	2000	2001
★★★★	★★★	★★	★★★	★★	★★★

recommended wines

NV Krug Brut Rosé 🍷   ★ ★ ★ ★ $$$$
dry, full-bodied, high acidity
Hints of hibiscus, glances of ginger, peaks of pomegranate, and slips of spice amaze and enthrall; this is one of the world's great wines.

1996 Nicolas Feuillatte Cuvée Palmes d'Or   ★ ★ ★ ★ $$$$
dry, medium-bodied, high acidity
Feuillatte's best Palmes d'Or ever, a paradise of ripe fruit and precious minerals.

**1995 Veuve Clicquot Ponsardin La Grande Dame
Brut Rosé** 🍷   ★ ★ ★ ★ $$$$
dry, medium-bodied, high acidity
Any Veuve wine offers a thrill but none more than La Grande Dame. It's superbly sophisticated and earthy at once, with mandarin orange, floral, and slight tropical flavors.

1996 Bollinger Grande Année Brut   ★ ★ ★ $$$$
dry, medium-bodied, high acidity
So laden with minerals, this is like a dip in the ocean. Great with oysters.

1996 Charles Heidsieck Brut Rosé 🍷   ★ ★ ★ $$$$
dry, medium-bodied, high acidity
One sip's like taking a walk through a souk, full of rose and orange flavors.

1995 Henriot Brut   ★ ★ ★ $$$$
dry, medium-bodied, high acidity
Creamy key lime and salty mineral flavors make a wine as refreshing as a margarita, but with lots more class.

NV Jacquart Brut de Nominée   ★ ★ ★ $$$$
dry, medium-bodied, high acidity
Yellow apple scents lead into a wine more mineral than fruity.

NV Philipponnat Cuvée 1522 Extra Brut   ★ ★ ★ $$$$
dry, medium-bodied, high acidity
Calvinist in austerity, this is Champagne for those who like their wine dry.

NV Jean Laurent Blanc de Noirs Brut   ★ ★ ★ $$$
dry, full-bodied, high acidity
Nut, brioche, and baked quince flavors, beautifully molded.

NV Moët & Chandon Brut Impérial   ★ ★ ★ $$$
dry, light-bodied, high acidity
This is regal and alive with chiffon-light floral and key lime flavors. Lovely.

WEB PARFUMÉ

Forget written wine recommendations. In the not too distant future you may be able to click your way to a whiff of whatever wine catches your fancy. Technology to transmit odors via the Internet is still in its infancy, but France Télécom has developed *web parfumé* far enough to share its technology with the Burgundy wine trade office (Bureau Interprofessionnel des Vins de Bourgogne). The office has set up a site (www.vins-bourgogne.fr/balade.htm) which offers a tour of the wine region, its vineyards, wineries, cellars, and wines, through images, narration, and scent—if you have the necessary diffuser. While it's unlikely that the subtleties of a vintage Champagne can be appreciated electronically, the idea is intriguing. Let's just hope hackers don't find a way to turn Web viruses into stink bombs.

NV Marquis de Vauzelle Brut ★★★ $$
dry, medium-bodied, high acidity
Dry apricot and marzipan flavors layered with minerals make this delicious.

NV Bonnaire Blanc de Blancs Grand Cru Brut ★★ $$$
dry, medium-bodied, high acidity
An explosion of orange flavors.

1994 Champagne Vranken Demoiselle Tête de Cuvée Brut ★★ $$$
dry, medium-bodied, high acidity
Herbs morph into flowers and berry flavors underlined by minerals.

NV Gosset Brut Excellence ★★ $$$
dry, full-bodied, high acidity
Plump bubbly—meaty in texture and ripe in flavors.

NV Louis Roederer Brut Premier ★★ $$$
dry, medium-bodied, high acidity
Caramel and green apple flavors offer reason to get excited.

NV Mumm Brut Rosé 🍷 ★★ $$$
dry, medium-bodied, high acidity
Austere yet inviting, this offers a patina of cherry over a base of light minerals.

NV Paul Bara Grand Cru Brut Réserve, Bouzy ★★ $$$
dry, medium-bodied, high acidity
Deliciously full of peaches, citrus, and cherries.

NV Perrier-Jouët Grand Brut ★★ $$$
dry, medium-bodied, high acidity
Sparkling minerals are rounded by peach and sweet oak flavors.

NV Piper-Heidsieck Cuvée Sublime Demi-Sec ★★ $$$
medium-sweet, medium-bodied, high acidity
Champagne as it used to be enjoyed: somewhat sweet, with flavors recalling Danish pastry in richness and layered flavor.

NV Pol Roger Brut Extra Cuvée de Réserve ★★ $$$
dry, light-bodied, high acidity
Pol Roger's always a fine choice when you want finesse.

NV Deutz Brut Classic ★ $$$
dry, light-bodied, high acidity
Nuts, citrus, and minerals, nicely combined, for a fair price.

other sparkling wines

Nearly every wine-producing country makes some version of sparkling wine. None carry the same prestige as wines from Champagne, but many are made using the same methods and sell for considerably less.

france

Champagne-like wines are made all over France, normally from whatever grape varieties are typical to the region. Those made in the same manner as Champagne are labeled *méthode tradition- nelle* or *Crémant*. Wines made using different techniques are often labeled simply *Brut* or *Mousseux* instead.

the bottom line Non-Champagne sparklers from France can be outstanding bargains, especially Vouvray Brut and Blanquette de Limoux wines. Expect to pay $8 to $24 for good-quality examples.

recommended wines

NV Sieur d'Arques Toques et Clochers, Crémant de Limoux ★ ★ ★ $
dry, medium-bodied, high acidity
The difference in flavor between this and good Champagne isn't much: this has it all, from tart, aromatic fruit to savory minerals.

NV Baumard Carte Turquoise Brut, Crémant de Loire ★ ★ $$
dry, medium-bodied, high acidity
A Chenin Blanc master offers this sparkling take, rich with earthy, ripe fruit.

1996 François Pinon Pétillant Sec, Vouvray ★ ★ $$
dry, light-bodied, high acidity
Utterly delightful, with garlands of apple and flower flavors.

NV Langlois-Château Brut Rosé, Crémant de Loire ❡ ★ ★ $$
dry, medium-bodied, high acidity
With peppery berry flavors, this is as good with dinner as it is before.

NV Jaillance Cuvée Impériale Tradition, Clairette de Die ★ ★ $
off-dry, light-bodied, high acidity
Thoroughly charming, these citrus blossom, honey, and spice flavors provide tonic for anything that ails you.

NV Willm Blanc de Noirs, Alsace ★ ★ $
dry, light-bodied, high acidity
Refreshment from Alsace, with crisp green apple and true pear flavors.

italy

With the ethos of *la dolce vita* extending throughout the peninsula, it is no surprise that Italy has a long tradition of *spumante* (sparkling) wines. They come in a variety of styles. Those from Franciacorta, in Lombardy, are made using the *metodo classico* of Champagne, and they are the driest and most serious. Piedmont's lightly sweet, flowery Moscato d'Asti is the most charming, while Prosecco, made near Venice, offers affordable refreshment. It's often drunk from tumblers at bars in the Veneto.

the bottom line Good Prosecco and Moscato d'Asti can be found for $10 or so. Impressive Franciacorta wines are priced comparably to Champagne, at $25 to $70.

recommended wines

1999 Bellavista Gran Cuvée Brut, Franciacorta   ★★★ $$$$
dry, medium-bodied, high acidity
Possibly Italy's finest sparkler, Bellavista shows much of the complexity of good Champagne with a dash of *la dolce vita*.

NV Ca' del Bosco, Franciacorta   ★★ $$$
dry, full-bodied, high acidity
Saucy and fresh, this is full of ripe fruit, caramel, and a few nuts.

NV Bisol Crede Brut, Prosecco di Valdobbiadene   ★★ $$
dry, light-bodied, high acidity
Far from insipid Prosecchi, Bisol rolls out a fruit basket of fun flavors.

NV Marwood Brut, Italy   ★★ $
dry, medium-bodied, high acidity
A simple sparkler, this hits all the right notes, from citrus to minerals.

NV Zardetto, Prosecco   ★ $
dry, medium-bodied, high acidity
Prosecco done dry, this will perk up your palate before dinner.

spain

CAVA

Spain's sparkling Cavas used to be more noteworthy for their very low prices than for their quality, but no more: quality is excellent, yet prices remain low. All are made using the Champagne method and local grapes.

the bottom line You can find $6 Cava, but spend $10 to $15 for far greater enjoyment.

recommended wines

2000 Huguet Reserva Brut Nature   ★★★ $$
dry, medium-bodied, high acidity
A springy Cava, with subtle floral flavors underlined by apple and minerals.

2000 Freixenet Brut Nature ★ ★ ★ $
dry, medium-bodied, high acidity
Great wine at great value, this offers a fine mousse of citrus, apple, and floral flavors for less than $15.

2001 Castillo Perelada Cuvée Especial Brut Nature ★ ★ $
dry, medium-bodied, high acidity
Puckery lemon and minerals are guaranteed to make your mouth water.

1999 Marqués de Gelida Brut ★ ★ $
dry, medium-bodied, high acidity
Like apples, sliced fresh and baked, sprinkled with nuts.

NV Segura Viudas Aria Brut ★ ★ $
dry, light-bodied, high acidity
These light, nutty apple and pear flavors are impressive—especially at $12.

NV Jaume Serra Cristalino Brut ★ $
dry, light-bodied, high acidity
Simple summer fruit and a little mineral flavor make this a no-brainer for inexpensive pleasure.

united states

Vintners throughout the U.S. produce sparkling wine, many using the same method and same grapes as in Champagne. California dominates, with the best of its sparklers made from grapes grown in the cooler regions of the state like Green Valley and Carneros. New York, the Pacific Northwest, Michigan, and New Mexico also craft some fine sparkling wines.

the bottom line Quality American sparklers sell for $9 to $80. Very good quality can be found for $12 to $25.

recommended wines

1998 Schramsberg J. Schram, California ★ ★ ★ ★ $$$$
dry, full-bodied, high acidity
Schramsberg's top wine doesn't hold back: this is an indulgence of ripe fruit, herbs, and minerals, with an appealing dose of bitter spice.

275

1998 Roederer Estate L'Ermitage Brut, Anderson Valley, California ★★★★ $$$
dry, full-bodied, high acidity

If P. Diddy ever gets tired of Cristal, he should try this glamorous Californian that has the stuff to please any lover of true Champagne.

1997 Domaine Carneros by Taittinger Le Rêve Brut, Carneros, California ★★★ $$$$
dry, full-bodied, high acidity

Dream, fantasy, or just luxurious reality, this oozes ripe citrus and berry spice.

1996 Iron Horse Brut LD, Green Valley, California ★★★ $$$
dry, medium-bodied, high acidity

Give this a few minutes in the glass and it will reveal its true dry spice and nut brittle flavors.

1999 Schramsberg Blanc de Blancs, California ★★★ $$$
dry, medium-bodied, high acidity

Racy wine: citrus flavors sear across the palate to a checkered-flag finish of mineral and sweet apple flavors.

1999 Wölffer Christian Wölffer Cuvée Brut, The Hamptons, New York ★★★ $$$
dry, full-bodied, high acidity

Forget the Hamptons' frolicking summer crowds, this sparkler has the depth for Manhattan's finest restaurants.

1995 Gloria Ferrer Royal Cuvée Brut, Carneros, California ★★★ $$
dry, full-bodied, high acidity

Modeled after a wine served to King Juan Carlos, this will surely please commoners with its herb-laden sweet lemon and mineral goodness.

1998 Pacific Echo Brut Rosé, Anderson Valley, California ♆ ★★★ $$
dry, medium-bodied, high acidity

From the cool Anderson Valley, this delivers juicy strawberry and peach flavors as flavorful as they are graceful.

1999 Handley Brut, Anderson Valley, California ★★ $$
dry, medium-bodied, high acidity

Handley takes full advantage of Anderson Valley's cool climate for a crisp, clean sparkling wine.

NV Mumm Napa Blanc de Noirs, Napa Valley, California ★★ $$
dry, medium-bodied, high acidity

Who cares if Mumm has its color wheel upside down? This decidedly rosé, not blanc, wine has loads of strawberry and spice.

other countries

Every wine-producing country seems to make sparkling wines. Some of the most reliable producers beyond the ones we've already covered are Germany and Austria, where sparkling *Sekt* is typically made from Riesling and Pinot Blanc. In the Southern Hemisphere, Argentina, Australia, New Zealand, and South Africa produce sparklers modeled after Champagne. Australia also offers dry, deeply red, sparkling Shiraz.

the bottom line South American sparklers run $9 to $12. Australian examples start at $8, but $20 to $40 buys better. A few Austrian and German sparkling wines run less than $20; luxury bottles cost $30 to $50.

recommended wines

1998 Georg Breuer Brut, Rheingau, Germany ★★★★ $$$
dry, medium-bodied, high acidity
One of the world's great sparklers, full of minerals, dry citrus, and honey.

1999 Huia Brut, Marlborough, New Zealand ★★★ $$$
dry, medium-bodied, high acidity
Hoo-ya!!! Peach melba flavors positively jump from the glass in this lovely wine.

1998 Yalumba D Black, Barossa, Australia ★★★ $$$
dry, full-bodied, high acidity
A red sparkler, spicy and savory with bitter chocolate and berry flavors.

NV Graham Beck Brut, Robertson, South Africa ★★ $
dry, medium-bodied, high acidity
Elegant and earthy at the same time, with fine minerals and tart fruit.

NV Banrock Station Sparkling Chardonnay, South Eastern Australia ★ $
dry, light-bodied, high acidity
Light and lemony flavors make one nice brunch sparkler.

2001 Spiropoulos Ode Panos Brut, Greece ★ $
dry, light-bodied, high acidity
A light melody of citrus flavors.

277

fortified & dessert wines

Whether a bone-dry fino Sherry before dinner or a lusciously sweet, late-harvest wine with or in place of dessert, fortified and dessert wines can be a memorable way to begin or finish a meal. Many fortified wines, such as Sherry and Madeira, can be enjoyed throughout the meal, too.

fortified wines

Sherry, Port, and Madeira all share a common feature—they have been "fortified" with a bit of extra alcohol (usually neutral-tasting grape brandy) before bottling. This helps preserve the wines from the effects of the warm climes in which they are made. The process can also produce a sweet wine if the alcohol is added before the wine has finished fermenting, as happens in the production of sweet purple Port wines.

SHERRY

Shakespeare's Falstaff may have sung the praises of sack, or Sherry, but today, regrettably, it has been virtually forgotten. The chalky soils around Jerez (also spelled Xérès) in southern Spain, together with the wild yeasts used to ferment it, make Sherry among the most distinctive wines in the world. With a wide range of styles, from palate-puckeringly dry to tooth-achingly sweet and unctuous, Sherry offers something for every taste.

grapes & styles

Most Sherry is made from Palomino grapes, though sweet styles are often made from or with the addition of Pedro Ximénez or Moscatel grapes. There are two basic categories of Sherry: Fino and Oloroso. Each has its own subcategories.

Fino Sherry is yeasty, floral, and slightly nutty. It gets its distinct flavor from *flor*, an oxygen-stifling yeast that grows on the wine's surface while it's maturing in wooden barrels. **Manzanilla** Sherry is a Fino aged around Sanlúcar de Barrameda, a seaside area especially hospitable to flor. Fresh as the salty ocean breezes that blow over the vineyards, Manzanilla's flavors also echo the flowery charms of chamomile (*manzanilla* in Spanish). **Amontillado** is a Fino that continues to age after its oxygen-inhibiting flor dies. Oxidation brings nutty qualities to the wine's inherent minerality. Most Amontillados are dry. **Pale Cream** Sherries are Finos sweetened by Pedro Ximénez wine or grape juice concentrate.

Oloroso Sherry doesn't develop flor, so it oxidizes faster as it ages, turning nutty and dark amber. Some Olorosos are dry, but most are sweet. **Cream** Sherry is an Oloroso sweetened with Pedro Ximénez wine. **Palo Cortado** is a rare type of Oloroso that happens to develop flor. Dark in color, it falls between Oloroso and Amontillado in style.

Pedro Ximénez gets its thick, treacle-sweet, dried fruit flavors from grapes of the same name grown mainly in the Montilla-Moriles region outside of Jerez. PX (its common nickname) is technically not Sherry, but several Sherry houses make it.

at the table

A dry Fino is everything you could hope for in an aperitif: light, mouthwatering, and delicious on its own. Dry Oloroso Sherry is delicious with Serrano ham or Manchego cheese, as well as with creamy soups—especially if you add a splash to the soup before serving. Sweeter versions are delicious with fruit and nut breads; or try sweet PX drizzled over vanilla ice cream.

the bottom line

Underappreciated and underpriced, Sherry is a terrific bargain. Many bottles cost less than $12; those from top producers are scarcely a few dollars more. Wines fetching $20 to $30 are generally superb. Older wines or special rare blends cost up to $125.

recommended wines

Lustau Almacenista Pata de Gallina Oloroso ★★★★ $$$
dry, medium-bodied, high acidity

Despite its name, these lightly spiced roasted apricot, baked apple, and wonderful mineral flavors are far from chicken scratch (*pata de gallina*).

Gonzalez Byass Noé Pedro Ximénez Muy Viejo ★★★★ $$
sweet, full-bodied, high acidity

With smoky dark coffee, orange, and dry fig flavors, this PX is way too good to pour over ice cream.

Hidalgo La Gitana Manzanilla ★★★★ $
dry, light-bodied, high acidity

As far as Manzanilla goes, there's no finer expression than La Gitana, with its sea breeze freshness and breezy chamomile notes.

Bodegas Dios Baco Cream Sherry ★★★ $$
sweet, full-bodied, high acidity

Pair this sweet, creamy Sherry with a pecan tart for a memorable dessert.

Bodegas Dios Baco Oloroso ★★★ $$
off-dry, medium-bodied, high acidity

This is at once creamy and caramel-rich, as well as dry and full of minerals.

Gonzalez Byass Apóstoles Palo Cortado Muy Viejo ★★★ $$
off-dry, medium-bodied, high acidity

Truffle aromas are so hypnotic you might forget to taste this, but do: it's deliciously rich with burnt sugar, sweet spice, and dried fruit.

Lustau Jarana Solera Reserva Light Fino ★★★ $
dry, medium-bodied, high acidity

Blanched almond flavors scented by acacia make this light but not austere.

Barbadillo Laura Moscatel Sherry ★★ $$
medium-sweet, medium-bodied, high acidity

Blended with Pedro Ximenez, Muscat plays things musky in this interesting Sherry variant, showing also its flowery charms.

Domecq La Ina Dry Fino ★★ $
dry, light-bodied, high acidity

Wispy wine, with sea breeze minerality.

Osborne Coquinero Fino Amontillado ★★ $
dry, medium-bodied, high acidity

A hive of flavor, with salty minerality and unexpected streaks of honey.

MADEIRA

From the island of the same name off Morocco's coast, Madeira was the wine of choice in the U.S. well into the 19th century. Today, it is inexplicably underappreciated. Like Sherry, Madeira comes in styles appropriate for before, during, and after a meal.

grapes & styles

Most Madeira wines are blends of grapes, but better versions will carry the name of one of four grape varieties: Sercial, Verdelho, Bual, and Malmsey (Malvasia). Sercial Madeiras are bone-dry; each variety listed after that gets progressively sweeter. Wines marked "Rainwater" are a common blend. Rare Vintage Madeiras age almost indefinitely and can be impressively old; bottles dating to the 1800s are still for sale today. Madeiras with an age designation, such as "five [or ten or fifteen] years old," are blends of vintages; the cited age is that of the youngest wine in the blend. Solera Madeiras, on the other hand, indicate the vintage of the oldest wine in the blend.

at the table

Sercial and Verdelho Madeira go nicely with salted nuts, dry cheeses, or baked oysters. Madeira is a classic match for hearty winter soups. The high acidity and rich sweetness of Buals and Malmseys make them great with crème brûlée and baked fruit-and-custard tarts.

the bottom line

Rainwater Madeira runs $10 to $15; far better five-year wines cost $17 to $25. Prices rise from there, with decades-old Madeira selling for $100 or more.

recommended wines

1934 Broadbent Verdelho ★★★★ $$$$
dry, medium-bodied, high acidity
Seventy years old, and this still smolders with powerful smoky, peppery herb, and dry apricot flavors.

Broadbent 10 Year Malmsey ★★★ $$$
medium-sweet, full-bodied, high acidity
Very fine Malmsey, full of orange marmalade, herbs, and toasted hazelnut flavors.

1986 Cossart Gordon Colheita Bual ★★★ $$$
medium-sweet, full-bodied, high acidity
Cedar and fresh tobacco notes are sweetened by apricot flavors, the whole heady as a humidor.

Blandy's 5 Year Verdelho ★★ $$
medium-sweet, full-bodied, high acidity
Delicious as a slice of gingerbread with a dollop of apricot jam.

Leacock's 5 Year Dry Sercial ★★ $$
dry, medium-bodied, high acidity
Savory Sercial with dry mineral and cirtus flavors—great with salty nibbles.

Blandy's 5 Year Rich Alvada ★★ $
medium-sweet, full-bodied, high acidity
Thoroughly enjoyable, this offers the thrill of Madeira for a modest price.

PORT

Port was a little-known wine local to Portugal's Douro region until English traders discovered it in the 17th century. Sweet and strong, it was a hit among the British, who began shipping it home to England from the port city of Oporto. Today, it's still loved for its warming, plummy flavors.

grapes & styles

More than eighty different grape varieties can go into Port wines, but the best known are Touriga Nacional, Touriga Franca, and Tinta Roriz (Tempranillo). These are never identified on the label. Instead, Port wines are labeled by style, which range from light White Port to long-aging, tannic, and sweet Vintage Port.

White Port, made from white grapes, has refreshing citrus flavors that make it a delightful aperitif. **Ruby Port,** the most common style, is usually a simple wine blended from wines aged for two or three years. More intense are **Reserve** or **Vintage Character Ports,** which are blends of Ruby Ports aged for four to six years. These wines often carry proprietary names like Warre's Warrior or Graham's Six Grapes. **Late Bottled Vintage (LBV) Ports** are Ruby Ports from a single vintage aged four to six years in barrels. They acquire some of the attributes of Vintage Ports without requiring further aging. **Vintage Ports** are wines from a single exceptional year. Aged in oak casks for two to three years before bottling, Vintage Port requires years, often decades, of aging before its potential is realized. **Single Quinta Vintage Ports** are made from the grapes of a particular vineyard (*quinta*). They are made in the same manner as Vintage Ports.

Tawny Ports are kept in barrels significantly longer than Vintage or other Ruby Ports. Long barrel-aging brings on dried fruit and nut flavors and a tawny color. The finest Tawnies are labeled with the average age of wine in the bottle, usually five to forty years. **Colheita Ports** are Tawnies from a single vintage (*colheita*). All Tawny Ports are ready to drink upon release. Tawny Ports without an indication of age are inferior wines that barely suggest how good aged Tawnies can be.

at the table

Chilled White Port is an excellent aperitif, alone or with a splash of tonic and a twist. Simple, juicy Ruby Ports are good companions to berry crumbles. The strong flavors of Vintage Port are traditionally savored alone or with strong, aged cheeses like Stilton. Tawny Port, with its dried fruit and nut flavors and high acidity, is terrific with tarte Tatin or pecan pie.

the bottom line
Ruby Ports cost $10 to $20; LBVs between $15 and $30. Young Vintage Ports sell for $35 to $100. Single Quinta Ports run about two-thirds the price of the same house's Vintage Port. Tawny Ports with age designations represent good value: ten-year Tawnies run $20 to $40 and increase with age. Some forty-year Tawnies hit $130.

recommended wines

1994 Broadbent Vintage ★ ★ ★ ★ $$$$
medium-sweet, full-bodied, high acidity
The wilds of the Douro region captured in a bottle: this is a menagerie of wild berry, animal, herb, and stone. First rate.

1992 Smith Woodhouse Late Bottled Vintage ★ ★ ★ ★ $$$
sweet, full-bodied, high acidity
A powerhouse LBV raging with intense cassis, minerals, and smoke.

Ferreira Duque de Bragança 20 Year Tawny ★ ★ ★ $$$$
off-dry, medium-bodied, high acidity
A smooth, dry Port, fascinating with orange, apricot, and almond notes.

fortified wines **port**

2001 Quinta de Roriz Vintage   ★★★ $$$$
sweet, full-bodied, high acidity
Dark, sweet berry flavors balance against sharp mineral and tobacco notes.

2001 Fonseca Quinta do Panascal Vintage   ★★★ $$$
sweet, full-bodied, high acidity
A battle royale rages in this Port as floral and lush fruit wrestles dry mineral and spice notes, all pinned down by licorice.

2001 Niepoort Secundum Vintage   ★★★ $$$
sweet, full-bodied, high acidity
Suave, sultry Port, its spicy berry flavors are no surprise, but the intense pear flavors…wow.

Graham's Six Grapes Unfiltered Reserve   ★★★ $$
sweet, full-bodied, high acidity
One of the best non-vintage Rubies around, Six Grapes offers plenty of grapey goodness with an abundance of herb and mineral flavors.

1997 Quinta do Crasto Late Bottled Vintage   ★★★ $$
medium-sweet, medium-bodied, high acidity
LBV that actually tastes like well-aged Vintage Port, this offers elegant berry flavors complemented by apple and smoke.

2001 Cockburn's Quinta dos Canais Vintage   ★★ $$$$
sweet, full-bodied, high acidity
Flavorful as a blueberry-apple crisp, velvety as good chocolate pudding.

Dow's Bottled 1998 Crusted Porto   ★★ $$
sweet, full-bodied, high acidity
Crushed berry flavors are given a tawny twist in this lovely, traditional tipple.

Warre's Otima 10 Year Tawny   ★★ $$
off-dry, medium-bodied, high acidity
More fruity than most Tawny, this is as flavorful as strawberry-rhubarb pie.

Warre's Fine Selected White   ★★ $
medium-sweet, medium-bodied, high acidity
A rare White Port with snappy green and cider apple flavors.

WINES WE WISH WE HAD MORE ROOM FOR
1976 Smith Woodhouse Colheita Tawny ★★★★ $$$ off-dry, medium-bodied, high acidity; **Graham's 20 Year Tawny** ★★★ $$$ medium-sweet, medium-bodied, high acidity; **1994 Rainha Santa Vintage** ★★★ $$$ medium-sweet, full-bodied, high acidity; **Cockburn's 10 Year Tawny** ★★ $$ sweet, full-bodied, high acidity

dessert wines

white wines

With sweet, hypnotic flavors that range from delicate floral notes to spice, nuts, honey, truffles, and smoke, sweet white wines are some of the most alluring in the world.

grapes & styles

Late-Harvest wines are made from grapes that have been left on the vine late into fall in order to attain especially high sugar levels. Made from a wide array of grapes, late-harvest wines are produced by nearly every winemaking country. Some of the most famous examples come from Germany (marked *Spätlese*, or the even sweeter *Auslese*), and Alsace (marked *Vendanges Tardives* (VT)). Excellent bottlings also come from California, Australia, South Africa, Chile, and the Greek isle of Samos.

Passito wines are made from grapes that have been dried before being pressed. A specialty of Italy, they are made from myriad grape varieties. Tuscan and Umbrian vintners use mostly Trebbiano grapes and call their wines *Vin Santo*. The island of Pantelleria off Italy's coast also makes lush Passito wines from Zibbibo, a local type of Muscat. The French make some Passito wines, too, which they call *Vin de Paille,* or "straw wine," for the straw mats on which the grapes are dried.

Botrytis wines achieve their distinctive flavors from a mold called *Botrytis cinerea,* affectionately called "noble rot" in English. The mold sucks the water out of the grapes, concentrating their luscious fruit flavors and adding smoky, spicy, truffle-like nuances. Waiting for botrytis is risky business, though: the wrong mold could attack and leave the vintner with rotten grapes, so botrytised wines are necessarily expensive. The most storied examples are Bordeaux's Sauternes, where Sémillon, Sauvignon Blanc, and Muscadelle meld for wines of exceptional flavor and longevity. Look also for wines labeled Barsac, a sub-

285

region of Sauternes. Neighboring Loupiac and Cadillac produce similar wines that often sell for less. In the Loire Valley, the regions of Quarts de Chaume, Vouvray, and Bonnezeaux produce superb sweets from Chenin Blanc. Wines from Coteaux du Layon and Montlouis are also good. Alsatian vintners use their finest grape varieties to make *Sélection de Grains Nobles* (SGN) wines. Germans and Austrians produce sublime wines from botrytised Riesling and other varieties, which they designate *Beerenauslese* or *Trockenbeerenauslese* according to the ripeness of the grapes (see p. 204). California, South Africa, and Australia also produce golden, botrytis-affected wines.

Ice Wine/Eiswein is made from grapes that have been left to ripen on vines until the first freeze. Then they are picked and pressed while still frozen, so that all that comes out is concentrated sweetness, and any water stays behind as ice crystals. German and Austrian producers excel at Eiswein, making examples from Riesling, Grüner Veltliner, and Scheurebe in particular. Vintners from Canada, New York, and Washington State use those and other grapes. California doesn't enjoy freezing temperatures, but some winemakers throw especially ripe grapes in the freezer and then press them.

Vin Doux Naturel (VDN) is a category of wines that are fortified with brandy to preserve the grape's natural sweetness. They are made primarily in the south of France, with the two most noteworthy examples, both made from Muscat grapes, hailing from Beaumes-de-Venise in the Rhône and Rivesaltes in Languedoc-Roussillon.

Tokaji is a wine of legend—capable, in its highest form, of bringing noblemen back from the dead, or so they say. Produced in Hungary and a small corner of Slovakia, Tokaji is made by combining a dry base of white still wine with a mash of botrytis-infected grapes (*aszù* in Hungarian). Tokaji is graded according to the quantity of crushed grapes that are added to the base, from three to six *puttonyos*, each puttonyo equaling a bin's worth of crushed grapes. The higher the puttonyo count, the sweeter the wine. The ultimate Tokaji is *Eszencia*, a wine made from the juice that oozes from the grapes crushed only by the pressure of their own weight. At every level, Tokaji typically offers flavors of dried apricot, orange, and almond, balanced with high acidity.

at the table

Sweet yet high-acid wines like Sauternes, Tokaji, VT, or Auslese Riesling are ideal for foie gras or salty, piquant cheese like Roquefort. The honey-and-blossom-scented Muscats of Samos and the nutty Passitos of Italy are great with Florentine cookies or almond macaroons. Pour a Vin Doux Naturel with a pineapple upside-down cake. Leave the clean, fresh flavors of ice wine unimpeded, or serve with slices of fresh summer fruit.

the bottom line Sweet white wines stretch from simple Muscats at $7 a bottle up to deluxe Sauternes that run $350. Samos Muscat is a bargain at $7 to $15; fortified versions from Beaumes-de-Venise run $11 to $30. Prized Passito wines run $20 and up for half bottles. Botrytis-affected wines like Sauternes, Alsatian SGNs, and German BAs and TBAs begin at $25 and run up to $350 per 375 ml. Fortunately the U.S. and Australia offer some superb substitutes at $14 to $25, and up to $75 for some Sauternes-like wines. France's Loire Valley offers very good botrytis wines for $18 to $75 per half bottle. Tokajis are in the same range, though revered Eszencia can pass $200.

what to buy SAUTERNES

1994	1995	1996	1997	1998
★★	★★★	★★★	★★★	★★★

1999	2000	2001	2002	2003
★★★	★★	★★★	★★	★★★

recommended wines

2001 Château Climens Premier Cru, Barsac, France ★★★★ $$$$
sweet, full-bodied, high acidity
Big, busty Barsac, with a décolletage of juicy fruit glittered up by diamonds and perfumed with spice.

2000 Domaine Weinbach Clos des Capucins Vendanges Tardives Tokay Pinot Gris Altenbourg, Alsace, France ★★★★ $$$$
medium-sweet, full-bodied, high acidity
Perfect Pinot Gris, this finds exceptional balance in powerful apple and pear flavors restrained by intense minerality.

dessert wines **whites**

2000 Dolce Late Harvest, Napa Valley, California
★★★★ $$$$ (375 ml)
sweet, full-bodied, high acidity
Smoky, earthy, and rich with baked pineapple flavors, Dolce always thrills.

1999 Feiler-Artinger Ruster Ausbruch Welschriesling, Burgenland, Austria
★★★★ $$$$ (375 ml)
sweet, full-bodied, high acidity
Wine as if painted by Gustav Klimt, mysterious, gilded, and unforgettable.

1999 Monarchia Tokaj-Hétszolo Szolobirtok Tokaji Aszú 6 Puttonyos, Hungary
★★★★ $$$$ (500 ml)
sweet, full-bodied, high acidity
Hungary's Eastern influences comes through in exotic spice and fruit flavors.

1998 Trimbach Vendanges Tardives Gewurztraminer, Alsace, France
★★★★ $$$$
medium-sweet, medium-bodied, high acidity
Loaded with minerals and expansive florality, this treasure hovers between savory and sweet. It could easily glide between main course and dessert.

1999 Brown Brothers Patricia Late Harvested Noble Riesling, King Valley, Australia
★★★★ $$$ (375 ml)
sweet, full-bodied, high acidity
Chestnut brown in color, burnt orange and ripe peach in flavor, superbly done.

2002 Domaine du Closel Les Coteaux, Savennières, France
★★★★ $$$
medium-sweet, full-bodied, high acidity
Spectacular wine, this shows Chenin's acrobatic abilities to the fullest, jumping from peppery flower notes to unexpected notes of chocolate before landing smoothly on a bed of ripe tropical fruit flavors.

1997 Fattoria Villa La Selva Vigna del Papa, Vin Santo del Chianti, Italy
★★★★ $$$ (500 ml)
medium-sweet, full-bodied, high acidity
Vin Santo, divinely inspired, with superb roasted fruit and salty mineral notes.

2002 Domaine des Baumard, Quarts de Chaume, France ★★★ $$$$
sweet, medium-bodied, high acidity
So intensely tropical, one could swear that Monsieur Baumard grows pineapples in the middle of France.

1999 Château de la Guimonière, Coteaux du Layon Chaume, France
★★★ $$$ (375 ml)
medium-sweet, full-bodied, high acidity
Wine that smokes, with bright citrus and thrilling herb flavors.

2001 Château de Rayne Vigneau, Sauternes, France ★★★ $$$
sweet, full-bodied, high acidity
This was made in Bordeaux but tastes of Hawaii, with plantation-fresh, grilled pineapple flavors garnished with a lei of flowers.

2000 Gsellmann & Gsellmann Gelber Muskateller Trockenbeerenauslese, Burgenland, Austria ★★★ $$$ (375 ml)
sweet, full-bodied, high acidity
Prepare yourself for this: its intense peppery herb, honeysuckle, and pineapple flavors are as startling as they are delicious.

2001 Heiss Traminer Eiswein, Neusiedlersee, Austria ★★★ $$$ (375 ml)
sweet, full-bodied, high acidity
Explosive flower and spice flavors introduce this wine; then autumn fruit flavors work their way in. It's sweet yet refreshing.

2002 Kracher Beerenauslese Cuvée, Burgenland, Austria ★★★ $$$ (375 ml)
sweet, full-bodied, high acidity
The basic wine from Austria's sweet-wine meister, this is a stunning study in simplicity. A pleasure.

2002 Louis Guntrum Pinguin Eiswein, Rheinhessen, Germany ★★★ $$$ (375 ml)
sweet, medium-bodied, high acidity
Sylvaner rarely smells (and tastes) so sweet as in this Eiswein, full of baked quince and haunting mushroomlike flavors.

2001 Martin Pasler Muskat-Ottonel Trockenbeerenauslese, Neusiedlersee, Austria ★★★ $$$ (375 ml)
sweet, full-bodied, high acidity
Forget that bouquet of roses: once poured, this elixir might not last as long as the flowers, but the memory of its intense florality and dry fruit flavors will certainly linger.

2003 Mount Horrocks Cordon Cut Riesling, Clare Valley, Australia ★★★ $$$ (375 ml)
sweet, full-bodied, high acidity
The Clare Valley excels at both dry and sweet Riesling, as exemplified in the heady yet delicate pear and lemon flavors of this wine.

1998 Samos Anthemis Muscato, Samos, Greece ★★★ $$$ (375 ml)
sweet, full-bodied, high acidity
This fortified muscat offers musky orange and spice flavors, well balanced and classically conceived.

dessert wines **whites**

2002 Joseph La Magia Botrytis Riesling Traminer, South Australia
★★★ $$ (375 ml)

sweet, full-bodied, high acidity

Two great grapes dance a bolero of floral apricot and spice flavors.

2000 Lawson's Dry Hills Late Harvest Semillon, Marlborough, New Zealand
★★★ $$ (375 ml)

medium-sweet, medium-bodied, high acidity

New Zealand isn't one of the Spice Islands, but you couldn't tell that from this peppery, peachy treat.

2001 Nico Lazaridi Moushk, Greece
★★★ $$ (500 ml)

medium-sweet, full-bodied, high acidity

Like a minimalist floral arrangement, this is singular in scent, yet universal in its fragrant beauty.

2002 Standing Stone Vineyards Cailloux, Finger Lakes, New York
★★★ $$ (375 ml)

sweet, full-bodied, high acidity

As the name suggests, this is awash with stones (*cailloux*), albeit heavily coated with dry fruit and herb flavors.

2002 Three Rivers Winery Biscuit Ridge Vineyard Late Harvest Gewürztraminer, Walla Walla Valley, Washington
★★★ $ (375 ml)

medium-sweet, full-bodied, high acidity

Honeysuckle on parade. Delicious.

2000 Weingut Erich Bender Bissersheimer Steig Huxelrebe Beerenauslese, Pfalz, Germany
★★★ $ (375 ml)

sweet, medium-bodied, high acidity

So what if it's hard to pronounce: this is spicy, floral, and delicious.

2002 Amity Vineyards Select Cluster Riesling, Oregon
★★ $$$ (375 ml)

sweet, medium-bodied, high acidity

Surprisingly floral for a Riesling, this should put a smile on anyone's face.

2001 Beringer Nightingale, Napa Valley, California
★★ $$$ (375 ml)

sweet, full-bodied, high acidity

Nightingale sings with smoky, spicy seduction.

2001 Martha Clara Vineyards Ciel, North Fork of Long Island, New York
★★ $$$ (375 ml)

sweet, full-bodied, high acidity

Apple pie flavors, courtesy of the Entenmann family, former maker of baked goods for Greater New York.

2002 Paumanok Late Harvest Botrytised Sauvignon Blanc, North Fork of Long Island, New York ★★ $$$ (375 ml)
medium-sweet, medium-bodied, high acidity
These lemony, stony flavors, lightly sweet and very refreshing, can make a summer dessert all by themselves.

1999 Pegasus Bay Finale Noble Chardonnay, Waipara, New Zealand ★★ $$$ (375 ml)
medium-sweet, medium-bodied, high acidity
Lovers of crème brûlée can enjoy their pleasure in a glass of this custard-smooth and burnt sugar–flavored Chardonnay.

2002 Amity Vineyards Bois Jolie Vineyard Late Harvest Riesling, Oregon ★★ $$ (375 ml)
sweet, medium-bodied, high acidity
Light apple blossom flavors make this very pretty Riesling.

2001 Babcock Cuvee Sublime Gewürztraminer, Santa Barbara County, California ★★ $$ (375 ml)
medium-sweet, full-bodied, high acidity
With spicy, piquant floral notes and lots of pear flavor, this is dreamy stuff.

2001 Château Bastor-Lamontagne, Sauternes, France ★★ $$
medium-sweet, medium-bodied, high acidity
Skirting the edge of dry, this offers pleasantly restrained orange, tropical, and herb flavors. A great deal, too.

2003 Handley Late Harvest Riesling, Anderson Valley, California ★★ $$ (375 ml)
medium-sweet, medium-bodied, high acidity
Handley plays it cool, with a good hand of limes and apples.

1999 Mas Cristine, Rivesaltes, France ★★ $$ (500 ml)
sweet, full-bodied, high acidity
The sunshine of the south of France is captured in this bottle, in flavors of dried apricot, orange peel, and peppery spice.

2002 Yakima Cellars Elerding Vineyard Late Harvest Viognier, Yakima Valley, Washington ★★ $$ (375 ml)
medium-sweet, medium-bodied, high acidity
Viognier, charmingly expressed, with ribbons of pear and floral flavors falling through its rich, satiny texture.

NV Achaia Clauss, Muscat de Patras, Greece ★ $
sweet, medium-bodied, medium acidity
A wave of lemon-vanilla flavors, gently presented.

dessert wines **reds**

2002 Navarro Vineyards Cluster Select Late Harvest Gewürztraminer, Anderson Valley, California ★★★ $$ (375 ml) sweet, full-bodied, high acidity; **2001 Wenzel Saz Ruster Ausbruch, Burgenland, Austria** ★★★ $$$$ (375 ml) sweet, full-bodied, high acidity; **2002 Macari Block E, North Fork of Long Island, New York** ★★★ $$$ (375 ml) sweet, full-bodied, high acidity; **2003 Wölffer Late Harvest Chardonnay, The Hamptons, New York** ★★★ $$$ (375 ml) sweet, full-bodied, high acidity; **2002 McCrea Late Harvest Viognier, Washington State** ★★ $$ (375 ml) medium-sweet, medium-bodied, high acidity; **NV Boutari, Samos, Greece** ★★ $ sweet, full-bodied, high acidity

red wines

There's more to red dessert wine than Port. From France to Australia, a host of noteworthy red dessert wines can be found in styles ranging from light and bubbly to chocolatey-rich.

grapes & styles

Grenache is the base of two rich, fortified wines from Roussillon in southern France, Banyuls and Maury. Northeastern Italy claims the relatively lighter, bittersweet Recioto della Valpolicella, the sweet sibling of Amarone (see p. 162). Also from Italy are sweet wines from red Muscat (Moscato Rosa) and Brachetto, which is made into a charming, lightly bubbly red equivalent to Moscato d'Asti. California and Australia make sweet late-harvest and Port-style wines from a range of grape varieties.

at the table

Lushly berried Banyuls and Maury are among the few wines that pair well with chocolate. Try them, too, with black or blueberry pies, or, a salty sheep's milk cheese. Recioto della Valpolicella is delicious with plum tarts. Serve Brachetto or Moscato Rosa with fresh berries. Use Port-style wines from California and Australia as you would the real thing: with blue cheese and walnuts.

the bottom line Banyuls and Maury run $20 to $50 per 750 ml bottle, but you can find them in half bottles. Recioto wines cost $20 to $100 or more per full bottle; Brachetto sells for $13 to $30 per full bottle. Moscato Rosa runs $15 to $35 for half bottles. Sweet California and Australian late-harvest and Port-style wines sell for between $12 and $50 per full bottle.

recommended wines

2003 Adelsheim Deglacé Pinot Noir, Yamhill County, Oregon ★★★ $$$ **(375 ml)**
sweet, medium-bodied, high acidity
Pinot Noir goes pink in this ice-box wine, full of lovely spice and orange notes.

De Bortoli 8 Year Tawny Port, South Eastern Australia ★★★ $$
medium-sweet, full-bodied, high acidity
Silky with wonderful dry fruit and vanilla flavors, this is a great bargain.

1998 M. Chapoutier, Banyuls, France ★★★ $$ **(500 ml)**
medium-sweet, full-bodied, high acidity
Smoky wild berry and herb notes backed by intense minerality provide good reason for Chapoutier to venture south of his Rhône domaine.

Tsantali 5 Year Cellar Reserve, Mavrodaphne of Patras, Greece ★★★ $ **(500 ml)**
medium-sweet, full-bodied, high acidity
Fascinating wine, this has the intensity of dark Jamaican rum; the chestnut, cherry, and leather of old Barolo; and the rancio notes of Armagnac.

Heitz Cellars Ink Grade Vineyard Port, Napa Valley, California ★★ $$
sweet, full-bodied, high acidity
What to drink after great Napa Cab? Napa port, full of blackberry and spice.

2003 Marenco Pineto, Brachetto d'Acqui, Piedmont, Italy ★★ $$
medium-sweet, light-bodied, high acidity
A fun, fizzy red wine, brimming with perfumed floral and berry flavors.

2001 Rosenblum Cellars Castanho Vineyard Zinfandel Port, San Francisco Bay, California ★★ $$ **(375 ml)**
sweet, full-bodied, high acidity
Zinfandel to the max, heady with bramble and spice flavors.

Wandin Valley Estate Muscat, Hunter Valley/Rutherglen, Australia ★★ $ **(375 ml)**
medium-sweet, medium-bodied, high acidity
A musky red Muscat, with fresh date and tobacco flavors.

50 best values

Finding a drinkable, affordable wine is a cinch. Finding one that offers great value for money spent is considerably more difficult. Great value doesn't necessarily mean low price; a beautifully aged Pinot Noir can be a bargain at $40. From more than 1,400 wines reviewed in the book, I give you my fifty best values:

WHITES & ROSÉS

Borgo Buon Natale Primogénito/First Born, Santa Maria Valley, California ★★★ $, p. 36

Bruno Hunold Gewürztraminer, Alsace, France ★★★ $, p. 92

Chappellet Dry Chenin Blanc, Napa Valley, California ★★★ $, p. 36

Claiborne & Churchill Dry Riesling, Central Coast, California ★★★★ $, p. 33

Cline Viognier, Sonoma County, California ★★★ $, p. 37

Clos Lapeyre, Jurançon Sec, France ★★★ $, p. 145

Conreria d'Scala Dei Les Brugueres, Priorat, Spain ★★★★ $$, p. 194

Cune Monopole, Rioja, Spain ★★★ $, p. 187

Domaine Langlois-Château, Saumur, France ★★★ $, p. 120

Domaine Les Hautes Noëlles Muscadet sur Lie, Côtes de Grandlieu, France ★★★★ $, p. 122

Domaine Marcel Deiss Muscat, Alsace, France ★★★★ $$$, p. 93

Frankland Estate Isolation Ridge Vineyard Riesling, Frankland River, Australia ★★★★ $$, p. 239

Hermann J. Wiemer Dry Johannisberg Riesling, Finger Lakes, New York ★★★★ $, p. 83

Hidalgo La Gitana Manzanilla, Jerez, Spain ★★★★ $, p. 280

Iron Horse Vineyards T bar T Rosato di Sangiovese, Alexander Valley, California ♥ ★★★ $, p. 38

La Pepière Cuvée Eden Muscadet sur Lie, Sèvre-et-Maine, France ★★★ $, p. 122

Mills Reef Reserve Sauvignon Blanc, Hawkes Bay, New Zealand ★★★ $, p. 250

Novellum Chardonnay, Vin de Pays des Coteaux de Fontcaude, France ★★★ $, p. 128

Primo Estate La Biondina, Adelaide, Australia ★★★ $, p. 240

Sieur d'Arques Toques et Clochers, Crémant de Limoux, France ★★★ $, p. 273

Sigalas, Santorini, Greece ★★★ $, p. 224
Tirecul La Gravière, Vin de Pays du Périgord, France ★★★★ $$, p. 145
Trimbach Réserve Personnelle Pinot Gris, Alsace, France ★★★★ $$$, p. 90

REDS

Arrowood Syrah, Sonoma County, California ★★★★ $$, p. 54
Bernard Baudry Les Grézeaux, Chinon, France ★★★★ $$$, p. 124
Casa Castillo Monastrell, Jumilla, Spain ★★★ $, p. 197
Casa Ferreirinha Vinha Grande, Douro, Portugal ★★★★ $$, p. 202
Château de Caraguilhes, Corbières, France ★★★ $, p. 129
Château de Parenchère Cuvée Raphael Gazaniol, Bordeaux Supérieur,
   France ★★★ $$, p. 101
Château d'Oupia Les Hérétiques, Vin de Pays de l'Hérault,
   France ★★★ $, p. 129
Château Lagrange Grand Cru, St-Julien, France ★★★ $$, p. 101
Cline Ancient Vines Zinfandel, California ★★★★ $$, p. 56
D'Arenberg The Stump Jump Grenache-Shiraz, McLaren Vale,
   Australia ★★★ $, p. 247
Domaine de la Brune, Coteaux du Languedoc, France ★★★ $, p. 129
Domaine des Roches Neuves, Saumur-Champigny, France ★★★ $, p. 125
Domaine du Roc Expression, Minervois, France ★★★ $, p. 129
Féraud-Brunel, Gigondas, France ★★★★ $$$, p. 140
Glen Fiona Syrah, Walla Walla Valley, Washington State ★★★ $$, p. 78
Guilhem Dardé Mas des Chimères, Coteaux du Languedoc,
   France ★★★★ $$, p. 128
Kalin Cellars Cuvee DD Pinot Noir, Sonoma County,
   California ★★★★ $$$, p. 50
Kir-Yianni Ramnista, Náoussa, Greece ★★★★ $$, p. 225
La Posta Estela Armando Vineyard Bonarda, Mendoza,
   Argentina ★★★★ $$, p. 257
Louis Jadot Château des Jacques, Moulin-à-Vent,
   France ★★★★ $$, p. 117
Miner Cabernet Sauvignon, Oakville, California ★★★★ $$$, p. 40
Nicolas Potel Maison Dieu Vieilles Vignes, Bourgogne,
   France ★★★ $$, p. 112
Pira Vigna Landes, Dolcetto di Dogliani, Italy ★★★★ $$, p. 158
Ridge Lytton Springs, Dry Creek Valley, California ★★★★ $$$, p. 56
Seven Hills Klipsun Vineyard Cabernet Sauvignon, Columbia Valley,
   Washington State ★★★★ $$$, p. 77
Tenuta Cocci Grifoni Le Torri, Rosso Piceno Superiore,
   Italy ★★★ $, p. 179
Wildekrans Pinotage, Walker Bay, South Africa ★★★★ $, p. 266

vintage chart

You've ordered a wine that's supposed to be great—but isn't? Maybe it's the vintage. This chart, which covers the wines that are commonly aged, will aid you not only in ordering wine but in

	1987	1988	1989	1990	1991	1992	1993
Bordeaux							
Right Bank	o	★★★	☆☆☆☆	☆☆☆☆	O	☆	★★
Left Bank (Médoc)	oo	★★★	☆☆☆☆	☆☆☆☆	★	★	★★
Red Graves	oo	☆☆☆	☆☆☆☆	☆☆☆☆	★	★	☆☆☆
Burgundy							
Côte d'Or Reds	☆☆	★★★	★★★	★★★★	☆☆	☆☆	☆☆☆
Chablis	oo	☆☆	★★★	☆☆☆	☆☆	☆☆☆	★★
Loire							
Chenin Blanc	o	★★	☆☆☆☆	★★★	O	☆☆	★★★
Cabernet Franc	o	☆☆☆	★★★★	★★★	O	O	★★★
Rhône							
Northern Reds	☆☆	★★★★	☆☆☆☆	☆☆☆☆	★★★	☆	☆
Southern Reds	oo	★★★★	★★★★	★★★★	☆	☆	☆☆
Italy							
Barolo & Barbaresco	☆	★★★★	☆☆☆☆	☆☆☆☆	★★★	☆	☆☆☆
Chianti	oo	★★★	★★	★★★★	☆☆☆	☆☆	★★★
Spain							
Rioja Reds	★★★	☆	★★★	★★★	★★	★★	★★
Ribera del Duero	★★★	☆☆	☆☆	★★★	★★★	☆	★★
Germany							
Riesling	☆☆	★★★	★★★	☆☆☆☆	★★	★★	★★★
California							
Cabernet Sauvignon	★★★★	☆☆	★★★	★★★★	★★★★	★★★★	☆☆☆
Chardonnay	oo	☆☆☆	☆☆	★★★	★★★	★★★	★★

o = Very bad vintage; a disaster

★ = Poor to average vintage; only the best wines are good quality

★★ = Good to very good vintage

★★★ = Excellent vintage

★★★★ = Outstanding vintage

evaluating those you already have and in choosing recent wines to purchase. The quality of the wine is indicated by the number of stars, just as in the "What to Buy" sections of this book. The color of the stars tells you where the wine is most likely to be in its progress, from "not ready" through "well past peak." For example, ★★ indicates a good wine at its peak, while ☆☆☆ signals an excellent wine whose time has almost passed.

1994	1995	1996	1997	1998	1999	2000	2001	2002	2003
☆☆☆	☆☆☆	☆☆☆☆	★★	★★★★	★★★	★★★★	★★★	★★★	★★
★★★	☆☆☆☆	☆☆☆☆	★★	★★★	★★★	★★★★	★★★	★★★	★★
☆☆☆	☆☆☆	☆☆☆	☆☆☆	★★	★★★	★★★★	★★	★★★	★★
★★	☆☆☆	☆☆☆☆	☆☆☆	☆☆	☆☆☆	★	★★	★★★★	★★★★
★★★	☆☆☆☆	☆☆☆☆	★★★	☆☆☆	☆☆☆	☆☆	☆☆	★★★	★★★
☆	★★★	★★★	☆☆☆☆	☆☆	☆☆	☆☆	☆☆☆	☆☆☆	★★★
★★	★★★	☆☆☆☆	☆☆☆☆	☆☆	☆☆	☆☆☆	☆☆	☆☆☆	★★★
★★★	☆☆☆☆	☆☆☆	★★★	☆☆☆	★★★★	★★★	★★★	★	★★
★★	★★★★	★★	★★	☆☆☆☆	☆☆☆	★★★★	★★★	★	★★
★★	☆☆☆	☆☆☆☆	★★★★	★★★	★★★	★★★	★★★	★	★★
☆☆☆	★★★★	★★★	★★★★	☆☆☆	☆☆☆	★★★	★★	★★	★★
★★★★	☆☆☆☆	☆☆☆	★★	☆☆☆	★★	★★	★★★	★★	★★
★★★★	☆☆☆☆	☆☆☆☆	☆☆☆	☆☆☆	★★	★★	★★★	★	★★
☆☆☆☆	★★★	☆☆☆☆	☆☆☆	☆☆☆	☆☆☆☆	☆☆	☆☆☆☆	☆☆☆	☆☆☆
☆☆☆☆	☆☆☆	☆☆☆	☆☆☆	☆☆	★★★	★★★	★★★★	★★★	☆☆☆
★★★★	★★★★	☆☆☆☆	☆☆☆	★★	☆☆☆	☆☆☆	☆☆☆	☆☆	★★

★ = Not ready; needs more time   ☆ = Past peak but still enjoyable
☆ = Can be drunk or held   ✿ = Well past peak
★ = At peak; perfect for drinking now   na = Not yet available

names you can trust

Faced with a shelf of unfamiliar bottles and no one around to guide you? Here's a tip: look for the importer's name on the back label. Some importers specialize in certain regions and consistently offer wines that are among the best of their type. Get to know the names of those who bring in wines you like, and you can be confident that you'll find nearly any of their wines enjoyable. Here are a few nationally available names to look for, grouped by specialty.

Australia The Australian Premium Wine Collection, Domaine Select Wine Estates, Epic Wines, Epicurean Wines, The Grateful Palate

Austria Terry Theise Estate Selections, Vin Divino

France Charles Neal Selections, Chartrand Imports, Eric Solomon/European Cellars, Europvin, Hand Picked Selections, Kermit Lynch Wine Merchant, Louis/Dressner Selections, Martine's Wines, Paterno Wines International, Robert Chadderdon Selections, Robert Kacher Selections, Rosenthal Wine Merchant, Vineyard Expressions, Weygandt-Metzler Importing, Wilson-Daniels

Germany Classical Wines, P.J. Valckenberg, Rudi Wiest Selections, Terry Theise Estate Selections

Italy Domaine Select Wine Estates, Empson, Leonardo LoCascio Selections/Winebow, Marc de Grazia Selections, Montecastelli Selections, Panebianco, Paterno Wines International, Summa Vitis, Vias Imports, Vin Divino, Vinifera Selections

Portugal Broadbent Selections, Tri-Vin Imports, Whitehall/Signature Imports

South Africa Cape Classics, Loest & McNamee

South America Banfi, Billington, Vine Connections

Spain Classical Wines, Eric Solomon/European Cellars, Jorge Ordonez/Fine Estates From Spain

index of wines

index

index

index

d

index

index

g

index

index

index

index

index

index